OCEAN

Revealing the secrets of the deep

OCEAN

Revealing the secrets of the deep

BRYAN RICHARD

SARAH RICKAYZEN　•　JOAN BARKER

This is a Parragon Publishing Book
First published in 2007

Parragon Publishing
Queen Street House
4 Queen Street
Bath, BA1 1HE, UK

Produced by Atlantic Publishing

Text © Parragon Books Ltd 2007
Photographs © see page 320

ISBN 978-1-4054-8790-0

Printed in China

CONTENTS

INTRODUCTION

From a certain point in outer space, above the Pacific Ocean, the Earth appears entirely blue. It is the presence of liquid water in such vast quantities that marks the planet out from its neighbors in the solar system. The oceans spawned the earliest life forms, and they continue to sustain all terrestrial creatures – mankind included. And not simply through the water cycle; the oceans also play a vital role in regulating the Earth's temperature; without them, the planet would be inhospitably hot by day and cold by night.

Much is already understood about the oceans, from the reason for their characteristic hue to the role they play in climatic phenomena such as tornadoes, tsunamis, and El Niño. But they are also the last great wilderness on Earth. Light penetrates only to a depth of around 600 feet; below lies a dark world of extraordinary topography and remarkable creatures. There are mountain ranges that dwarf the Andes, and trenches so deep that if Mount Everest were deposited there, it would still find itself covered by over a mile of sea water. The coelacanth, thought to be extinct before 1938, can claim the title of the "ocean's dinosaur" since fossil records show it to be at least 400 million years old. And textbooks had to be rewritten when the megamouth shark was first sighted in 1976. What other, as yet undiscovered, species inhabit the depths?

Ocean examines every facet of this remarkable environment, from plate tectonics to the effects of the moon, phytoplankton to blue whales. It traces Man's efforts to probe the deep in aid of scientific discovery; it also covers his less worthy activities regarding the environment, the ramifications of which remain uncertain.

Mankind began to look outward with the dawn of the space era in the 1950s. This book shows that seventy percent of the Earth's surface is a source of wonder whose secrets have yet to be fully revealed.

The giver of life

Water is one of the most familiar and ubiquitous substances on Earth, with an estimated total volume of some 333 million cubic miles. Of this, more than 97%, covers over 70% of the planet's surface in the form of our oceans, whilst the remaining three percent of freshwater is held mainly in glaciers and the icecaps (69%), in groundwater in the subterranean lithosphere (30%), in terrestrial surface waters such as swamps, rivers and lakes (0.03%), and in our atmosphere as water vapor (0.04%), which is constantly being transported and recycled by the hydrological cycle. Additionally, water is contained within the tissues of all living organisms, sometimes accounting for over 90% of their weight; yet this biological water, which is also subject to continuous recycling, accounts for a tiny percentage of the total found on Earth, at around just 0.0001%.

In some ways, water is one of the simplest of all compounds, and in its purest state, it is colorless, tasteless and odorless, and yet it can also be seen as one of the most complex, with a range of unusual, and even unique, chemical and physical properties, which govern the world's chemical and physical conditions, and which are essential for the existence of life.

Physical properties

Water has the simple chemical formula H_2O, meaning that a single molecule of water is comprized of two hydrogen atoms, and one of oxygen, which results in one of the smallest and lightest of all molecules. The way in which hydrogen and oxygen atoms attach to one another also results in the molecule being positively charged on the hydrogen side and negatively charged on the oxygen side, which in turn creates hydrogen bonds between water molecules, that causes them to be brought together. Hydrogen is the most common of all elements in the universe, thought to account for some 92.7% of all matter, and it readily, and tightly, binds to oxygen.

However, whilst recent discoveries have suggested that water may not be as exceptionally rare in the universe as was once believed, there are few places where it is thought to occur in liquid form, and so it is perhaps even more remarkable that the Earth is home to so much of it. Moreover, water is found here in all three physical states under normal conditions; liquid, solid and gas.

We tend to take for granted that liquid water becomes a gas or vapor at 212°F (depending on altitude), and freezes at 32°F, to become solid ice. Yet, unlike any other substance, its maximum density is achieved in liquid form (at around 40°F), rather than when it is solidified.

As with other substances water tends to expand when heated and contract when cooled, but on account of the forms of the hydrogen bonds, and the rigid geometric arrangement of the molecules, as water freezes beyond its maximum density, it begins to expand, with its volume increasing by approximately 9%, whilst conversely, its density decreases. This property enables water in its solid form, ice, to float on water in its liquid form, which has important ramifications for the planet. Floating ice forms a protective layer that insulates the water and organisms below, and slows freezing, but if the ice was to sink and to continue to contract, away from the sun's heat, then polar waters would freeze solid, with far-reaching consequences for deep water circulation within the oceans, and for the global climate above. The fact that water expands as it freezes also enables certain organisms to survive within it, rather than simply being crushed to death.

Below: Floating ice forms a protective layer that insulates the water and organisms below.

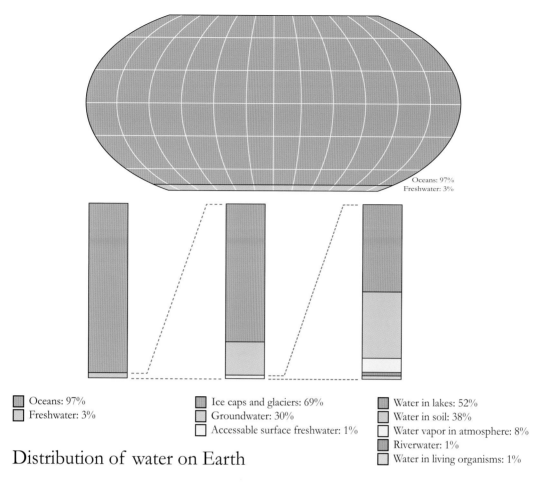

Oceans: 97%
Freshwater: 3%

■ Oceans: 97%	■ Ice caps and glaciers: 69%	■ Water in lakes: 52%
▢ Freshwater: 3%	▨ Groundwater: 30%	▢ Water in soil: 38%
	☐ Accessible surface freshwater: 1%	☐ Water vapor in atmosphere: 8%
		■ Riverwater: 1%
		▢ Water in living organisms: 1%

Distribution of water on Earth

Regulating the earth's climate

Water also possesses other important thermal properties. It conducts heat more readily than any other liquid, with the exception of mercury, and it has a very high specific heat, which refers to the amount of energy that is necessary to change its own temperature. In fact, aside from ammonia, water has the highest known specific heat amongst naturally occurring compounds. This means that it is able to slowly absorb a large amount of heat energy before its own temperature is raied, and that this energy is retained and released slowly as it cools.

In this way, large bodies of water such as the oceans help to regulate the Earth's climate; storing heat by day and during the summer months, and releasing it at night and in the winter. Similarly, lakes may have a moderating effect on local climatic conditions, whilst the phenomenon is also important in the regulation of body temperature amongst living things.

Water is sometimes referred to as a universal solvent or super-solvent, as it demonstrates an extraordinary propensity for dissolving other substances and carrying them in solution. This includes both organic and inorganic materials, and is an essential process for life. It represents the means by which nutrients are transferred to, from and within, living things. No known organisms can exist without water, which is essential for countless biological and biochemical processes to take place, such as photosynthesis in plants, which is the dominant form of primary production on Earth.

In the oceans, a huge range of elements and compounds, minerals and dissolved gases occur, including sodium and chloride, which form salt, and elements that are thought to represent the basis of life, such as carbon, nitrogen, phosphorus, hydrogen, and oxygen, from which organic compounds are formed, as well as essential nutrients such as phosphates, nitrates, and silicates. Despite this however, seawater is chemically very pure, being comprized of around 95% water, and yet it seems that for every substance contained within it, there is probably an organism that is capable of utilizing it in some way, and that water itself, with all of its remarkable properties, is fundamentally both life-giving and life-sustaining.

OCEAN DYNAMICS

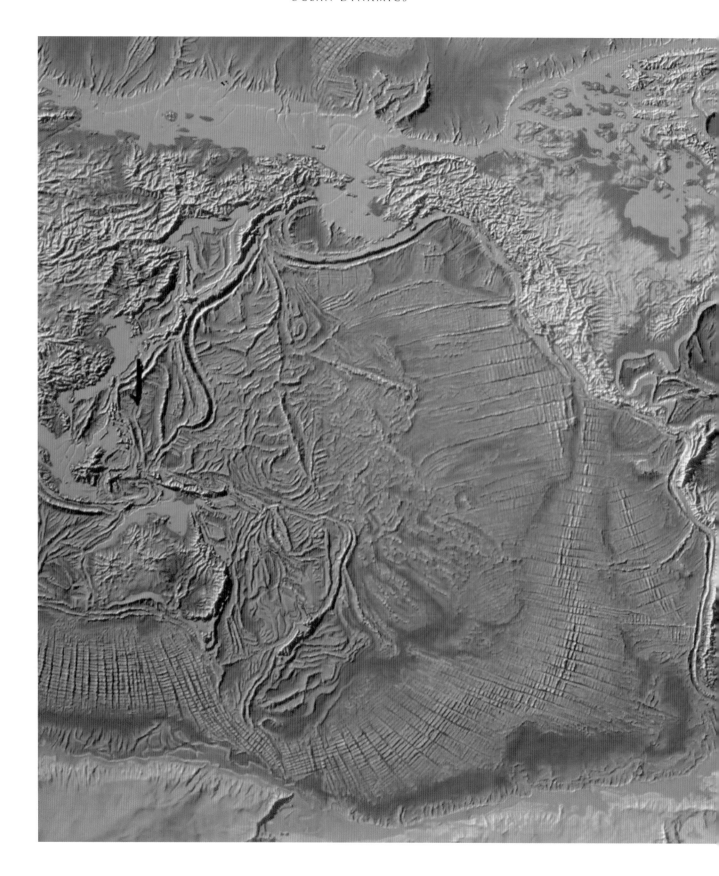

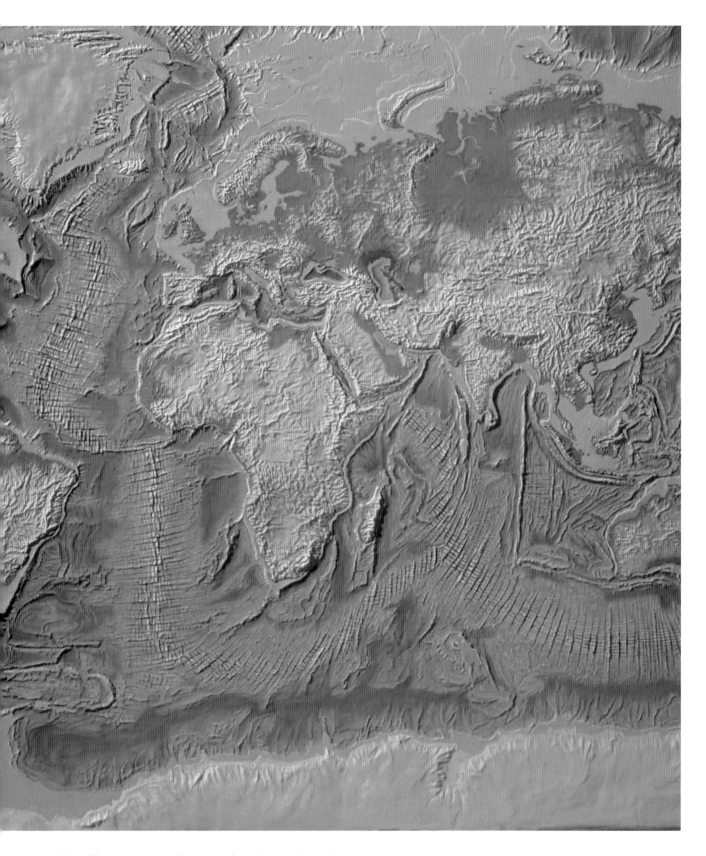

Above: The topography of the ocean floor, showing the continental
shelves, ocean basins, ridges and trenches.

Ocean formation

Plate tectonics

Earth as we know it – with its various oceans and continents – has taken billions of years to evolve. Formed as a molten ball of gas and metals 4.6 billion years ago, it cooled over tens of millions of years to form a hard outer skin called the crust; composed of igneous rock, it reaches depths ranging from 5 miles beneath the oceans to over 40 miles on land. Below the crust are three further layers: the mantle, measuring about 1900 miles; the outer core made from nickel-iron is 2200 miles thick; in the center of our planet, with a 750 miles radius, is an inner core of molten metal.

The crust is not one continuous layer wrapped around the Earth, but rather a number of tectonic plates – 13 major ones – which fit together rather like a jigsaw puzzle. All the plates float on top of the mantle which is in a semi-molten state. A distinction is made between the oceanic and continental plates, the latter being responsible for continental drift.

The ocean basins and the first water

Once the Earth's crust had formed, about 4.5 billion years ago, the ocean basins began to form. The oceanic crust, being heavier than the continental plate, pushed down on the mantle to a greater degree, causing depressions in the Earth's surface which eventually became the ocean basins, and over time, filled with water. The first water on the planet originated about 4 billion years ago from the gases produced by volcanic activity within the mantle. As the Earth cooled, the water vapor condensed to fall as rain, running under gravity into the ocean basins. Water also came from space in the form of icy comets which evaporated as they hit our atmosphere and condensed when cool to form rain.

Below: Today just over 70% of the Earth's surface is covered with water. If the surface of the Earth was flat and even, the depth of water would be 2¼ miles. Fortunately the complicated topography of the Earth, with deep ocean basins, means that almost 98% of the planet's water is stored there.

Continental drift

The tectonic plates are constantly on the move to reshape the map of the continents and oceans. It is thought that convection currents in the mantle upon which they rest, cause such movement. Known as continental drift, the idea was first proposed in 1912 by a German scientist called Alfred Wegener, but not proved or universally accepted until the 1960s.

Around 200 million years ago, Earth had one large ocean – Panthalassa – which surrounded a large continental mass known as Pangaea and the smaller Tethys Sea. Pangaea began to break up about 50 million years later to form two land masses: Laurasia to the north, which eventually formed North America and Eurasia; and in the south, Gondwana which became South America, Africa, India, Australia and Antarctica. As these two continents began to move apart on their separate plates, a stretch of water, now the North Atlantic, opened up. It was at this time that the Mid-Atlantic Ridge began to form.

Similarly, the Indian Ocean was formed from a rift in Gondwana. As Pangaea widened and broke apart, the Arctic Ocean took shape. The South Atlantic Basin began to develop and meet with the North Atlantic, their mid-ocean ridges joining as a result. The super-ocean of Panthalassa was shrinking to become part of the Pacific Ocean of today.

By 15 million years ago, the oceans and continents had moved, more or less, to their present positions. The plates are still on the move: the Pacific Ocean is still shrinking, and the Atlantic is expanding at a rate of about one inch a year.

Right: Pangaea was a supercontinent that included all the landmasses of the world before the Triassic period when it spit into Laurasia and Gondwana. This movement is known as continental drift. The continents are still moving today.

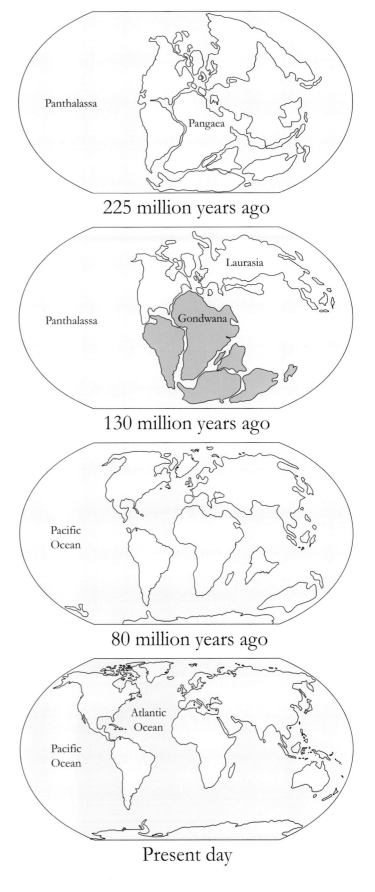

225 million years ago

130 million years ago

80 million years ago

Present day

Topography of the ocean floor

It wasn't until after the Second World War, when sonar was introduced to survey the ocean floors, that the topography of the seabed became known. Rather than the flat, featureless plain previously envisaged, undersea mountain ranges, rift valleys, trenches and plateaux were discovered. These features exist in all of the world's oceans and are the result of tectonic plate activity.

Volcanic activity

At the edge of the ocean, the continental shelf reaches out under the sea. This is the last few miles (generally about 40 miles, but it can be as little as half a mile and as great as 560 miles) of the continental plate that at one time would have been above sea level. At the shelf break, the terrain drops away rapidly to the continental slope which continues downward until it meets the oceanic crust. This is where the deep ocean floor begins, and is known as the abyssal plain. Covered in an ooze made up of dead organic matter, the plain is permeated with underwater volcanoes – seamounts and guyots. These volcanoes are a result of the hot magma from the mantle layer pushing up through the crust. If the seamounts rise above the water, they form volcanic islands, such as those in Hawaii. Guyots are flat-topped seamounts which have been eroded.

Trenches

Trenches are another feature of the ocean floor. Where two plates converge, one gives way to the other. Known as subduction, one of the plates will descend into the mantle, thus creating the trench. These features reach incredible depths: the deepest, and thus the most famous, is the Marianas Trench; measuring a little over 36,000 feet it is deeper than Mt Everest is high. Sited in the western North Pacific off the coast of Japan, it was formed when the Pacific Plate was subducted beneath the Philippine Plate. Trenches are most commonly found in the Pacific Rim, where the oceanic plate is forced below the continental plates around its edge. Where this occurs near the coast, a trench will form in the ocean where the plate is subducted, whilst inland the continental plate may buckle to form a mountain range. The Andes were formed in this way by the Pacific Plate pushing the Nazca Plate toward the continent of South America.

Below: A map of known lithospheric plates. The surface of the Earth is divided into 13 major plates and a number of smaller ones which all float on the partly molten layer of the mantle beneath. Some of these plates are oceanic, others carry continents and are responsible for continental drift.

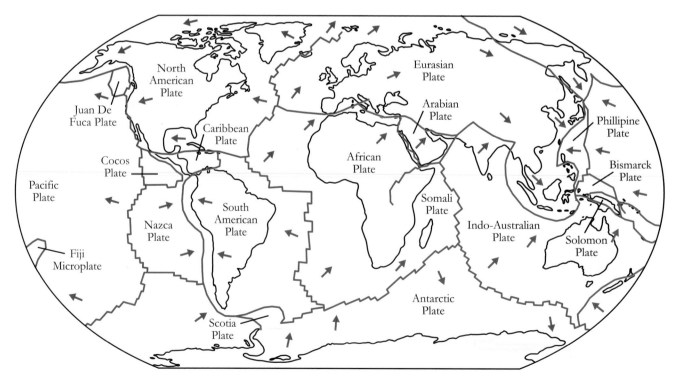

Division of Earth into lithospheric plates

Mid-ocean ridges

Where magma rises up between two oceanic plates and forces them apart, mid-ocean ridges form. At the gap between the plates a valley is formed and the nature of the seabed changes. The area is already unstable because of the magma pushing through the Earth's crust; sea water percolates down through the crust and is heated in the mantle below to very high temperatures before being forced back up again. These hydrothermal vents, as they are called, are home to a great deal of life on the seabed, despite the lack of sunlight. The minerals from the vents nourish bacteria present in the water through a process of chemical synthesis, allowing them to grow and support other life.

The Mid-Atlantic Ridge is an example of tectonic plates in the east and west moving apart. Running from the Arctic Circle in the north to sub-Antarctica, it is a massive submarine mountain range, breaking through the sea at its highest points to form islands such as Iceland, the Azores and Ascension Island. Discovery of the ridge in the 1950s led to the general acceptance of Wegener's theory of continental drift.

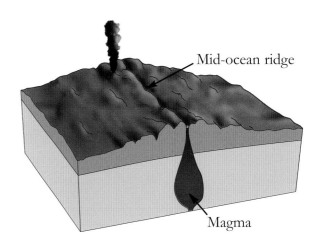

Above: A cross section of a mid-ocean ridge showing magma pushing up through th Eart's crust. A mid-ocean ridge is an underwater mountain range formed by plate tectonics. The mid-ocean ridges of the world are connected and form a single mid-oceanic ridge system that crosses all the major oceans except the North Pacific. The mid-oceanic ridge system is the longest mountain range system in the world with a total length of 28,000 miles. It is up to 30 miles wide and 10,000 feet high.

Below: Undersea volcanoes are found all along the mid-ocean ridges. Volcanoes sometimes grow large enough to form volcanic islands such as the Galapagos Islands and those on the Hawaiian ridge. When molten lava from an erupting volcano flows into the sea, it is cooled by the ocean and accumulates on the seafloor.

Above: The sea level is much higher today than 18,000 years ago. This means that all the margins of continental crusts have been flooded and new shallow, underwater habitats have been created. These regions are called continental shelves and are ideal for colonization by a variety of plants and animals.

Opposite above: The Arctic ice sheet reaches its maximum size in winter. As the spring thaw progresses, the periphery of the ice sheet breaks up, and the resulting floes drift southward. Although the dynamics of ice movement are not fully understood, it is known that ice floes move under the influence of winds, unlike icebergs which move with ocean currents.

Opposite below: The early breaking up and melting of ice during unusually warm winters (possibly caused in the longer term by climate change and global warming) has in recent years resulted in increased mortality of seal pups born on the ice. Inadequate and thin ice floes mean fewer places for the mothers to give birth; pups also drown or are crushed due to the breaking up of ice beneath them.

Changing sea levels

During the peak of the last ice age – about 18,000 years ago – sea levels were more than 400 feet lower than they are today. During this time, for example, what is now the Bering Strait between Alaska and Asia, was dry land and it is believed that humans migrated across this connection to North America.

Much of the rise since then happened before 6000 years ago. For the last 3000 years, levels have been more or less constant, except that over the last century they have risen at a rate of 0.3-0.12 inches/year, and over the last decade at 0.12 inches/year.

The rise since the ice age has meant that previously exposed stretches of land at the edges of all the continental crusts have been flooded to form large areas of shallow submarine habitats around the globe.

Short-term changes in sea level can be the result of many factors such as tides, storm surges, evaporation, rainfall, floods, run-offs from rivers and tsunamis. The major influences on longer term changes are temperature and the amount of water "locked up" as sea ice, polar ice caps, glaciers and fresh water. It is estimated that the rise in sea level due to temperature increase is about 0.03 inches/year.

Global warming

Temperature rises are, however, a major concern in the issue of global warming. Some predictions put sea levels rising by as much as 3 feet by the end of this century. At the heart of the global warming phenomenon is the increase in levels of greenhouse gas emissions, most notably carbon dioxide, which have risen by 25% in the last 100 years.

Carbon dioxide prevents heat from the sun being radiated back out and away from the Earth, thus increasing the overall global temperature. If temperatures continue to rise, polar ice caps will begin to melt and sea levels will rise. Figures vary substantially on the extent of this change, but some estimates put it at about 2 feet if smaller glaciers and ice caps melt, 20 feet if the Greenland ice sheet were to disappear and a staggering 200 feet if there was a whole-scale melting of the Antarctica ice sheet.

If global warming continues, the latter two scenarios are likely to be hundreds, if not thousands of years in the future. The melting of the ice caps, however, could have a significant effect within the next century.

The impact on coastal areas would be world-wide: the loss of natural habitats, coastal settlements and property would be extensive; erosion; increased flood risk in low-lying areas and changes in water quality would be inevitable, as would the adverse effects on tourism, recreation, transportation and coastal and maritime industries.

Coastal landscapes

The coastlines of the world are shaped by the waves and the weather and produce a wide variety of environments for marine, air and land animals to live and breed: sandy beaches and mudflats, rocky cliffs, river estuaries and salt marshes all attract different species of flora and fauna.

These various habitats form essentially from one of two types of coastline – rocky or sandy.

Rocky coasts are characterized by high energy waves crashing against tall cliffs or rocky outcrops. The cliffs have usually been formed from uplifted layers of rock which are still being eroded or which might still be rising. Erosion by the waves is a major feature here and the resultant debris and sediment are washed away quickly and deposited in quieter, less frenzied waters.

As well as cliffs, other features such as arches, blow-holes and sea stacks add a dramatic effect. Arches form when rocky outcrops are eroded by the sea into familiar arched structures; Durdle Door on the Dorset coast in England is a good example of this, as is London Arch off the coast of Victoria in South Australia. Formerly known as London Bridge because of its similarity to it, part of the arch collapsed in the 1990s to form a stack. Famous examples of sea stacks are The Needles off the coast of the Isle of Wight and Old Harry Rocks in Dorset, England. All are formed from the erosive action of the waves and the wind.

Below: Limestone sea stack formations. These make up part of the Twelve Apostles formation in the Port Campbell National Park, Australia. The sea stacks are pillars of sedimentary rock that were once part of the adjoining coast. They were formed when parts of the coast were isolated by wave erosion.

Low-energy coastlines

Where there are weaknesses in the cliffs, water will force its way in and erode the rock, until, over time, the cliff face collapses into the sea. Pebbles and larger pieces, even boulders might be deposited around the remaining cliff, whilst finer sediment is moved by waves, tides and currents to more sheltered spots.

Sandy shores are generally sheltered to a certain extent from the highly powerful forces of the ocean and are known as low-energy coastlines. Waves and the weather will still affect the shape of the land which often changes through the seasons. Winter storms, for example, will move sediments and deposited material around the beach or further up the coast; it will eventually return over the year.

The material eroded from the rocky coasts will be washed away and deposited around sandy shorelines; where wave action is weak or not sustained then muddy shores will result, whereas stronger wave action will give sandy beaches. The amount of erosion and deposition will usually be fairly balanced, but if more material is deposited than washed away, the beach or shore will extend further out to sea. This may take many hundreds of years, but there are examples of towns "moving" inland from the coast over time. Some sand will be brought further onto the beach by the wind or sea; further action by the wind drives it into small ripples and eventually dunes will develop behind the main stretch of beach.

Above Right: View of Durdle Door on the Dorset coast, England. This landform is the product of coastal erosion where less resistant rock has been eroded to leave a promontory of more resistant rock. The arch has formed from a hole at a weak spot in the promontory and will eventually collapse to form a stack.

Right: Lower Coastal Plain, Georgia USA. Salt marshes form on coastal mud flats such as estuaries and bays. Much of the marsh is completely submerged in seawater twice a day. Salt marshes are a threatened habitat due to pressure for land being drained and reclaimed from the sea for human use.

Deep water circulation, currents and climate control

Surface currents of the world's oceans are driven by the winds, but the deep and bottom waters are not subjected to air movements; early studies of the oceans thus assumed that the deep ocean was static in nature.

This has since been proven not to be the case and – although slow – deep water circulation occurs on a massive, indeed a global, scale, linking the waters of the world. Because this movement of water transfers energy, in the form of heat, it also has a significant impact on the planet's climate.

In the deep ocean, water movement is driven by changes in water density, which in turn is affected by variations in temperature and salinity (salt content): the cooler the water, the denser it becomes; high salinity will also produce dense water. Being dense, the water is also heavier than that surrounding it and it will sink.

It is in areas of high latitude that the dense water masses sink into the deep ocean basins. As the Gulf Stream heads north and east into the Atlantic Ocean, it cools and becomes known as the North Atlantic Drift; reaching Greenland the effects of evaporation and further cooling make it saltier; polar water is also saltier because when it freezes the salt remains in the unfrozen water. This dense water mass – known as the North Atlantic Deep Water (NADW) – slowly sinks and starts to push other dense water ahead of it southward.

This same process occurs in the Weddell Sea off the coast of Antarctica to produce Antarctic Bottom Water (AABW), which flows north into the Atlantic Basin. This is the densest water on the planet, being cold and highly salted, and as it meets the NADW it underflows it.

The global conveyor belt
This scale of movement of truly massive amounts of water – 100 million cubic feet enter the flow every second – is known as the Great Ocean Conveyor or sometimes, the global conveyor belt.

The belt moves slowly eastward around South Africa, some peeling off to form currents running up the western side of South America (the Humboldt) and western Africa (the Benguela). Continuing eastward toward the Pacific, upwellings of the cold water occur in the Indian and northern Pacific Oceans. On rising to the surface, the water warms and begins to flow back

westward along the southern Indian Ocean, into the Atlantic and north toward Greenland again, where the process will repeat itself. It is estimated that such a journey will take up to 1200 years to complete, but it ensures a mixing of the Earth's oceans and transfers heat on a global scale, helping to regulate the planet's climate.

An example of this is the Gulf Stream/North Atlantic Drift. The warm equatorial waters of the Stream will cool as they move northward and out into the Atlantic; the heat is lost to the air which warms and is carried eastward by the trade winds to reach the shores of western Europe. The climate here is relatively mild, with fewer extremes of temperature between winter and summer than the rest of the continent.

Above: Eastern shore of the Dead Sea, with a salt concentration of over 20% sodium chloride; it is also rich in magnesium, calcium and potassium chlorides. The water in the Dead Sea is so dense, it is impossible for the human body to sink in it.

Right: Sea water is 1.03 times heavier than the same volume of fresh water at the same temperature. Different bodies of water have different amounts of salt mixed in, or different salinities. Salinity is expressed by the amount of salt found in 1,000 grams of water. Therefore, if we have 1 gram of salt and 1,000 grams of water, the salinity is 1 part per thousand, or 1 ppt. The average ocean salinity is 35 ppt. This number varies between about 32 and 37 ppt. Rainfall, evaporation, river runoff, and ice formation cause the variations. For example, the Black Sea is so diluted by river runoff, its average salinity is only 16 ppt. The Dead Sea has an average salinity of 300 ppt.

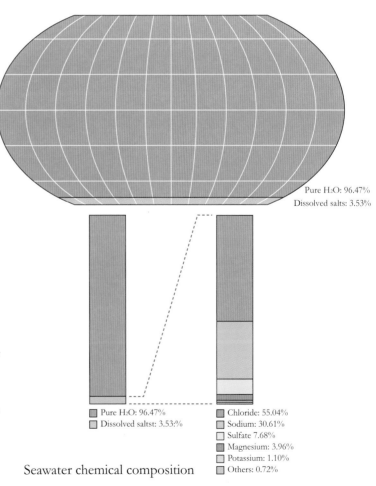

Pure H₂O: 96.47%
Dissolved salts: 3.53%

Seawater chemical composition

- Pure H₂O: 96.47%
- Dissolved saltst: 3.53:%
- Chloride: 55.04%
- Sodium: 30.61%
- Sulfate 7.68%
- Magnesium: 3.96%
- Potassium: 1.10%
- Others: 0.72%

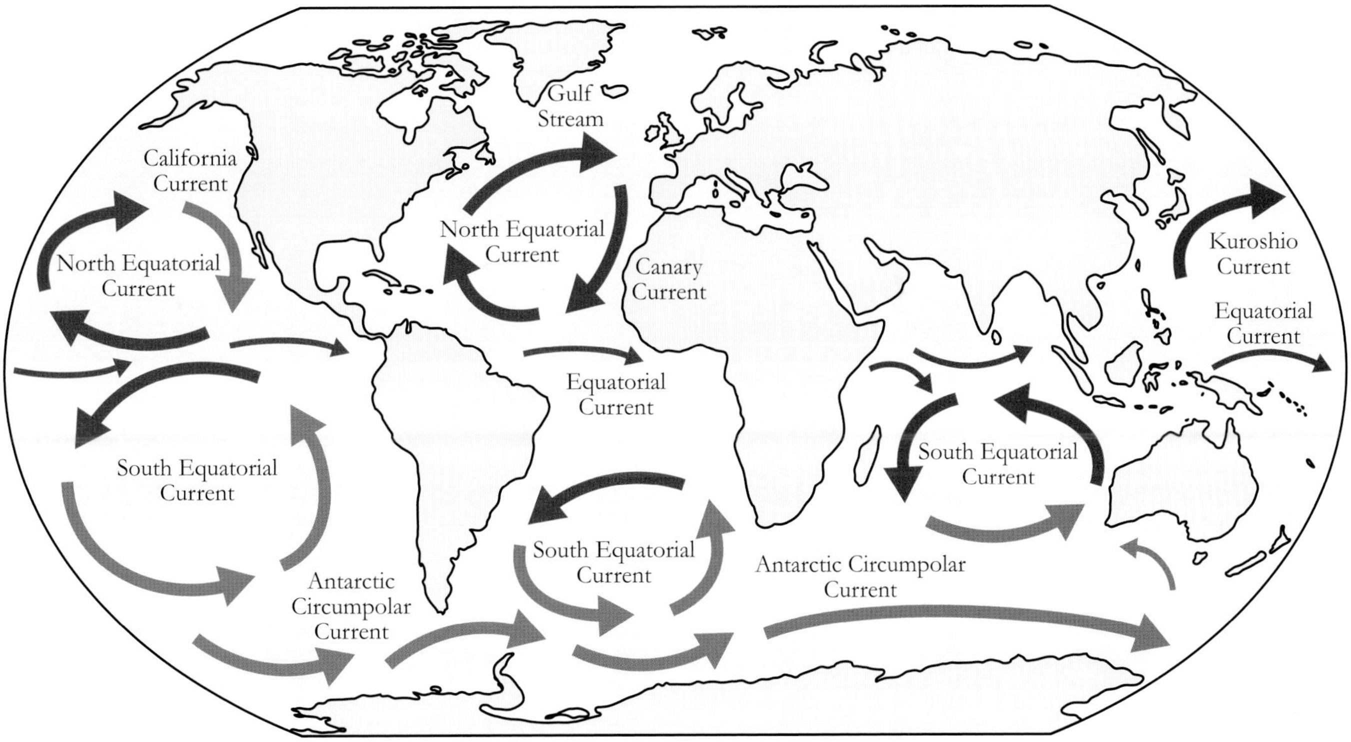
Gulf Stream
California Current
North Equatorial Current
North Equatorial Current
Canary Current
Kuroshio Current
Equatorial Current
Equatorial Current
South Equatorial Current
South Equatorial Current
South Equatorial Current
Antarctic Circumpolar Current
Antarctic Circumpolar Current

Above: There are two types of ocean currents: surface currents and deep water currents. Surface currents occupy the top 1300 feet and about 10% of the water in the ocean. Deep water currents occupy the remaining 90%. These waters move around the ocean basins by density-driven forces and gravity. The density difference is a function of different temperatures and salinity. These dense waters sink into the deep ocean basins at high latitudes where the temperatures are cold enough to cause the density to increase.

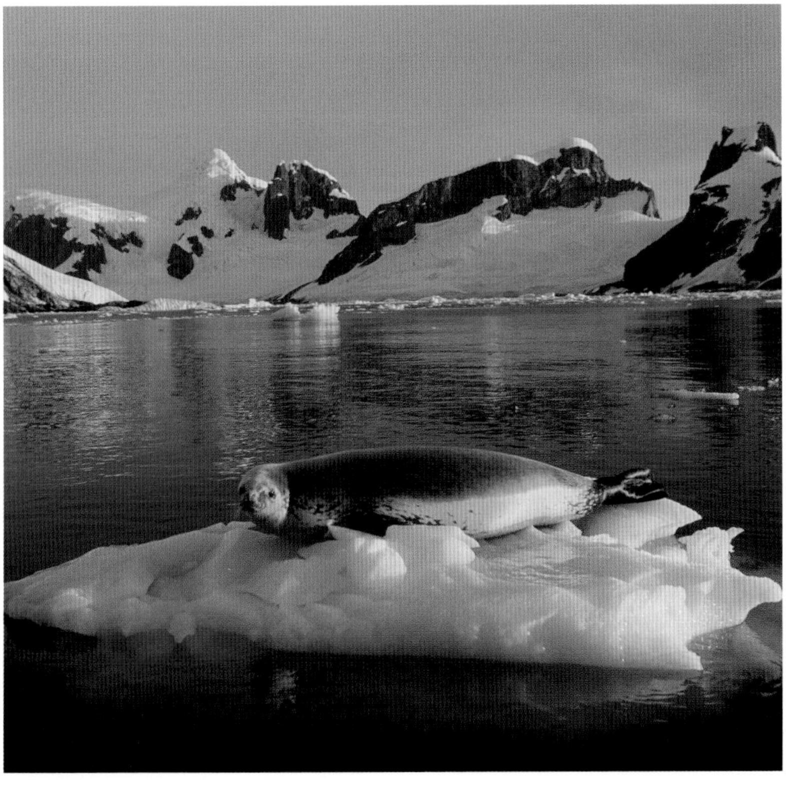

Left: Polar water is saltier because when the water freezes the salt remains in the unfrozen water. This produces water with high salinity which has a high density and will therefore sink. Ice is less dense than liquid water and therefore it floats. If this did not happen the polar oceans would be frozen solid.

Opposite: Mangrove trees or shrubs grow in shallow, muddy water along sheltered, tropical or subtropical shorelines and estuaries. They are able to survive inundation by salt water twice a day and in "soil" which is unstable and poor in oxygen. To deal with the salt in the water they have tangled masses of roots which help to trap mud particles and bind them together. Some mangrove roots, called pneumatophores, grow upward to collect oxygen from the air. This is because the mud in which mangroves grow is typically poor in the oxygen needed by the roots. By trapping mud particles, mangrove plants help to prevent coastal erosion.

Polar ice sheets

Unlike other materials which contract as they cool, water expands as it freezes and becomes less dense. As a consequence, it floats on the denser mass of liquid water. If this were not the case, the ice sheets of the Arctic and Antarctica – which cover about 12% of the planet's oceans – would not exist; instead the ice would sink into the ocean depths away from sun's heat and remain there frozen solid. There would be no deep ocean circulation to balance and regulate the world's climate: the poles would remain frozen throughout the year, temperate zones would also be much colder and endure freezing conditions for much of the year, and the tropics would be much hotter than they are today.

Polar ice is found at both poles, but the Arctic and the Antarctica are distinct from each other in that the one is a small ocean covered by a thick layer of ice, and surrounded more or less by the great land masses of Greenland, Eurasia and North America; and the other is a continental landmass covered in snow and ice with a surrounding sea – the Southern Ocean – which will also be covered by greater or lesser amounts of sheet ice depending on the time of year.

Polar ice

In the depths of winter in the Arctic Ocean, sea ice covers about 9 million square miles; this reduces to about 4 million square miles during the summer months, so roughly half of the ice will remain permanently frozen. This is known as polar ice or multi-year ice and is generally about 20 feet thick, although the effects of global warming on the climate could mean that this permanent layer will begin to melt. The sea ice or pack ice that comes and goes each year around the pole is not static, but moves with the Transpolar Drift in a south-westerly direction around the Arctic Circle, ending up where it began, with some breaking off and drifting down into lower latitudes.

The Southern Ocean

The Southern Ocean which surrounds the continent of Antarctica is larger than the Arctic Ocean and warmed to a certain extent by the neighboring Pacific and Indian Oceans. Formerly part of central Gondwanaland 290 million years ago, Antarctica drifted slowly southward as the single landmass began to break into the individual continents. As it did so, it cooled and by 25 million years ago it was covered with ice.

Sheet ice begins to form at the edges of the Antarctic landmass in March each year, extending northward by as much as 8 miles a day. At its peak, in September, it will have reached 400-1900 miles from the coastline, covering an area of sea twice as large as Antarctica itself.

Ice formation

Water in the Arctic and Antarctic freezes at 35.24°F. As ice forms in the polar seas, most of the salt is left in the surrounding water. Crystals of ice, known as frazil ice will float near the surface of the water, congealing to form a thicker textured ice as it cools further.
As temperatures drop further still, more solid flat ice is formed in between the textured "soup", until eventually the soup itself freezes and the sea becomes solid. Freezing continues slowly beneath the insulating surface layer until it reaches a thickness of between 3-6 feet by the end of the winter. In rough seas, polar ice may break into large pieces known as ice floes, which may then refreeze as pack ice.

In Antarctica, where ice sheets and glaciers meet the sea, large chunks may break off to form icebergs. The largest of these are tabular bergs, which can measure several miles across and over 650 feet deep. As they drift north, they will be subject to the wind, sun and waves and may disintegrate into smaller pieces. The harvesting of ice bergs – for the massive amounts of fresh water they contain – has been considered in the past, but the vastness of the Southern Ocean and its relative isolation have proved economically and logistically prohibitive.

Opposite: Seals often use slabs of ice as a resting and breeding platform. Seals are streamlined, highly specialized marine creatures that have adapted to life in cold waters with a thick layer of blubber and fur.

Above: A polar ice cap is a high-latitude region of a planet or moon that is covered in ice. Polar ice caps form because high-latitude regions receive less energy in the form of solar radiation from the sun than equatorial regions, resulting in lower surface temperatures. Seasonal variations of the ice caps take place due to varied solar energy absorption as a planet and its moons revolve around their sun.

Right: Antarctica is an isolated continent that is no longer home to any terrestrial animals, with the exception of a few insects and other small invertebrates. However, there is a diverse and abundant community of animals living within the Antarctic shelf. Several varieties of penguins live on the ice around the edge of the Antarctic peninsula as well as the larger icebergs that break off from the Antarctic ice. To withstand the harsh conditions of the Antarctic, their bodies are insulated by a thick layer of blubber and a dense network of waterproof plumage.

El Niño and La Niña

This phenomenon occurs off the coast of Central and South America, but has consequences for weather patterns further afield; indeed on the other side of the globe.

In the coastal waters of Peru, the warm surface waters are normally blown offshore by the trade winds, allowing colder, nutrient-rich water to move up to the surface. This is known as upwelling and is important for the livelihoods of the fishing community in that region. The nutrients attract and support vast blooms of plankton, which in turn are fed upon by massive populations of anchovy.

In El Niño years, for reasons which are not entirely clear, the trade winds die down and the warm water is left near the shore. The lack of nutrients means a dearth of plankton; the anchovy themselves also need cold water and with no food the fish are unable to survive in such conditions. The fishing industry is severely affected or, in years when the El Niño effect is particularly pronounced, is decimated.

La Niña is the return of the upwelling, usually the following year when the trade winds again push the warm water out to sea.

El Niño's global effect on weather patterns is now widely recognized; its influence is now felt far and wide. The trade winds that would normally carry moisture-laden air to Pacific islands such as Hawaii and Papua New Guinea die down in El Niño years and without them these areas will often suffer drought conditions. The warm waters remaining at the South American coast will heat air masses as they move northward, producing conditions conducive for tornadoes seen in the states of the American south-west.

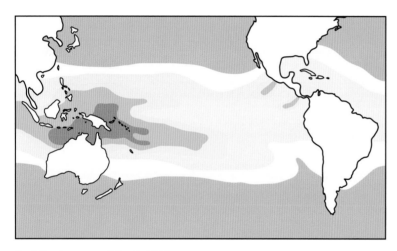

La Niña January - March 1989

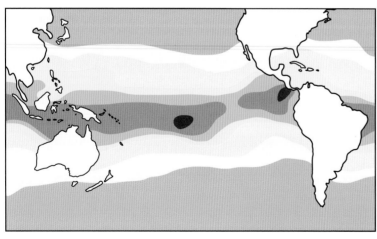

El Niño January - March 1998

68°F   77°F   86°F

Left: El Niño and La Niña alter the temperature of the surface waters across the Pacific. During an El Niño year, the trade winds in the Pacific die down or reverse direction. The upwelling currents in the east subside, and the pool of warm water in the western Pacific spreads out over the entire basin. The phytoplankton in the central Pacific all but disappear, and the populations in the eastern Pacific are lowered significantly. The opposite occurs during La Niña. The easterly trade winds pick up and blow even more hot water into the west. The upwelling increases in the central and eastern regions, causing the phytoplankton concentration to explode.

Opposite: Cold water upwelling from the depths along the coast of South America normally makes for good fishing conditions since it contains nutrients that attract large colonies of anchovy and other types of fish. During an El Niño, fish become scarce due to the dearth of plankton in the warmer water; this can have a significant impact on local fishing economies.

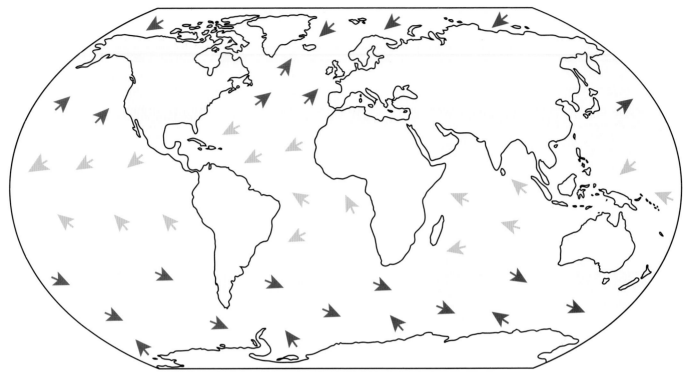

Global wind patterns

◄ Polar Easterlies

➤ Westerlies

◄ North East Trades & South East Trades

Above: The region of Earth receiving the Sun's direct rays is the equator. Here, air is heated and rises, leaving low pressure areas behind. Moving to about thirty degrees north and south of the equator, the warm air from the equator begins to cool and sink. Between thirty degrees latitude and the equator, most of the cooling sinking air moves back to the equator. The rest of the air flows toward the poles. The air movements toward the equator are called trade winds – warm, steady breezes that blow almost continuously. The trade winds coming from the south and the north meet near the equator. These converging trade winds produce general upward winds as they are heated, so there are no steady surface winds. This area of calm is called the doldrums.

Left and opposite below: Damage to coastal property from El Niño in Pacifica, California. El Niño events produce changes in global weather patterns and can cause massive floods in some areas and catastrophic droughts in others.

Above: During the El Niño of 1997 and 1998, the warmed waters covered an area the size of the United States. Vast amounts of heat were pumped into the air above, and the result was a shift in weather patterns that cascaded across much of the world. It also spawned a string of deadly tornadoes that ripped through central Florida. The conditions that El Niño bring are particularly conducive to the formation of tornadoes.

The Moon and tides

The daily, or sometimes twice-daily, ebb and flow of the waters around our coasts has been going on for billions of years. It is only in the last few centuries, however, that man has come to an understanding of the complex nature of this phenomenon.

The occurrence of tides is governed by the gravitational pull of the Moon and the Sun, combined with the rotation of the Earth and the Moon; they may also be affected by water depth and the particular shape and size of the coastline.

As the Moon is closer to Earth than the Sun, its gravitational pull is greater; the Earth also exerts a centrifugal force as it spins on its axis and this will balance the pull of the moon to a greater or lesser extent depending on their relative positions. The oceans on the side of Earth facing the Moon will experience a stronger pull and be moved that bit further. On the opposite side, the centrifugal force will be stronger and will pull the waters on that side to the same degree. These two movements are the high tides that most seas and oceans experience twice a day; low tides will occur in the waters in between these two areas as the centrifugal and gravitational forces will have pulled the water away from them.

The tidal range

The cycle of tides is related to the lunar day which lasts 24 hours and 50 minutes, i.e. the time it takes the Moon to make one orbit of the Earth. The most common tide pattern is the one that occurs twice a day – high tide (or water) is followed by low tide every 6 hours 12 minutes. Most of the Atlantic and Indian Ocean tides follow this pattern. In some places, such as the Gulf of Mexico and a lot of Antarctica, there is one tide per day – high and low water are separated by 12 hours 25 minutes. Around the Pacific, tides are generally diurnal, but one of the high tides is much greater than the next one.

The tidal range – the vertical difference in the height of the water at high tide and low tide – will vary around the world, but the usual range is 3-9 feet. The greatest tidal range on Earth – 50 feet – takes place in the Bay of Fundy in Nova Scotia on the east coast of Canada where 100 billion tons of water is moved in and out of the bay twice daily. The strong tidal currents here thoroughly mix the nutrients in the water to provide perfect conditions for phytoplankton to thrive. These blooms attract zooplankton, which in turn attract larger predators such as humpback whales which feed on a daily diet of krill.

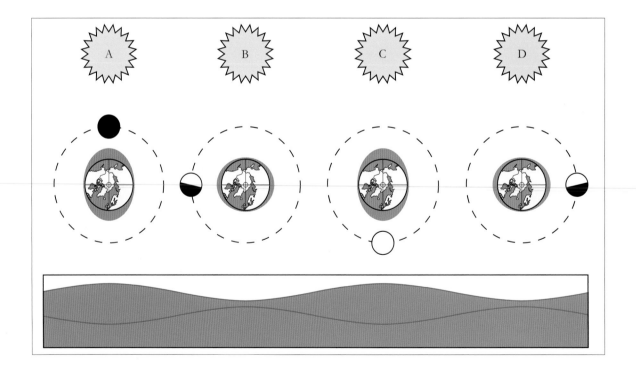

The lunar month

Opposite: Twice during every lunar month (28 days) the tides will change in nature. Spring tides (the name relating to the height of the tide and not the season of the year) are those that give the greatest tidal range and occur when there is a new or a full moon. For such a circumstance, the Moon and the Sun must be aligned; then the gravitational pull of both will work with the Earth's centrifugal force to give a greater high tide (see A and C opposite).

     The position of the Moon in relation to the Earth when it is in the first or last quarter of its cycle means that it will exert a gravitational pull that is at 90° to the Sun's pull (see B and D opposite). This will have the effect of cancelling out each pull to a certain extent and so the height of the high tide will be reduced. These are known as neap tides.

Above: The gravitational pull of the Moon on the Earth is twice that of the Sun because, although the Moon is much smaller, it is 400 times closer to the Earth.

Waves and tsunamis

Created by and deriving their energy from the wind, waves can be a mighty and destructive force, responsible for the loss of human life around the world, not to mention the sinking of boats and the washing away of houses and settlements around our coasts.

Although looking at waves on the open ocean it appears as if the water is moving in a ridge across the surface, this is not the case. It is instead the energy transferred from the wind into the wave that is being transported, through the circular motion of the water. The energy is released as the wave breaks; the bigger the wave, the more energy released.

As the wind blows across the open sea it causes ripples; these begin to form a crest as the wind pushes at the top of the ripple, and eddies of water at the front of the nascent wave help it to take on its familiar shape. Within the wave, the water is moving in circles: up and forward to the crest and then down and backward. In this way, the energy stored in the water is moved along.

The distance over which the wind blows across the water is known as the fetch, and it is this which determines the height of a wave. The longest fetch is in the Pacific, and so it is here that the biggest waves are usually to be found, reaching heights of up to 50 feet. The highest ever recorded wave was 112 feet high.

Waves break as they reach the shore. This is because the seabed rises up as it nears land to meet the shoreline; the waves will be slowed by the resulting friction and therefore get closer together; as they back up, the height of the wave increases and the length shortens. The water at the top of the wave is not affected by the friction of the seabed as much as that at the bottom and will therefore move faster, causing the crest to spill over itself. It is at this point that the wave breaks, releasing its energy onto the shore.

Above: It is only when a tsunami reaches the shore that its full destructive forces are unleashed. The after effects are not just confined to coastal areas. The force and speed of the wave and huge volume of water give the tsunami enough momentum to carry seawater and debris a long way inland.

Opposite: Waves are characterized by their dimensions. The highest part is called the crest or peak; and the lowest part, or hollow, is called the trough. A wave's dimensions are its height, which is the vertical distance between the crest and the trough; its wavelength, which is the distance between one wave and the next, measured from crest to crest or trough to trough; and its period, which is the time required for a wave to pass a fixed point.

Tsunamis

Derived from the Japanese meaning "Harbor wave", tsunamis have also been known as tidal waves, although they have nothing to do with tides. They are in fact triggered by the shock waves from earthquakes and volcanic activity beneath the oceans. Starting as a fairly small wave, usually less than 3 feet high, a tsunami will gather speed as it radiates outward until it meets the continental slope where it will slow down. Again, as it slows, and because of the huge amount of power pushing it, it will grow massively in height very quickly, rushing inland with devastating results.

Tsunamis commonly occur in the Pacific Ocean, because of the instability of the tectonic plates around its rim. When Krakatoa in Indonesia erupted in 1883, tsunamis traveled half way round the globe, killing 36,000 people.

The most recent tsunami catastrophe occurred on 26th December 2004 as a result of an earthquake (measuring 9.5 on the Richter Scale) in the Indian Ocean. As well as striking Indonesia, Thailand and parts of Malaysia, a series of tsunamis reached Sri Lanka, India, Bangladesh and the Maldives. They wrought destruction on a truly massive scale, with over 230,000 lives being lost and millions left homeless. As a result, there has been a call for the establishment of a global tsunami monitoring system, similar to that already in existence in Hawaii.

LIFE IN THE OCEANS

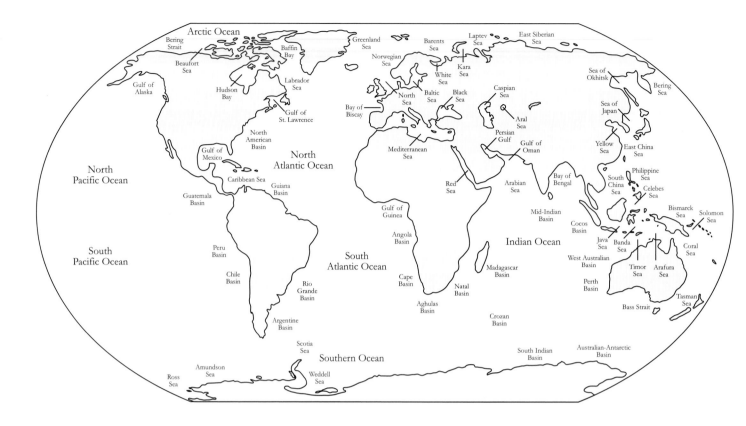

The largest habitat

The world's oceans represent the largest habitat for life on Earth; a space around 250 times greater than that offered by the terrestrial environment, and yet, of the approximately 1.5 to 1.75 million species so far described by science, fewer than a quarter are marine. However, it is estimated that there are several million more species on the planet, and many of these are expected to inhabit the oceans; a realm that remains largely unexplored. In fact, new species are constantly being discovered in the marine environment, particularly in its as yet uncharted depths. The oceans have acted as a laboratory for the evolution of life for most of our planet's history, and today it is widely recognized that they contain the greatest diversity of life on Earth: from ancient microbial forms to the largest animal the world has ever known, and from mammals and reptiles that have made an evolutionary return to the sea to a whole host of organisms that have no closely related terrestrial counterparts.

The origin and evolution of life

The precise origins of life on Earth may never be fully understood, and speculative theories about where life first occurred range from the extraterrestrial to within volcanic rocks or terrestrial ponds, at coastal hot springs, the ocean's surface, or at deep sea hydrothermal vents. However, it is thought that around four billion years ago – within the first billion years of the Earth's history the conditions were exactly right, with the necessary mixture of chemical elements such as hydrogen, oxygen, carbon and nitrogen for the formation of the first organic compounds to take place. Driven by intense heat, lightning or radiation this process, which also required water in order to occur, resulted in the appearance of amino acids: the building blocks of life.

Thus it is almost certain that the primordial oceans became a chemical soup, awash with simple organic molecules, which combined and recombined over millions of years to form increasingly complex substances, such as proteins, ribonucleic acid (RNA), and deoxyribonucleic acid (DNA). These developments led in turn to the ability for self-replication and the possibility for mutation and ultimately, through a process of natural selection, to the organisation of early organic molecules into the first simple lifeforms: single-celled prokaryotes, such as archaea and bacteria, which lacked specialized structures such as a true nucleus, or a protective membrane around their DNA. They probably metabolized such substances as methane, hydrogen, sulphates and carbon dioxide in order to drive their life processes.

In time however, more complex organisms developed, such as cyanobacteria, or blue-green algae, which contained chlorophyll and were able to photosynthesize, harnessing the sun's energy to produce food. It is thought that such organisms may have dominated the Earth for over one billion years, and that during that time they essentially functioned as rudimentary plants, gradually increasing the amount of oxygen that was available in the atmosphere and the oceans. This change is likely to have been detrimental to most other forms of life, but in time would lead to the formation of the ozone layer, which would protect the Earth and its inhabitants from the Sun's damaging ultraviolet radiation, and would eventually result in the proliferation of respiration, which is used by the majority of plants and animals known today.

However, initially, the evolutionary pressures created by these atmospheric changes may well have prompted symbiotic relationships and the merging of various microbial forms to form more complex organisms such as the precursors of multi-celled lifeforms. These were the eukaryotes, which first appeared around 2.1 billion years ago, and led to a diverse range of protists and protoctists, all of which are thought to have possessed a nucleus and other complex cell structures. A further, highly significant development then occurred around 1.8 billion years ago, with the advent of sexual reproduction. This dramatically speeded up the process of evolution by combining the genetic material of two parents by means of specialized sex cells or gametes, thereby increasing the genetic diversity of the offspring.

Multi-cellular life
The next major development, and a further step toward true multi-cellular life, is thought to have taken place approximately 1.4 billion years ago, with the appearance of the first colonial animals, such as sponges. They comprised a variety of inter-dependent single-celled organisms that performed particular tasks, so that the colony functioned, in essence, as a single entity. This was followed by the first metazoans, around 680 million years ago, which may well have been similar to the most simple multi-celled animals alive today – the cnidarians or jellyfish, sea anemones, corals and sea firs. They all possess a radial symmetry and two layers of

Opposite: The world's oceans represent the largest habitat for life on Earth; a space around 250 times greater than that offered by the terrestrial environment.

Below: Sirenians, such as the West Indian Manatee, (*Trichechus manatus*), are the only herbivorous marine mammals.

years, evolution would give rise to the cartilaginous fish and bony fish, amphibians, reptiles, birds and mammals. Meanwhile, an even greater profusion of invertebrates – which in fact are thought to account for some 97 percent of animal species in existence today were also evolving.

Regardless of the habitats in which it occurs today, be they terrestrial, freshwater or marine, the huge diversity of life on Earth can be traced back to oceanic origins; it is believed that for perhaps three of the four billion years over which life has been evolving, it remained there. Moreover, it seems certain that an incredible wealth of species have always remained there, multiplying and mutating in the unseen depths, still awaiting discovery.

Left: A tiny, transparent crustacean forages amongst coral polyps.

Below: Corals, anemones and their relatives, are thought to be similar to some of the earliest multi-cellular life on Earth.

Opposite: Distribution of marine life. The vast majority of marine organisms feeding on phytoplankton and zooplankton will use the darkness as a means of escaping attention. During the day, they will swim deeper in the twilight zone where predators find it tricky to detect them in the gloom.

cells, typically surrounded by nematocysts or stinging cells.

This is thought to have been followed firstly by the development of a central, third layer of cells, in which muscles and organs were formed; resulting in early worm-like animals and flatworms, and later the additional development of the body cavity, which gave rise to the nematode and segmented annelid worms. Following on from this, around 570 million years ago, there began a massive diversification of multi-cellular animals in the oceans, which is sometimes referred to as the Cambrian explosion, during which, examples from the vast majority of all animal phyla known today, first appeared on Earth. The majority of these animals were invertebrates, which significantly, began to develop exoskeletons, hard shells and jointed legs, but there were also chordates.

Vertebrate animals

The phylum *Chordata* contains primitive, invertebrate-like chordates such as the tunicates or sea squirts which belong to the subphylum *Urochordata*, as well as the seemingly fish-like lancelets of the subphylum *Cephalochordata*. The third subphylum of the group is *Vertebrata*, or the vertebrate – those animals which possess a backbone. The earliest known vertebrate animal from the fossil record is Myllokunmingia, which is thought to be a primitive, jawless fish much like a hagfish. From these humble beginnings over millions of

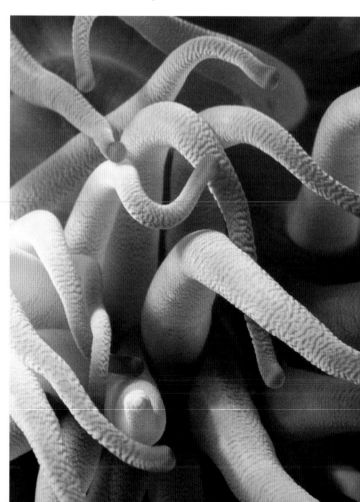

The diversity of marine life and ocean food webs

Today, six kingdoms are widely accepted at the top level of scientific classification: the microbial, single-celled *Archaea* and *Bacteria*, which are the most numerous, diverse and pervasive of all organisms; the *Protista*, which incorporates a range of lifeforms that seem to lie somewhere between animals and plants, and which are an important element of the ocean's plankton; the *Plantae*, or plants, which is generally taken to include the seaweeds, although some forms of algae are often regarded as either protists or bacteria; the *Fungi*, which are actually more closely related to animals than plants, and like the bacteria are important decomposers; and the *Animalia*, which includes all of the invertebrate and vertebrate animals. Representatives of all of these kingdoms inhabit the oceans today, and all have their roles to play within the intricate cycle of life: participating in both the global recycling of energy, chemicals and nutrients, and the complex, but perhaps

more localized food webs of particular ocean habitats, ecosystems and communities.

In a simplified food chain, organisms are represented sequentially as connective links, from the primary producers to the herbivores and carnivores. Whilst such systems do represent part of the process, the actual feeding relationships tend to be far more complex and diverse. With rare exceptions, the primary producers, or autotrophs, which are capable of producing their own food, are indeed consumed by herbivorous organisms, which are then consumed by carnivorous ones. All of them occur in a stunning array of forms that demonstrate particular physical and behavioral adaptations appropriate to their roles. However, a food web more accurately describes the variety of associations between species, which may occupy different niches or levels at different times in their development, or feed on a variety of other species that fulfil different positions within the web. In such a system it is also essential to consider the detritivores and decomposers, which break down dead organic material, and in so doing release inorganic compounds back into the system to be recycled by the primary producers.

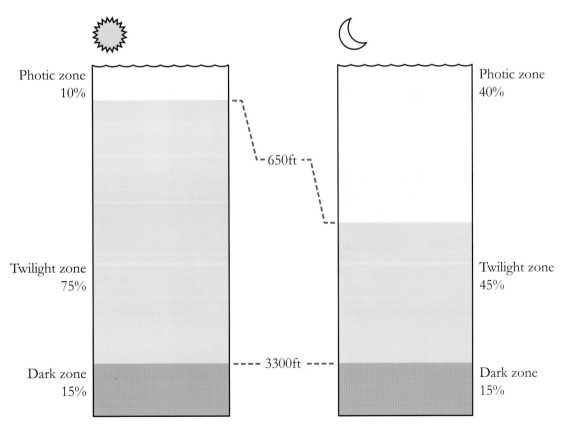

Photic zone
10%

Twilight zone
75%

Dark zone
15%

650ft

3300ft

Photic zone
40%

Twilight zone
45%

Dark zone
15%

Distribution of marine life

Plankton:
The foundation of ocean life

With the exception of certain autotrophic archaea and bacteria, which are capable of manufacturing their own food in the absence of sunlight, the ocean's primary producers are photosynthesising plants, which create their food using the energy of the Sun. However, whereas on land these plants tend to be relatively large, in the oceans the majority of these primary producers, which represent the base of almost all known food webs, and thus support almost all of the other marine lifeforms, are the billions of microscopic single-celled plants, known as phytoplankton. These in turn are largely consumed by vast numbers of tiny free-swimming herbivorous animals (mainly copepod crustaceans, which make up part of the zooplankton; with the remainder of that group consisting of vertebrate and invertebrate eggs, known collectively as the meroplankton) and carnivorous planktonic animals that may prey on the herbivorous zooplankton, each other or in some cases, even larger animals such as small fish. The zooplankton meanwhile fall prey to, and sustain, animals that may be as small as themselves or as large as the huge planktivorous sharks and whales.

Phytoplankton

The phytoplankton fall into two main groups, the diatoms, which are predominantly found drifting in temperate waters, and the dinofagellates, many of which are capable of active swimming, and which occur mainly in tropical waters. Both groups contain numerous species, which, given sufficient sunlight and nutrients, are all capable of incredibly rapid reproduction, resulting in vast seasonal swarms or blooms that frequently turn the surface waters, where they live and photosynthesize, cloudy with their presence and sheer numbers. For whilst they are generally transparent, each contains the colored pigments necessary for photosynthesis. The blooms of some dinoflagellates for example, can result in a phenomenon known as a red tide, which colors the water brown or red. Whilst phytoplankton blooms are essential to the perpetuation of ocean life, some red tides can be devastating to other organisms, as the plankton species involved may deplete the available oxygen and nutrients. They also contain potent toxins, which are capable of polluting the surrounding water or rapidly entering directly into the food chain, killing invertebrates and fish, and being potentially hazardous to man.

Zooplankton

A huge diversity of animal forms make up the zooplankton: from the eggs and larvae of mollusks and fish, to both single-celled and multi-cellular organisms which are planktonic throughout their often short-lived existences. The herbivorous copepod crustaceans are amongst the most numerous and important, and may in fact be amongst the most abundant animals on the planet. Following closely behind the phytoplankton blooms, these shrimp-like animals rapidly reproduce as they graze, consuming thousands of diatoms each day and producing several hundred eggs each week. The larvae then hatch and mature at an astonishing rate, maintaining the vast swarms for as long as food is available. Despite their diminutive size, they are fairly complex animals, which often possess an array of sensory equipment to detect the phytoplankton, and are typically equipped with hair-like cilia on their legs to draw in and trap their food. Other copepods meanwhile may be carnivorous, even feeding on their own kind; these in turn often fall prey to other carnivorous planktonic animals such as the gelatinous jellyfish, siphonophores, swimming pteropod snails, larvaceans and salps, which may trail deadly stinging tentacles or retractable mucus webs into the water to ensnare their prey, or simply draw in water as they swim, filtering their food as they do so.

The vast quantities of zooplankton, herbivores and carnivores alike, go on to feed a huge range of fish, mammals and seabirds, many of which migrate seasonally over long distances to reach these food sources, and time their reproductive cycles to coincide with the availability of food that is ensured by the plankton blooms. In the complex ocean food webs, it is not only the planktivores that are sustained by such blooms, but a host of carnivores that feed on those animals as well.

Above: Marine zooplankton, magnified x 16. These are various shrimp-like crustaceans at different larval stages.

Opposite: Marine phytoplankton, magnified x 20.

Feeding

The methods of feeding employed by marine animals are truly diverse. The very nature of the ocean, as an aquatic environment, ensures that some of these methods, such as filter-feeding, are unlike any that are encountered in terrestrial habitats, although it has its equivalent in freshwater. Additionally, marine organisms display a wide range of strategies and sensory adaptations for locating their food, and an equally varied assortment of defensive methods for avoiding predation: from camouflage, to armour and venom.

Filter-feeding

With such an abundance of planktonic food available in the oceans, as well as suspended particles of organic detritus, it is perhaps not surprising that many disparate animals have evolved methods of filter-feeding: straining or siphoning such material from the water column as they swim, or adopting sedentary lifestyles, where they simply wait for passing food. Some animals, such as the baleen whales, sieve vast quantities of zooplankton from the water through their baleen plates; whilst others, such as tubeworms and feather stars

Below: The ocean consists of different layers. From the sunlit surface waters of the photic zone, down to the deep sea trenches of the Hadal zone, where no light ever penetrates.

extend feathery tentacles or arms into the current; still others, including certain copepod crustaceans, may trap their food with hair-like cilia on the outsides of their bodies, or like sea squirts and sponges, draw in food and water by beating cilia within their bodies. Similarly, many bivalve mollusks possess two siphons: one through which water and food is brought in, and another through which the water is expelled.

Detritivores and sediment-swallowing

Much of the particulate food, including dead organic matter and faecal waste that is not extracted from the water column, descends to the sea floor, where it is rapidly broken down by bacteria. These in turn, along with any remaining organic material, and fine inorganic sediment such as sand and mud, provide a source of food for numerous worms, sea cucumbers, crabs and even fish; they often simply ingest the sediment and digest any organic material from it, expelling the inorganic matter as waste, or else they may pick though it with specialized mouthparts. Other detritivores meanwhile include a host of invertebrates, hagfish and other carrion-eaters, which may begin the process of breaking down animal carcasses into smaller parts as they feed.

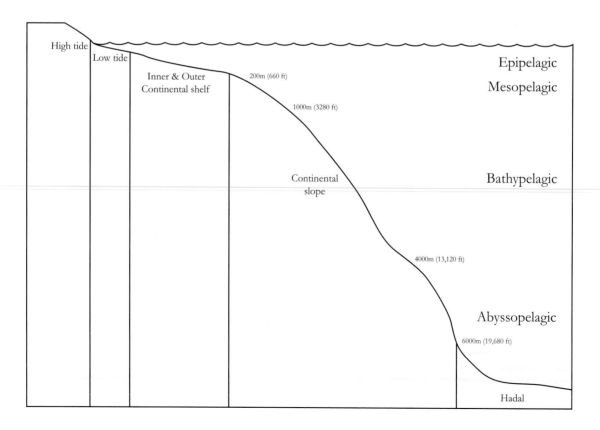

Grazing

In sunlit shallow waters, where algae and seagrasses are able to photosynthesize and grow, they may form blanketing mats, dense seaweed forests or meadows, all of which may be directly grazed by a huge variety of animals. These include gastropod mollusks, or sea snails, which use their rasping mouthparts, known as a radula to strip away the vegetation, and sea urchins, which possess tooth-like structures on their undersides that perform a similar function. Meanwhile, many larger animals, including fish, turtles and mammals such as sirenians, also graze large quantities of marine vegetation. Additionally, there are several animals, including echinoderms and fish, which "graze" upon soft-bodied sedentary invertebrates, such as corals and similar polyp animals.

Predation

Searching and hunting for prey often involves expending a great deal of energy, and so many larger animals, such as penguins and other diving birds, pelagic fish, including billfish and sharks, as well as seals and sea lions, and the toothed whales, have become highly efficient at doing so. They are often capable of great speed and maneuvrability, and possess heightened senses, sharp bills or powerful teeth and jaws, in order to maximize the potential for securing a meal. In more sheltered habitats, many free-swimming predators opt for the sit-and-wait tactics of stealth and camouflage; perhaps hiding in crevices, amongst vegetation, or half-buried in the sediment on the sea floor, before lunging to grasp their prey.

Some fish and all of the sea snakes, are capable of killing their prey with venom, as are the jellyfish and cone snails amongst the invertebrates. However, most slow-moving carnivorous invertebrates tend to feed on sedentary ones such as mollusks, sometimes forcing open their protective shells or drilling through them, and digesting the soft body parts with enzymes or their own everted stomachs.

Remarkably, some sea cucumbers are able to eviscerate their internal organs in order to distract or even entangle would-be predators, whilst many starfish can easily regenerate lost limbs. Other unusual marine defence mechanisms include the release of clouds of inky, bioluminescent or toxic liquids.

Above: Scalloped Hammerhead Shark (*Sphyrna lewini*). Sharks are highly efficient predators, capable of great speed and maneuvrability in order to maximize the potential for securing a meal.

Movement

Whilst there are many sedentary and sessile invertebrates to be found in the marine environment, which after a drifting larval stage may live permanently attached to the substrate, there are also those that burrow and creep into or over it. They may move with muscular contractions of the body, as in many worms, or with a modified muscular foot, as in many bivalves and gastropods. There are also echinoderms such as starfish that are able to walk over the ocean floor, using the thousands of tube-feet present on their arms, and the arthropods, such as crabs and lobsters, which walk on jointed legs. Even some fish possess modified pectoral fins that provide them with the ability to walk on the sea bed.

However, the density of water brings increased buoyancy, supporting weight and enabling many animals to float with relative ease. Some do so more or less passively, perhaps beating tiny hairs to effect some degree of control as they float, but a common characteristic of ocean movement, particularly amongst larger animals, is powered swimming, which is evident in the fishes, marine reptiles, diving birds and mammals. Most of them possess a streamlined body shape and a smooth surface in order to reduce drag, and are able to

power themselves through the water with undulations of the body and fins or paddle-like flippers. In order to improve buoyancy, many fish also possess gas-filled swim bladders or hold reserves of fatty oils within their bodies, but there are also species that must swim constantly to avoid sinking.

Relatively few invertebrates are well adapted for powered swimming, although there are crustaceans such as swimming crabs, which have flattened, paddle-like limbs, and mollusks such as the pteropods, or wing-footed snails, which are able to swim by beating the edges of their modified mollusk foot like a pair of wings. The most effective method however, is perhaps that of other mollusks, the cuttlefish and squid, which use a continuous, rippling fin in order to effect forward motion, and are able to move backwards by drawing in and rapidly expelling water from their bodies.

Above: Many fish possess a swim bladder, which provides them with neutral buoyancy, allowing them to remain afloat effortlessly.

Left: Echinoderms, such as these starfish, move over the sea floor using tiny tube-feet.

Opposite above: A female octopus will guard her eggs without feeding, and will die of starvation shortly after they hatch.

Opposite below: Different fish use a variety of different breeding methods, from broadcast spawning to the bearing of live young.

Reproduction

For more than one billion years all life in the ocean reproduced by asexual methods, with organisms simply dividing their single cell in two, in a process of splitting or budding, to give rise to new individuals; to this day, certain invertebrates, such as corals, sea fans and anemones, continue to do so. The benefits of such a system include the speed and ease with which it can take place; there is no need for finding or attracting a mate, for example. However, asexual reproduction limits genetic variation, which, according to the principles of natural selection, can better insure the survival of individuals and species under changing environmental conditions. Additionally, the process also tends to limit the dispersal, and therefore the distribution of new individuals.

The development of sexual reproduction, by which the genetic material of two parents is combined, dramatically increased genetic variability, and in the case of oviparous, or egg-laying organisms that fertilize their eggs externally, the potential for dispersal was also increased. However, in such cases, the possibility of

predation of the eggs and larvae can be a major risk. In order to combat this, many fish and invertebrates are broadcast spawners, producing and releasing hundreds, thousands or even millions of eggs at a single time. As few as one percent of the young produced in this way may survive to adulthood, but the vast quantities ensure that at least some individuals will survive to perpetuate the species; those that do not, help to sustain a myriad of other marine organisms as food. Other animals may instead guard their eggs, as in the case of certain fish and octopus, whilst others still are viviparous, giving birth to live, often well developed young. This is practised by various species of sharks and other fish, as well as mammals. Many animals may abandon their young shortly after birth, but mammals will look after their offspring for a protracted period, generally until the juveniles are capable of fending for themselves.

Some marine animals use a combination of sexual and asexual methods, seemingly taking advantage of the best each has to offer: being able to sustain their species when mates may not be available, but also able to benefit from genetic variability. Many marine organisms are also hermaphroditic, producing both male and female gametes, and some are able to self-fertilize. This is particularly prevalent amongst colonial animals such as corals, but remarkably, certain fish also possess this ability, especially some of those encountered in the deep sea, where finding a mate may be highly difficult. Other fish meanwhile, tend to change sex as they develop, or may do so in order to redress an imbalance in population dynamics.

ABOVE THE TIDELINE

At home on land and sea

On sea cliffs and amongst sand dunes, we may find numerous hardy, terrestrial plants, such as lichens, mosses and dune grasses. They are adapted to withstand the high stresses of the coastal environment, such as a lack of freshwater and the effects of corrosive, wind-borne salt carried from the surface of the sea. But with the exception of hardy periwinkles and some amphipod and isopod crustaceans, almost no animals associated with the marine environment are ever found beyond the supralittoral fringe, that is, out of the reach of the ocean's spray, or above the limit of the high tide. For on the landward side of this border, we essentially enter the realm of the terrestrial. Yet here, even terrestrial fauna tends to be limited to insects, and perhaps amongst well established dunes and on cliff tops, to lizards and grazing rabbits. Larger terrestrial mammals

may visit as opportunistic scavengers, picking amongst the debris left high up the beach after storm tides, but there are few animals resident here.

However, at certain times of the year, such locations may be transformed by a bustle of activity, as marine mammals and reptiles, whose ancestors were once terrestrial, return to the land to give birth or to lay their eggs, out of the reach of the sea. Similarly, seabirds, some of which may spend almost their entire lives out on and over the open oceans, often congregate in vast breeding colonies on cliffs to lay their eggs and raise their young.

Above: An Estuarine crocodile (*Crocodylus porosus*) seizes a bird, Australia.

Opposite: Land crabs on Clipperton Island in the Pacific. Long adapted to the terrestrial environment, these must still return to the sea to spawn, and some do so in their millions, providing a dramatic spectacle for the human observer, and a welcome meal for numerous hungry predators.

Sea turtles

Modern sea turtles are thought to have evolved about 120 million years ago and are highly adapted to a marine existence, with their relatively light, streamlined shells, and limbs which are modified into large flippers for swimming. Some are even able to supplement their oxygen supply, which is normally obtained by breathing air at the water's surface, through the lining of the pharynx, which operates as a gill, and although some turtles will occasionally haul out on the beaches of remote islands, most spend almost their entire lives in the sea. However, turtles reproduce by laying leathery eggs, which require incubation, and the females of all species must come ashore in order to bury their eggs in the sand.

The breeding season

At the start of the breeding season, the sexually mature turtles migrate into the coastal waters of their breeding grounds, along the shores where they themselves were hatched. In the case of the Green Turtle (*Chelonia mydas*), which typically feeds in the shallow tropical waters of the Atlantic, along the coasts of the Americas, this can entail a journey of over 1,000 miles to the tiny Ascension Island in the middle of the Atlantic Ocean, where some 5,000 Green Turtles are known to lay their eggs. Other highly pelagic species, such as the Olive Ridley Turtle (*Lepidochelys olivacea*), may undertake comparable migrations. The Olive Ridley is also thought to be the most abundant marine turtle species, and breeds in huge numbers off the Pacific coast of Mexico and Costa Rica, and also in India, where hundreds of thousands of females lay their eggs simultaneously, an event which is known as an arribada.

Mating occurs at sea, following which the males will return to their feeding grounds, leaving the females as they prepare to nest. The females are usually ready to lay their eggs about two weeks after fertilization has taken place, at which time they will leave the sea and begin to haul themselves up the nesting beaches, which are also known as rookeries.

Nesting in the sand

The females emerge from the sea at night, under the cover of darkness, and drag themselves far up the beaches until they are above the tideline. Being highly cumbersome on land, this in itself can be an exhaustive process for the turtles, but once they are far enough from the sea, they must then dig a nest in the sand. This is executed with the rear flippers, and nests may be surprisingly deep, at about 32 inches. Once the nest has been excavated, the female will lay a clutch of between 50 and 180 eggs, depending on the species, before burying them in the sand, and heading back to sea.

The entire process may take several hours, and be performed up to seven times during the breeding season, with successive clutches of eggs being fertilized with stored sperm at approximately two-week intervals. The females will often eat very little during this period, and instead will rely predominantly on their reserves of fat, but once egg-laying is completed, they will return to their feeding grounds and resume eating. Unusually for reptiles, some turtles are almost entirely herbivorous, feeding on algae, but many also consume benthic or free-floating invertebrates. The Hawksbill Turtle (*Eretmochelys imbricata*) feeds almost exclusively on sponges.

Adult turtles do not care for their young, leaving the eggs to incubate and hatch alone. Hatching occurs after about two months, although in higher temperatures the incubation period may be shorter. Temperature also has a bearing on the gender of the hatchlings, with more females being produced in warmer temperatures.

Running the gauntlet

Once hatched, the young turtles dig themselves out of their nests, and must then run the gauntlet of predators, including birds, mammals and crabs as they attempt to make it to the sea. Hatching usually occurs at night, in order to reduce predation, but despite this, it has been demonstrated that the hatchlings rely on light to guide them to the water, and at night instinctively head towards the reflective surface of the sea. Once they have entered the water, the baby turtles swim out in the direction the waves are coming from, heading toward deeper water.

No one is certain where the young turtles spend the first months, or even years, of their lives, but it is thought that they may drift with rafts of floating sargassum seaweed, which provide food and shelter, and disperse widely with the currents. Juvenile turtles will then typically move into coastal waters, although the unusual Leatherback Turtle (*Dermochelys coriacea*), which is the only member of the family *Dermochelyidae*, and has a leathery, rather than bony shell, remains pelagic throughout its life.

Turtles can be extremely long-lived, but of those that hatch, relatively few will make it to adulthood to return to breed in the waters that they first entered. Quite how adult turtles are able to find their way back to these nesting sites remains something of a mystery, but it is thought that they may orient themselves and navigate according to the Earth's magnetic field. Males may sometimes breed annually, but females will usually reproduce every two to five years.

Above: A Pacific Ridley Turtle (*Lepidochelys olivacea*) buries its eggs on a Mexican beach.

Opposite: The Hawksbill Turtle (*Eretmochelys imbricate*) was once widely hunted for its beautiful shell.

Land crabs

When the first arthropods emerged from the sea to begin to colonize the land around 450 million years ago, eventually giving rise to the arachnids and insects, it was primarily their exoskeletons, comprising protein and chitin, which guaranteed their success. This hard outer casing provided the support which enabled improved mobility on land and offered protection from desiccation and predators. It is thought that the first terrestrial arthropods were most likely early predecessors of the centipedes or scorpions, rather than crustaceans, a group of arthropods which remain largely aquatic. Along with developments to their gill structures, it is the arthropod exoskeleton that has enabled land crabs to migrate directly to land from the marine environment, without first evolving through stages of brackish and freshwater existence, and they are the only decapod crustaceans to have done so.

The search for water

Most land crabs excavate deep burrows in order to reach the water table, and even those that cannot survive prolonged periods of submersion require water in order to moisten their gill structures so that they can breathe on land. Moreover, every species goes through an aquatic larval stage, and the adults must return to water in order to release their eggs or newly emergent young.

Two crab families

The land crabs belong to two distinct families; *Gecarcinidae*, or the true land crabs, and *Coenobitidae*, the terrestrial hermit crabs. This latter group is composed of eight species, including the only representative of the genus Birgus, the Coconut, or Robber Crab (*Birgus latro*), which is the world's largest terrestrial arthropod. This species is an inhabit of humid tropical islands in the Indian and Pacific oceans, and may attain a length of some 16 inches, with a leg span of around 3 feet, and a weight of as much as 9 pounds, although much larger specimens have been reported. It is also thought to be extremely long-lived, with a lifespan of perhaps 30 years or more.

When young, it utilizes empty snail shells in much the same way as other hermit crabs, and may even use discarded coconut shells, but it rapidly outgrows even these. By adulthood its carapace is strong enough not to require additional protection of this kind. However, it tends to remain in its burrow during the day in order to stay moist, and may do so for extended periods when moulting. It typically emerges at night to forage for food, and is omnivorous, with a diet consisting of fruit, leaf-litter, other vegetation and carrion. At times it may also feed on small animals, but it is perhaps best known for feeding on coconuts, being able to climb trees in order to reach them, and with claws powerful enough to break their shells.

Coconut crab

The adult Coconut Crab (*Birgus latro*) may be found far inland, and is able to breathe out of water using modified gills known as branchiostegal lungs, but these must be kept moist with either fresh or salt water. Its rudimentary gills, once used to breathe underwater, no longer function adequately however, and it will quickly drown if submerged.

Mating occurs on land following which, the females produce a number of eggs, which they secure to their abdomen. These are carried on the body for some months until they are ready to hatch, when the females make their way down to the ocean's edge to release their larvae into the water. The young are carried by the tide for about one month, before settling on the seabed, where they will remain for about a further month, protecting their soft bodies with mollusk shells. At the age of about three months, the crabs will emerge on to land, where they will then remain, only venturing to the water's edge to obtain water or to spawn.

The Red Crab (*Gecarcoidea natalis*), of Christmas Island in the Indian Ocean is a true land crab, and is much smaller, at around 6 inches in length, but in certain respects its behavior is similar to that of the Coconut Crab. It tends to inhabit areas of humid rainforest, where it dwells in a burrow to retain moisture, and during the dry season, may remain in its burrow for long periods. However, when active, the Red Crab is usually diurnal. It forages amongst the vegetation of the forest floor, and is also omnivorous, consuming green vegetation, leaves, fruit and flowers, carrion and small invertebrates.

The Red Crab (*Gecarcoidea natalis*) is solitary except when breeding, when it forms huge aggregations. At the start of the rainy season, a spectacular, synchronized migration is undertaken from the forest interior to the coast, involving perhaps hundreds of millions of crabs. This is sparked by the onset of the rains, and timed to coincide with the retreating high tide following the moon's last quarter, when the sea level is most constant, and the adult females are at less risk of drowning.

Mating occurs close to the sea, in burrows excavated by the males, where the females will remain as they produce as many as 100,000 eggs in a brood pouch, over the course of a few days. The eggs will then be released into the ocean, where they immediately hatch, releasing millions of larvae. Those that survive will gather along the shore after about a month, and leave the water after about five days to begin heading inland. Similar mass spawning and migrations are undertaken by other Red Crab species across Cuba, the Bahamas and the Caribbean.

Above: Land crabs are closely related to hermit crabs, and when young, will protect themselves by dwelling in empty shells.

Left: The Coconut Crab (*Birgus latro*) has extremely powerful claws, which are strong enough to break coconuts apart.

Pinnipeds: seals, sea lions and walruses

The pinnipeds, or "fin-footed" animals, which belong to the superfamily Pinnipedia, which includes the true seals of the family *Phocidae*, the eared seals, or fur seals and sea lions, of the family *Otariidae*, and the walruses of the family *Odobenidae*, are carnivorous marine mammals. They are thought to have evolved from terrestrial ancestors during the late Oligocene or early Miocene epochs.

All are well adapted to life in the sea, with feet that have become modified into flippers and a streamlined body shape, but there are also various differences between the families, such as the inability of the true seals to use their hind limbs to move on land, their lack of external ears, and their relatively shorter period of weaning and caring for their young. These factors have led to the suggestion that the true seals may be more highly advanced in their development toward an entirely aquatic existence. Despite their adaptations however, all pinnipeds must still return to land, or in some cases ice, in order to breed.

The young of the Common, or Harbor Seal (*Phoca vitulina*), are born with a waterproof coat and are capable of entering the water just hours, or even minutes after birth, and so are often born on tidal sandbanks, but other pinnipeds are born with a downy, natal coat, and must undergo a moult before they are ready to enter the sea. For this reason, the females must give birth above the reach of the tides.

It was formerly believed that the true seals evolved from an otter-like mammal, whilst the others evolved independently from a bear-like creature around 20 million years ago. Recent genetic analysis suggests that all pinnipeds are descended from a common, bear-like ancestor, and probably diverged into their current families around 25 million years ago.

Below: The California Sea Lion, (*Zalophus californianus*) is a member of the family Otariidae, and is quite mobile on land.

Colonial breeding

Due to the constraints of finding suitable breeding grounds, and in order to maximize the potential for securing a mate and to minimize predation of their young, most pinnipeds breed colonially and synchronously, with females coming into oestrus at the same time. In order to circumvent the need to come ashore twice, for mating and birthing, females give birth to pups which have resulted from the previous year's mating, due to delayed implantation, and then become receptive to males. Breeding is polygynous, with males mating with several females, and as a result, males will usually attempt to secure a territory, or establish their dominance over a harem of females, often with aggressive displays. In some species, such as the elephant seals, vicious fights frequently occur, which may result in bloodshed and even fatalities.

Southern Elephant seals

The male, or bull, Southern Elephant Seal (*Mirounga leonina*), is the largest of the world's pinnipeds, weighing up to 8,800 pounds, and measuring around 20 feet in length. Females, or cows, weigh approximately 2,200 pounds, and attain a length of about 13 feet; the greatest sexual dimorphism in terms of size amongst mammals. The name "elephant seal" is not derived merely from the huge bulk of these animals however, but also from the fact that the males possess an enlarged, trunk-like proboscis, which is used to amplify their roars, particularly during breeding displays.

This species breeds on Antarctic and Subantarctic shores, notably on South Georgia, where an estimated 350,000 individuals, or around half the entire population, come ashore to mate. The bulls arrive first, some weeks before the females, and begin to establish territories, with the largest bulls typically securing the largest territories and the breeding rights to large numbers of females. Once the females arrive, a highly successful male, or "beachmaster," may be able to defend and mate with a harem of perhaps 50 or more females. Less successful, subordinate males may attempt to mate with females on the peripheries of these large groups.

The females give birth to a single pup about a week after their arrival, which possesses a dense black coat, may be over 3 feet in length, and weigh around 100 pounds. These pups are suckled for about three or four weeks, on incredibly rich milk, during which time they may quadruple in weight. The females mate as the young are weaned, and then return to the sea, leaving their pups to fend for themselves.

After a few weeks, the juvenile seals, now with gray, sleek, waterproof coats, make their way to the sea and disperse. The females may become sexually mature after about three years, and males at about six, but it may be several more years until males are powerful enough to command a large harem.

The Northern Fur seal

The Northern Fur Seal breeds in the North Pacific, with huge, well-established colonies on the Pribilof and Commander islands in the Bering Sea, which may number well over one million individuals. These species are also polygynous, with males establishing territories in order to mate with large numbers of females. The eared seals, however, wean their pups for a much longer period, around three to four months. The pups are born within a few days of the female's arrival at the breeding sites, following which the cows will mate, and feed their young for around ten days, before going to sea to feed themselves. They will then alternate between going to sea and nursing their young until the pups are weaned.

Vast well established colonies

The largest pinniped breeding colonies are established not by true seals, but by fur seals, namely, the Northern Fur Seal (*Callorhinus ursinus*) and the Antarctic, or Kerguelen Fur Seal (*Arctocephalus gazella*). Like the Southern Elephant Seal, the Antarctic Fur Seal also breeds on the island of South Georgia, and it does so in vast numbers, with up to an estimated four million individuals coming ashore to reproduce.

Above: Crabeater Seal, Antarctic.

Seabird colonies

Many seabirds are highly pelagic, spending several months at a time wandering over the open oceans in search of food, and often traveling great distances as they do so. A number of species even migrate between the North Atlantic and the Southern Ocean. However, with the exception of the Emperor Penguin (*Aptenodytes forsteri*), which breeds on the Antarctic ice, seabirds must all come to land when breeding, in order to nest, lay their eggs and rear their young, and most do so colonially.

Colonies may vary in size and composition according to species and location, but as seabirds are reliant upon the sea for their food, and are typically not competing for such resources at their chosen nesting sites, where space allows, they can afford to nest in large numbers, and many do so. This is a strategy that not only minimizes predation of eggs and hatchlings by birds such as the Great Black-backed Gull (*Larus marinus*), and the Great Skua (*Stercorarius skua*), but also helps to protect adult birds from raptors such as the Peregrine Falcon (*Falco peregrinus*), and the giant Steller's Sea Eagle (*Haliaeetus pelagicus*), which often patrol the skies close to such colonies in search of stragglers. Additionally, colonial nesting may also help individuals in finding both a mate and food. As the birds are solitary for much of the time, it is also thought that socialization helps to promote both the incentive and physical developments required for successful breeding.

The world's largest breeding colonies
Some of the world's largest breeding colonies are to be found on island cliff faces in the North Atlantic and North Pacific, where there is easy access to the sea and a scarcity of terrestrial predators. Similarly, remote islands tend to be selected by ground-nesting birds in the southern hemisphere, where large cliff faces are less numerous.

Mixed colonies
Seabirds often nest in mixed colonies, and at certain locations these combined aggregations can be vast. In parts of Russia, Iceland, Europe and North America, literally millions of birds crowd the cliff faces, whilst similar numbers nest on southern coasts and islands, at such places as the Falkland Islands, the aptly named Bird Island, South Georgia, and the Tristan da Cunha and Gough Island groups in the mid-South Atlantic Ocean. Smaller but no less significant colonies are to be found on numerous tropical islands in the Pacific, such as the Cook and Pitcairn groups.

The North Pacific

In the North Pacific, some 80 million seabirds are estimated to breed along the coasts of Alaska and far eastern Russia each spring and summer, with between about two and four million birds nesting on the Russian island of Talan alone. In the North Atlantic, Labrador and Newfoundland in Canada and the Island of St Kilda in the Scottish Hebrides are home to some of the largest and most diverse bird colonies in the world, consisting of numerous petrels, terns, gulls, skuas and auks, amongst others.

Auks, such as the Common Guillemot, or Murre (*Uria aalge*), the Thick-billed Murre (*Uria lomvia*), and the Razorbill (*Alca torda*), are often amongst the most numerous species crowding the rocky ledges of North Atlantic cliffs during the breeding season, and are some of the most distinctive, being somewhat penguin-like, with an upright stance and black and white plumage. Like penguins, these birds are also skilled underwater swimmers, and they dive from the surface in search of small fish and invertebrates.

Unlike penguins however, they are capable of flight, and often nest high up on almost vertical cliff faces. Females typically produce a single egg when breeding, which is usually laid on a bare ledge, sometimes surrounded by stones or a small amount of vegetation. In the case of the Common Guillemot, the egg is protected from rolling from its precarious position by its almost conical shape. Although these birds generally pair-up before breeding, males may be left to incubate alone whilst the females go on to mate again, and will then care for their young alone following hatching. The young will typically leave the nest at about three weeks of age, before they are capable of flight, by simply plunging to the water below.

Puffins

The puffins are closely related, also belonging to the auk family *Alcidae*, and are colonial breeders, but the birds tend to excavate burrows on grassy clifftops when nesting. The Tufted Puffin (*Fratercula cirrhata*) and Horned Puffin (*Fratercula corniculata*) are found in the North Pacific, whilst the North Atlantic is home to just one species, the Common or Atlantic Puffin (*Fratercula arctica*). All possess large, distinctive bills, which become particularly colorful when breeding.

Northern Gannet

Also distinctive, with its yellow head, is the Northern Gannet (*Morus bassanus*), which breeds in its largest numbers on St Kilda, and on Bonaventure Island,

Canada. This species may pair for several years, and bonds are reinforced during the breeding season by elaborate courtship displays, which involve preening, bowing and bill-tapping.

Storm Petrol

In the Southern Ocean Wilson's Storm Petrel (*Oceanites oceanicus*), which may be the most abundant bird in the world, nests in colonies of millions, from the coast of Antarctica north to the Falklands, whilst those islands are also home to the largest breeding colonies of one of the largest and most pelagic of all seabirds, the Black-Browed Albatross (*Thalassarche melanophris*).

Boobies

In the tropical Pacific the closely related Boobies, such as the Blue-footed (*Sula nebouxii*), Red-footed (*Sula sula*), Masked (*Sula dactylatra*) and Brown Booby (*Sula leucogaster*), breed on remote islands. There has typically been a lack of native terrestrial predators on their traditional nesting grounds; but in some cases introduced species, such as rats and mice, domestic cats, dogs and pigs have taken a heavy toll on population numbers and hampered breeding success.

Above: The Masked Booby (*Sula dactylatra*).

Opposite: Northern Gannet (*Morus bassanus*), nesting on Bass Rock, Scotland.

ESTUARIES, SALT MARSHES AND MUDFLATS

Where freshwater and sea water meet

Like all coastal habitats, estuaries, with their surrounding salt marshes and tidal flats, represent a meeting of the land and the ocean. However, perhaps more importantly, as the places where rivers flow into the sea, they are defined by the meeting of freshwater and seawater, forming a unique habitat where the terrestrial, freshwater and marine converge.

Having been formed as the result of the flooding of river mouths, valleys and their adjacent lands by the sea, by glacial retreat or geological movements, and by the build-up of sediments deposited by rivers, most estuaries are relatively sheltered from extreme wave action and strong currents, but they are nonetheless dynamic environments, which are subjected to both the daily influence of the tides, and the constant input of inland waters. As a result, they are typically characterized by changing water levels, highly variable salinity and a range of temperatures, all of which must be tolerated or overcome by the organisms that live there.

Despite this, estuarine habitats can be counted as being amongst the most productive ecosystems on Earth; rich in a diverse array of nutrients from both rivers and the sea that supports an abundance of plant and animal species, from photosynthesizing algae and phytoplankton, to invertebrates and fish, birds and mammals, all linked in a complex web of life. In addition to being important feeding grounds, estuaries are also used as nurseries by numerous fish and as breeding and overwintering sites by many birds. Furthermore, their tidal flats and wetlands not only filter large amounts of nutrients, but also potentially harmful pollutants, whilst deposited sediments help to stabilize coastal habitats, protecting them from erosion and flooding.

Variable salinity

The changing salinity of the water is one of the most significant factors in determining the kinds of organisms able to survive and thrive in estuarine environments, as most plants and animals are stenohaline, meaning that they can tolerate only a narrow range of variation in salinity, and so tend to be either exclusively marine or freshwater species. Conversely, those that are tolerant of a wide variety of salinities are known as euryhaline organisms, and it is these plants and animals that dominate in estuaries.

The relative amounts of seawater and freshwater in an estuary are constantly changing with the rise and fall of the tide, and also with the degree of flow of the river, which may be swollen by rainfall or melting snow for example. Salinity also tends to vary in different parts of the estuary, increasing further from the shore and the mouth of the river, and may be dramatically affected by the lie of the land. Where the slope of a river entering the sea is negligible, or the mouth

of a river narrows abruptly, the degree of tidal inundation into that river may be dramatic, affecting the salinity of the water far inland.

Furthermore, as freshwater is less dense than seawater, it may float above it as it enters the estuary, causing a variation in salinity according to depth, and allowing higher salinity water to penetrate upstream below the flow of freshwater. This has enabled benthic, or bottom-dwelling, marine organisms to establish themselves further inland, and to adapt to freshwater conditions. Most of the plants associated with estuaries and salt marshes are terrestrial species which have evolved to tolerate higher salinities.

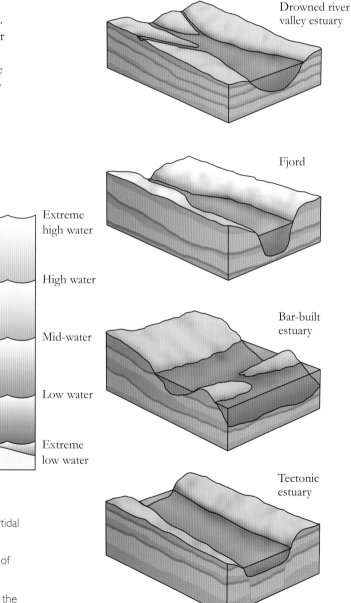

Drowned river valley estuary

Fjord

Bar-built estuary

Tectonic estuary

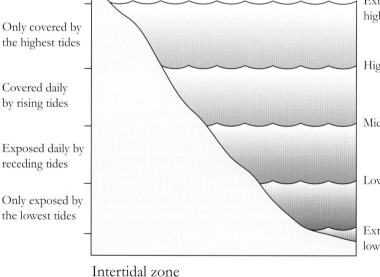

Only covered by the highest tides

Covered daily by rising tides

Exposed daily by receding tides

Only exposed by the lowest tides

Extreme high water

High water

Mid-water

Low water

Extreme low water

Intertidal zone

Above: Levels of immersion and emersion throughout the intertidal zone.

Right: Different types of estuary result from different processes of formation.

Opposite: The Oystercatcher (*Haematopus ostralegus*) is one of the most distinctive of estuarine birds.

Salt marshes

In tropical and subtropical regions, river deltas are typically dominated by mangrove swamps and forests, but in temperate regions, estuaries are often bordered by extensive salt marshes. These are formed by the accumulation of sediments deposited by the river, which are then colonized by low-lying, salt-tolerant plants, or halophytes, and criss-crossed by creeks and channels, through which the sea flows into and out of the marsh with the tides.

As in other tidal habitats which experience highly variable conditions, salt marshes tend to be populated by fewer species than either fully terrestrial or marine environments, which are more stable, but because they are relatively well protected and rich in nutrients, they are very productive, and tend to support large numbers of those organisms that are present.

Being transitional environments from the terrestrial to the marine, they also generally display distinct patterns of zonation, or the grouping of species, from the higher levees on the landward side, across the marsh flats or plains, sloping to the lower-lying mudflats that are subjected to the greatest extent and highest frequency of tidal inundation.

Accordingly, salinity varies throughout the marsh in relation to the reach of the tide, and therefore plants and animals that are able to tolerate the highest levels of salinity are found closest to the sea in the lower marsh, whilst those that are less tolerant occur in the upper parts of the marsh, where they may be submerged by the sea only at the highest tides.

The animals found in the upper marsh tend to be mainly terrestrial species, such as insects, amphibians and rodents, whilst plants of the upper marsh include the Sea-aster (*Aster tripolium*), Sea-lavender (*Limonium vulgare*), and Sea-milkwort (*Glaux maritima*). These tend to have narrow leaves to reduce water resistance during periods of immersion, and many also possess salt glands through which excess salt can be excreted.

Further down through the marsh, grasses such as Salt Hay (*Spartina patens*), and Spike Grass (*Distichlis spicata*), may dominate, along with Glasswort, or Marsh Samphire (*Salicornia europaea*), which lacks salt glands, and instead is succulent, and therefore able to dilute its salt intake with a high water content. Marine amphipods and isopods, as well as larger crustaceans such as crabs, increase in number in the lower parts of the marsh, as do various worms, and snails such as the Marsh Periwinkle (*Littorina irrorata*), whilst the tidal creeks may be home to fish, including gobies, juvenile flatfish and eels.

Cord grasses, such as *Spartina anglica* and *Spartina alterniflora*, dominate from the lower marsh to the edge of the tidal flats, and are highly important in stabilizing the sediment and contributing detritus into the food chain. However, whilst this muddy sediment is highly rich in nutrients and organic material, it is also lacking in oxygen and may quickly become stagnant.

Right: Sea lavender, (*Limonium vulgare*), West Sussex, UK.

Mudflats

At the lower edge of the salt marsh, which is subjected to daily tidal inundation and the highest salinity, marsh plants become increasingly sparse, until they are absent altogether, and the retreat of the tide reveals a flat expanse of seemingly barren mud, perhaps broken only by small clumps of Eelgrass (*Zostera marina*), or seaweeds that have managed to establish a foothold. As at the marsh's edge, the muddy sediment here is nutrient-rich, but it is almost constantly waterlogged, and therefore resistant to water and oxygen exchange. It is dominated by bacteria, which further reduce oxygen levels, so that just a few inches beneath the surface layer, the sediment is anaerobic or deoxygenated and high in hydrogen sulfide. However, these bacteria also break down organic matter, producing a nutrient-rich detritus that is capable of supporting an abundance of life.

Whilst at first glance the mudflat may appear bleak and desolate, the activities of wading birds, probing into the mud with their bills, or a closer inspection of the mud itself, might reveal a host of hidden organisms. These burrowing animals, which are referred to as the infauna, seek refuge in the sediment to avoid exposure to the air, changing water conditions, and to escape predation, but must be capable of withstanding, or otherwise adapting to, the lack of oxygen and the variable salinity of the mudflat habitat in order to do so.

This infauna is comprized largely of small detritus-feeding invertebrates such as marine worms, bivalve mollusks and tiny crustaceans, which provide an essential resource for scavengers and predators, including larger invertebrates, fish and birds. Additionally, the infauna play an important role in encouraging water exchange in the sediment via the holes and tunnels that they make within it.

Below: Mudflats may sometimes appear desolate, but traces of activity such as worm casts reveal a hidden world of wildlife.

Infauna

Worms are typically amongst the most numerous of infaunal species, and range from the Lugworm (*Arenicola marina*), which lives a sedentary existence in a U-shaped burrow, digesting organic matter by swallowing the sediment, to errant, or highly mobile species such as the Ragworm (*Nereis diversicolor*), and King Ragworm (*Nereis virens*), which may scavenge for detritus or prey on other worms. The King Ragworm in particular, may be a fearsome predator, attaining a length of some 36 inches, and possessing powerful jaws.

Other carnivorous worms include the paddleworms, such as *Anaitides maculata* and *Anaitides mucosa*. Both lack jaws, but have a modified proboscis that may be everted through the mouth to consume their prey. One of the most distinctive estuarine worms however, is the Sea-mouse (*Aphrodita aculeata*). Its name is derived from its dense covering of chaetae, or hairs, which gives it a somewhat furry appearance, but whilst

those on its back tend to be gray-brown, those along its sides are colorful and iridescent. This species is also predatory, and shows a preference for Nereis species, which are commonly three times its own length or more. Scale worms, of the family Polynoidae, tend to be smaller still, perhaps attaining a length of between 1/2 and 3 inches, but these too are carnivorous on small worms and other invertebrates. Despite this however, some, such as *harmothoe lunulata*, may live commensally in the burrows of larger invertebrates such as the bivalve *Mysella bidentata*, the Burrowing Brittle-star (*Amphiura brachiata*), or burrowing sea cucumbers such as labidoplax digitata. This worm-like holothurian, which may grow to a length of about 12 inches, lacks the tube feet of more mobile sea cucumbers, and burrows into the sediment, leaving its tentacles exposed in order to collect detritus.

The Cotton Spinner (*Holothuria forskali*), however, is epifaunal or benthic, living on the surface of the sediment, and able to crawl along on its well developed tube feet. Its name is derived from its practice of discharging part of its gut in long, cotton-like threads when threatened by potential predators.

Above: The Willet (*Catoptrophorus semipalmatus*) is a large sandpiper, which feeds on worms and crustaceans.

Left: The coastal plant, Rock Samphire (*Crithmum maritimum*).

Tidal flats

Mollusks are also numerous on the tidal flats,
particularly bivalves, but the aptly named Mudsnail or
Laver Spire Shell (*Hydrobia ulvae*), is often the most
numerous of all, reaching densities of between 20,000
and an astonishing 300,000 per yard square. It feeds on
tiny organic particles, which it rasps from the sediment,
but at high tide, it floats upside down at the water's
surface by producing a raft of mucus, which may also
trap food.

   Common bivalves of the mudflats include the
Peppery Furrow Shell (*Scrobicularia plana*), the Common
Otter Shell (*Lutraria lutraria*), and gaper shells, such as
the Sand Gaper, or Soft-shelled Clam (*Mya arenaria*), and
the Blunt Gaper (*Mya truncata*), which possess extremely
long siphons, enabling them to bury themselves deeply
in the mud. In fact, the gaper shells get their name
because their siphons are so large that their shells
cannot fully close when retracted.

Other siphon-feeders include the venus or
carpet shells, such as the Banded Carpet Shell (*Tapes
rhomboides*), Chequered Carpet Shell (*Tapes decussates*), the
Cross-cut Carpet Shell (*Venerupis cerrusata*) and the
Quahog, or American Hard-shelled Clam (*Mercenaria
mercenaria*), which are often consumed by humans and
therefore of commercial importance.

Oyster

At one time the most commercially important bivalves
that were found and cultivated in estuarine waters were
the Blue, Edible, or Common Mussel (*Mytilus edulis*) and
the Common, Edible or European Oyster (*Ostrea edulis*),
but overfishing, competition from introduced species,
and decimation by predatory mollusks and starfish have
led to severe population declines. The largest bivalve
found in European waters is the Fan Mussel (*Atrina
fragilis*), which may attain a length of around 12 inches;
this too has experienced a severe decline.

Crustaceans

In addition to worms and mollusks, crustaceans are also common on mudflats. These range from fairly large species such as the Edible Crab (*Cancer pagurus*), Blue Crab (*Callinectes sapidus*), and the Common Prawn (*Palaemon serratus*), to various shrimps, such as the Pink Shrimp (*Pandalus montagui*), and tiny amphipods such as *Gammarus duebeni*, *Gammarus tigrinus*, *Gammarus salinus* and *Corophium volutator*, which are commonly known as mudshrimps. Despite the small size of these animals, they can occur in incredibly high densities, and so whilst at low tide they may be the main food source for numerous species of probing waders, particularly sandpipers and plovers, at high tide they sustain a wide variety of fish.

Opposite: An errant polychaete worm traverses the muddy sea floor at high tide, whilst mollusks extend their siphons to trap food particles.

Right: The Common Mussel (*Mytilus edulis*) can form dense beds on tidal flats.

Below: The Edible Crab (*Cancer pagurus*).

Estuarine fish

There are many different species of fish that are commonly found in estuaries. Those that are permanent residents in euryhaline conditions form only one of several groups associated with this habitat, which is frequented by both marine and freshwater fish that may enter brackish waters either seasonally or opportunistically in order to feed, to breed, or as passage migrants, which may pass through estuaries en route to either marine or freshwater spawning grounds. One of the largest groups, however, is that of juvenile fish, which may have hatched upstream, offshore or in the estuary itself, and which use estuaries as nurseries. They benefit from the abundance of plankton, invertebrates and other organic material available as food, as well as from the relative protection that the semi-enclosed shallows provide from larger, predatory fish, before entering the open ocean as adults.

These include species such as rocklings, mullets and rays, numerous flatfish, such as Dab (*Limanda limanda*), Sole (*Solea solea*), Plaice (*Pleuronectes platessa*), various flounders, and also Cod (*Gadus morhua*), Poor Cod (*Trisopterus minutus*), Whiting (*Merlangius merlangus*), Pout (*Trisopterus luscus*), basses, herrings and shads, many of which are of commercial importance as adults.

Seabass

The European Seabass (*Dicentrarchus labrax*), for example, is often a solitary, offshore fish as an adult, but it is amongst the most common of estuarine nursery fish when young, and will form large shoals, which prey on other small fish, fry and invertebrates. However, it will also enter estuaries and even freshwater, as an adult, particularly during the summer months. Mullets, such as the Thick-lipped Gray Mullet (*Crenimugil labrosus*), may also enter rivers seasonally in spring and summer, and can sometimes be found in estuaries for much of the year; they tend to spend the winter months in deeper offshore waters.

Fresh water species

Relatively few freshwater species descend rivers in order to breed in estuaries, but in the southern hemisphere, several members of the family *Galaxiidae* are well known for doing so, incorporating a marine cycle in their development. The Common Jollytail (*Galaxias maculatus*), for example, migrates downstream to spawn in estuaries, laying its eggs amongst vegetation. When these hatch, the larvae do not remain in the estuary, but enter the open sea for about five or six months, before entering freshwater, where they will spend their adult lives. Interestingly, the Common Jollytail is found in both Australasian and South American waters, and is thought to demonstrate the widest natural distribution of any freshwater fish. Other Galaxiids may hatch in rivers, but be washed downstream to estuaries as larvae, where they will develop for a time before returning upstream.

Opposite: Bass are common in estuaries as both juveniles and adults.

Below: Birds of prey such as the Osprey (*Pandion haliaetus*) are often attracted to estuaries by the large numbers of fish.

Best of both worlds

Some species, such as the Three-spined Stickleback (*Gasterosteus aculeatus*), seem to thrive equally well in freshwater, estuarine or marine conditions, and may remain in, or move between these habitats, as does the Flounder (*Platichthys flesus*). Like other flatfish, the Flounder begins life upright, before turning on to one side, which effectively becomes its underside. The eye on that side then migrates to the upper side as a result of the disproportionate growth of one side of the head. However, whilst most flatfish species are either right or left-sided, both the Flounder, and its North American counterpart, the Starry Flounder (*Platichthys stellatus*), are unusual in displaying the least constancy in the position of their eyes, and therefore their sidedness. Along with the Hogchoker (*Trinectes maculatus*), they are

also unusual in being the only flatfish to be found in freshwater. The adults typically spawn at sea or in estuaries, following which, the eggs, larvae and fry are pelagic, but the juveniles will commonly gather in estuaries, and individuals are common in the tidal creeks of salt marshes. Some however, penetrate far upriver, and may remain there until they too are ready to spawn at about three years of age.

Displaced by flooding

Fish such as Pike (*Esox lucius*), Crucian Carp (*Carassius carassius*), Dace (*Leuciscus leuciscus*), and Grayling (*Thymallus thymallus*), which are almost exclusively freshwater species, may sometimes be displaced by the sudden flooding of rivers, or else enter estuaries from freshwater in order to feed.

Passage migrants

Passage migrants occur in two forms; anadromous and catadromous. The former means that the adults enter rivers from the sea in order to spawn, whilst the latter group comprizes of species that spend most of their adult life in rivers and spawn at sea.

The Atlantic Salmon (*Salmo salar*), is undoubtedly one of the most familiar anadramous species on both sides of the Atlantic, being highly prized by both recreational and commercial fishermen. It begins its life in freshwater, where it may remain and grow for around three or four years, before migrating downstream toward the sea, often in early summer. Once clear of the estuary, the Atlantic Salmon will then enter the open sea, which it will inhabit for a further year or more, feeding on small fish, crustaceans and other invertebrates, before it is ready to spawn itself. It will then return to the river in which it hatched in order to breed, at which time it may be over 3 feet in length.

Marine species such as the Monkfish or Angel Shark (*Squatina squatina*) and the Conger Eel (*Conger conger*) may visit estuaries opportunistically in search of prey, whilst large shoals of Atlantic Mackerel (*Scomber scombrus*) will enter estuaries seasonally, in late spring and early summer, as they pursue fish fry into shallow waters.

Opposite: Conger Eel (*Conger conger*).

Below: The Monkfish, or Angel Shark, (*Squatina squatina*).

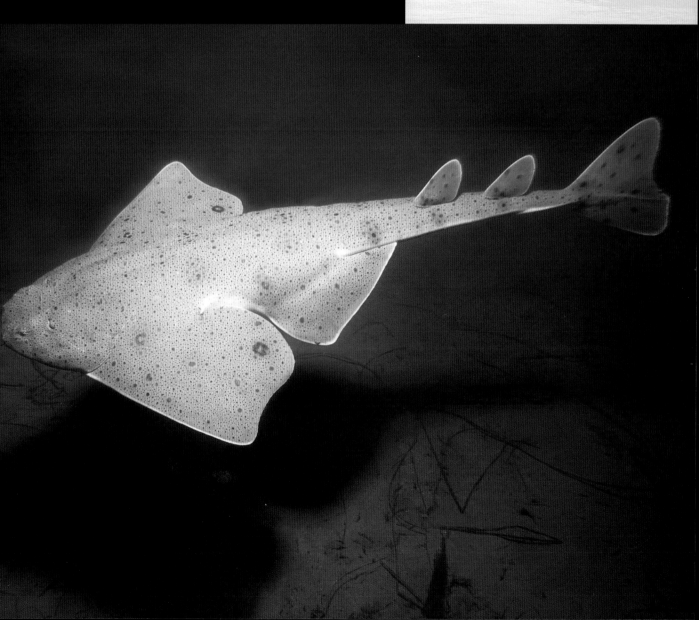

The European Eel

The most well known of the catadromous fish are probably the European Eel (*Anguilla anguilla*) and American Eel (*Anguilla rostrata*), which undertake remarkable migrations from their birthplace in the Sargasso Sea to spend much of their lives in freshwater, before returning to the sea as adults to breed and die. For the European Eel, this may mean a journey of perhaps 5,000 miles, and several years. The eels begin life as microscopic, leptocephalous larvae, transforming first to transparent "glass eels," and then to pigmented juveniles, or elvers, at around four years of age. On reaching the estuary, these elvers then head upstream, to spend several years in freshwater, until they are ready to undertake the arduous return journey to their breeding grounds. Some eels however, may remain in freshwater for life, often becoming landlocked owing to their ability to travel over ground from rivers to enclosed bodies of water. It has also been suggested that males may remain in estuaries, never entering freshwater.

Opposite above: Juvenile eels are known as "glass eels," as they are almost entirely transparent.

Opposite below: The Atlantic Salmon, (*Salmo salar*), begins its life in freshwater, but heads out to sea as an adult.

Below: The European Eel, (*Anguilla anguilla*) is spawned at sea, but travels to inland waterways as it develops.

Rainbow trout

Familiar anadramous species include the Rainbow Trout (*Oncorhynchus mykiss*), smelt, and the shads, such as the American Shad (*Alosa sapidissima*), Allis Shad (*Alosa alosa*), and the Twaite Shad, (*Alosa fallax*), which are members of the herring family, *Clupeidae*. For this reason, and on account of their spawning behavior, they are sometimes known as "river herrings". They are typically found in shallow coastal waters and around estuaries, but will enter rivers in order to spawn in freshwater, and may swim far upstream to do so. The young will then spend some time in freshwater before entering the sea, where they will live their adult lives. Isolated, non-migratory populations also exist in inland waterways, whilst others may sometimes dwell permanently in the lower reaches of rivers or in estuaries, except when breeding.

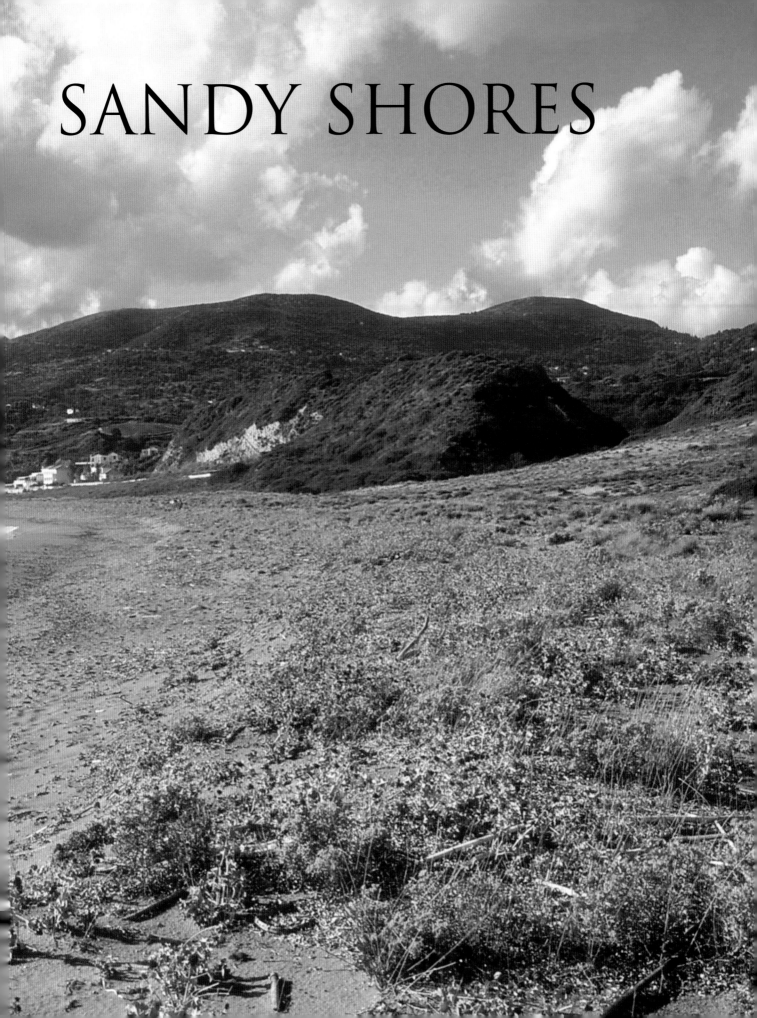

SANDY SHORES

Adapt and survive

With the exception of a few plants that may establish themselves above the high-water mark and therefore beyond the usual reach of the sea, the sandy shore might easily appear as a desolate landscape that is essentially devoid of life and the means to sustain it. However, whilst this environment is indeed harsh and demanding, it is populated by a number of species of plants and animals that have developed particular adaptations in order to survive its rigors.

Transient organisms and organic detritus that might typically occupy other terrestrial and marine habitats are often deposited, or may otherwise accumulate, on a sandy shore. These contribute to the diversity of its ecosystem and fulfil important roles within it.

Shifting sands

Most sandy shores are commonly classed as low-energy coastlines, and are not generally subjected to the pounding waves associated with rocky shores. They are nonetheless highly unstable habitats, which experience high levels of wave action, large variations in temperature and moisture, a lack of shelter and freshwater. Perhaps most importantly, a continually moving substrate causes problems of abrasion and presents difficulties in terms of attachment for both animals and plants. This means that animals are at risk of being swept out to sea, whilst seaweeds and other vegetation that might otherwise offer food and shelter to animal life, cannot establish a foothold and so are largely absent.

Many of these factors not only vary during the course of a day, because of periodic tidal exposure, but also along the slope of the foreshore, according to the depth of exposure. Although sandy beaches typically slope gently, this nevertheless results in vertical zonation, whereby various organisms populate different areas of the shore. Each of these presents its own problems to would-be inhabitants, which in turn display particular adaptations to those conditions. These zones include the strandline, where the high tide deposits organic material, through the intertidal zone, that is, the area between low and high tides), which is subjected to daily inundation by the tide and thus to varying degrees of marine and aerial exposure, and the lower beach, incorporating the subtidal zone, or shallows. Furthermore, the intertidal zone may be subdivided into upper, middle and lower areas, and also includes the swash or surf zone, where the waves run up the beach and break.

Microflora, meiofauna and macrofauna

Life on a sandy shore can be broadly divided into the microflora, or microscopic plantlife, such as diatoms and algae, the macrofauna, or larger animals, and the meiofauna or microfauna, tiny, often microscopic animals and larvae. These last are also collectively known as the infauna, or interstitial fauna, as they actually inhabit the spaces between the grains of sand on the beach. These spaces, and thus the presence of meiofauna, vary according to the size of the sand grains. Where fine silt occurs, it may fill the interstitial spaces, impacting upon the meiofauna, whilst very coarse sand will tend to drain quickly, and may not retain enough moisture to support an abundance of life. The meiofauna are also affected by the tidal level, and many make distinct vertical migrations through the sand in response to light, moisture and temperature variations. In fact, some diatoms even perform vertical migrations to the surface

in order to take advantage of sunlight, before retreating downward to escape being washed out to sea by the approaching tide. This is accomplished by the expulsion of mucus, which also protects against desiccation, but quite how the "body clock" of a diatom functions is yet to be understood.

The micro-community

There is no major primary production on the sandy shore habitat, with the exception of diatoms and other algal forms which may support the micro-community of the meiofauna. Aside from this, energy is contributed to the ecosystem by phytoplankton and organic detritus originating from adjacent terrestrial, marine and intertidal habitats.

The meiofauna consists of both herbivorous and carnivorous animals, including ciliate protozoans, polychaete, oligochaete and nematode worms. It includes tiny crustaceans such as copepods, which fulfil an important role in the sandy shore ecosystem by breaking down organic matter, providing food for the resident macrofauna, such as larger invertebrates of various types. These also face the same sorts of problems that are presented by the shifting substrate and lack of shelter, and they have a similar means to overcome those problems, namely, they burrow.

Dynamic habitat

Diatoms, or planktonic plant-life, that may be washed ashore from the shallows, will nourish various small invertebrates. These will provide food for larger invertebrates, numerous fish and shorebirds such as waders. Far from being barren and lifeless, the sandy shore is a dynamic habitat supporting a thriving community of life.

As is typical of such a variable and difficult environment, the diversity of species is usually quite limited. However, there tend to be relatively large numbers of individuals of those species that are present, and have adapted to survive in and exploit particular niches within their ecosystems.

Opposite above: Empty scallop and cockle shells washed up on a sandy beach in California.

Right: A variety of diatoms.

Previous Page: The beach at Katelios Bay, Kefalonia, the Greek Island. A Nesting Beach for the Loggerhead turtle

Life in the sand

Several types of animals burrow beneath the sand at various levels on the beach, in order to seek shelter from turbulent tides, extremes of temperature, desiccation and potential predators. But burrowing also presents its own difficulties, particularly with regard to obtaining food and oxygen, and different animals have developed specific strategies in order to solve these problems.

In general, the upper intertidal zone is the most sparsely populated. It has the greatest range of temperature variation, so that desiccation in summer and freezing in winter can be significant difficulties. Minimal tidal inundation is a year-round problem and restricts the available marine resources. Food sources here consist largely of marine detritus at the strandline, which is typically populated by terrestrial insects and their larvae, and marine amphipods, including sand-hoppers such as *Talitrus saltator*.

Further down the beach, in the mid-intertidal zone, which experiences moderate periods of inundation, there is a greater diversity of species. Whilst scavengers are present here too, several other methods of feeding are employed by the burrowing invertebrates found here, including siphoning, deposit-feeding, and sediment-swallowing.

Sediment-swallowing animals

Amongst the sediment-swallowing animals, the Lugworm (*Arenicola marina*), and related species, are probably amongst the most common on many beaches, their presence being betrayed by the worm-casts of coiled sand

Sand-hoppers

As juveniles, sand-hoppers – tiny, laterally-flattened, shrimp-like crustaceans – are most commonly found beneath stranded wrack, but the adults may burrow to depths of up to three feet, particularly when breeding. They are highly mobile and generally nocturnal animals, emerging at night to hop and crawl their way down the beach to scavenge for food, consuming both animal and plant matter. They also require immersion in water in order to wet their gills, but cannot survive complete submersion for long periods.

Above: A sand hopper (*Gammarus sp*)

Opposite above: The Peacock Worm (*Sabella pavonina*) is a suspension feeder.

Opposite below: The Atlantic Ghost Crab (*Ocypode quadrata*)

which are often a familiar sight at low tide. This polychaete worm behaves in much the same way as an earthworm, consuming the sediment in order to digest organic matter that is contained within. It lives in a U-shaped burrow in moist sand, and ingests sand at one end, depositing the waste sediment at the other.

Suspension feeding

Some polychaete worms, such as *Amphitrite johnstoni* live in membranous, sand-coated tubes, from which a crown of tentacles extends with which to collect detritus that is deposited on the sand surface. In some species these tentacles are modified to filter food directly from the water at high tide, a process known as suspension-feeding. Still others, such as the Ragworm (*Nereis diversicolor*), may feed on organic matter that is trapped in their mucus-lined burrows, but are also free-living predators, which will actively hunt for other worms at high tide.

Certain bivalve mollusks are also to be found in the sand on the middle shore, such as the Thin Tellin (*Tellina/Angulus tenuis*), which may occur in high densities. This animal uses its muscular foot to burrow rapidly into the sand as the tide recedes, but at high tide obtains both food and oxygen by means of siphoning. It has two siphons, one of which is used to draw water, containing food and oxygen to its gills, whilst the other returns water and waste back into the sea.

Left: The Sea Potato or Heart Urchin (*Echinocardium cordatum*).

Opposite: A Sea Cucumber (*Actinopyga obesa*).

Below: Starfish on the beach at Queen Charlottes, British Columbia, Canada

The subtidal shallows

The lower intertidal zone, which extends into the subtidal shallows, is exposed to the air only briefly at low tide, and is the most stable habitat on the sandy shore in terms of moisture and temperature variation, and is characterized by the greatest species diversity. However, this area is almost continuously subjected to the action of currents and waves, and the animals here must be able to burrow rapidly or deeply, or be well protected against wave turbulence in order to survive. Some species, such as the Catworm (*Nephthys hombergi*), which makes temporary burrows, are also active swimmers.

As in the mid-intertidal zone, various burrowing worms and bivalves tend to dominate here, including several species of clam and fast-burrowing razor shells.

Anemones, such as the Daisy Anemone (*Cereus pendunculatus*), and worm-like burrowing anemones, which lack an adhesive basal disc, such as *Halcampa chrysanthellum*, may also be found buried in the sand, with their tentacles exposed in order to feed. Tube-footed echinoderms, including the Sea-potato (*Echinocardium cordatum*), sand dollars, brittle-stars and sea cucumbers, also inhabit the lower shore and shallows. Whilst some, such as the Burrowing Brittle-star (*Amphiura brachiata*), are largely solitary, sand dollars may be highly abundant in some locations, forming dense beds, with individuals partially buried in the sand, angled so as best to obtain food. These animals may trap water-borne food particles on their short spines, or use their tube feet to collect them from the sand.

Larger crustaceans

Crustaceans, such as the Common Shrimp (*Crangon vulgaris*) and Glass Shrimp (*Archaeomysis grebnitzkii*), also thrive in the lower intertidal zone, burrowing into the upper layer of sand when in need of shelter, and emerging at high tide in order to feed on zooplankton and other small animals.

The Masked Crab usually forages nocturnally, and during the day will avoid predation by burying itself in the sand, leaving only the tips of its long, hairy antennae exposed at the surface. It uses these in much the same way as a bivalve uses its siphon, holding them together to form a breathing tube. Mole crabs, which are sometimes also known as sand crabs, possess similar antennae with which they are able to trap particles of food. They also employ their antennae like underwater sails, using them to transport themselves with the currents and waves in order to remain in the surf zone. Similarly, some types of mollusk are able to spread out their foot to migrate with the tides.

Masked crab

Larger crustaceans include numerous species of crab which spend time burrowed in the surface sediment between feeding, but some crabs, including the Masked Crab (*Corystes cassivelaunus*) and Spiny Mole Crab (*Blepharipoda occidentalis*), are specialized burrowers.

Below: This mole crab. which is known as the Atlantic Sand Crab (*Emerita talpoida*) emerges from the sea floor.

Opposite: The Masked Crab (*Corystes cassivelaunus*) uses its elongated antennae as a snorkel.

Fish of the sandy shallows

Several types of fish inhabit the shallow waters over sandy beds, and the flatfish, such as the Plaice (*Pleuronectes platessa*), and Turbot (*Psetta maxima*), which belong to the order Pleuronectiformes, are amongst those best adapted for a benthic existence; that is, living on the seabed itself. However, they begin their lives swimming in an upright position, transforming as they grow. The body becomes flattened, and they begin to swim on one side, before they settle on the bottom, where as a result of the disproportionate growth of one side of the head, one eye and nostril migrate to the uppermost side. The eyes also protrude, in order to optimize their vision in this new position, whilst the mouth twists, to allow easier bottom-feeding. Their prey typically consists of polychaete worms, bivalve mollusks and crustaceans, but larger species like the Turbot will also consume smaller fish. Flatfish frequently burrow into the upper layer of sediment, and are generally well camouflaged against the sand. Some are able to change their color to match the substrate, but they are preyed upon by other fish, notably sharks and the closely related rays, both of which possess highly developed sensory organs. These are known as the ampullae of Lorenzini, after their discoverer, the biologist Stefano Lorenzini, and are incredibly sensitive to electricity, allowing sharks and rays to detect the minute electrical signals emitted by other fish, even those buried in the sand.

Opposite: The shape and mottled patterns of the Turbot (*Psetta maximus*) make it ideally suited to a life on the sea floor.

Above: Lesser-Spotted Dogfish (*Scyliorhinus canicula*)

Below: An egg sac, commonly known as a mermaid's purse, with developing embryo visible inside.

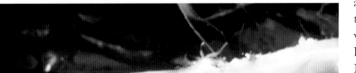

The Lesser-spotted Dogfish

The Lesser-spotted Dogfish (*Scyliorhinus canicula*), which is also sometimes known as the Rough Hound or Rock Salmon, is a small and common shark that is found over sandy beds in European waters, whilst the Thornback Ray (*Raja clavata*) is the most common and widespread ray in these habitats. Like the flatfish, rays are benthic and flattened, and often sandy in color, but unlike them, they do not undergo a transformation to become that way. Both the Lesser-spotted Dogfish and Thornback Ray are oviparous, producing the egg sacs known as Mermaid's Purses that are often washed up on sandy

The California Grunion: a fish out of water

Whilst many fish spawn in the shallow waters along sandy shores, the California Grunion (*Leuresthes tenuis*) is unique in its spawning behavior, actually coming out of the water to lay its eggs in the moist sand on the beach.

These small, iridescent fish inhabit the coastal waters off California, and breed between late February and early September, coming onto the beaches at night in the days following the highest spring tides. They travel with the breaking waves, before wriggling as far up the shore as possible, where the females, often attended by several males, will burrow backward into the wet sand to lay their eggs about 2 inches below the surface. The males attempt to wrap themselves about the female in order to fertilize the eggs as they are deposited. The fish then return to the sea with the next wave, leaving the eggs buried in the sand, out of the reach of successive waves and marine predators, such as other fish.

Around ten days later, when the tides next reach the same height up the beach, the eggs are disturbed by the surf and hatch, and the newly emerged grunions are then carried out to sea.

A living fossil

Despite its name, the Horseshoe Crab (*Limulus polyphemus*) is actually more closely related to spiders and scorpions than to other crabs, being a descendant of the ancient sea scorpions that inhabited the Palaeozoic oceans hundreds of millions of years ago. It is thought to have remained unchanged for around 350 million years.

It typically lives over sandy seabeds in relatively shallow waters, where it feeds on worms, mollusks and other invertebrates that it digs from the sand. In spring it comes onto the sandy shore in order to breed, often in huge numbers.

The smaller males appear first, and await the arrival of the females, to which they then attach themselves with their bulbous claws. At high tide, the crabs swarm up onto the sand, where the female will excavate a cavity in which to deposit several thousand eggs, and the male is then dragged over the nest to fertilize them. Unpaired males meanwhile will throng around the attached animals in an attempt to fertilize any exposed eggs.

Once spawning has taken place, the adult crabs return to the sea, leaving the young to hatch alone. These take the form of free-swimming larvae, which will settle about a week after hatching to undergo their first moult, a process that will continue throughout their lives as the hard external carapace, from which their name is derived, develops and grows.

The Horseshoe crab

In areas such as Delaware Bay on the North American Atlantic Coast, where Horseshoe Crabs breed in vast numbers, their eggs have become an extremely important foodstuff for migratory shorebirds such as the Sanderling (*Calidris alba*) and Red Knot (*Calidris canutus*), which undertake vast journeys from Brazil on their way to their Arctic breeding grounds.

Opposite: The California Grunion (*Leuresthes tenius*) spawns out of the water during high spring tides, burying itself into the sand.

Below left: The Horseshoe Crab (*Limulus polyphemus*) is an ancient form of arthropod, which breeds on sandy shores.

Below right: In some places, birds such as the Sanderling (*Calidris alba*) rely on the eggs of the Horseshoe Crab, in order to fuel their migrations.

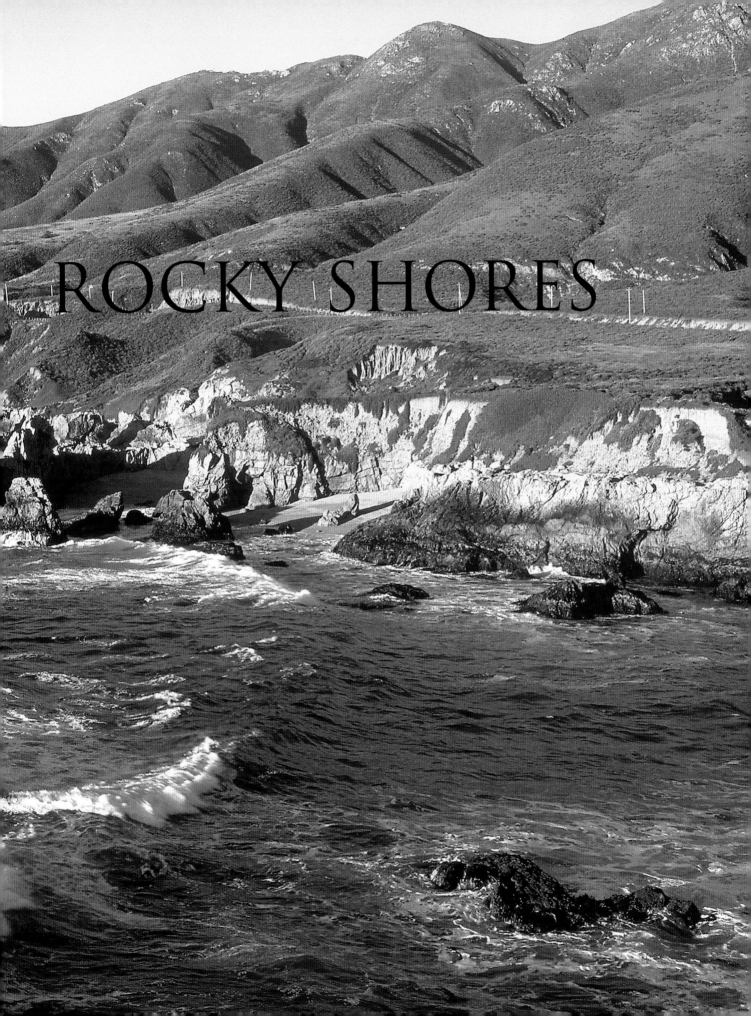

ROCKY SHORES

Adapt and survive

The rocky shore, be it in the form of an exposed headland or a more sheltered cove or bay, can be a rugged, imposing and seemingly inhospitable place, where plunging cliffs and rocky outcrops are subjected to the continual assault of the wind and waves that shape them. The rocky coast also experiences the extreme conditions and stresses that occur in almost all tidal habitats: the sharp contrast between exposure to air and water, and the associated variations in moisture, temperature, salinity and light that this brings on a daily basis. However, as in all these habitats, there are lifeforms present that have adapted to survive such extremes. At some rocky shores, where cliffs descend straight into the sea, there may be little or no intertidal zone, a factor greatly affecting the type and abundance of life that may be found there. Yet even where the land and sea meet sharply, there are often wave-cut platforms of bedrock that are revealed at low tide, which are pocked and scarred with craters and crevices, and scattered with rocks and boulders. These offer the possibility of shelter to a wide range of species,
and in fact, the rocky shore is home to some of the most productive and diverse ecosystems of any coastal habitat.

Productivity and energy flow on the rocky shore

The rocky shore is an example of a high-energy coastline, which is directly exposed to the abrasive power of the waves and the eroded sediment contained within them. Whilst the bedrock itself may often be very hard and unyielding, it is slowly but surely being eroded.

However, whilst few animals could survive being dashed against the rocks, it is their very presence that enables life to thrive, providing a stable foundation upon which plants and animals are able to establish themselves and their communities. Unlike a sandy beach, where the substrate is in constant motion, making it almost impossible for plants to become established, the rocky shore presents the opportunity of attachment to numerous plants. They form the basis of the rocky shore ecosystem as the main producers, converting water and carbon dioxide by means of photosynthesis into the carbohydrates upon which all animals depend for survival. Whilst on sandy shores microscopic diatoms dominate, on rocky shores algal forms of various types are present. Some of these, such as the macro-algae, or seaweeds, can grow rapidly and become surprisingly large. With the micro-algae and lichens they provide food for herbivorous grazers, filter-feeders and scavengers, which in turn support all manner of carnivorous predators, from invertebrates to fish, birds and mammals.

Zonation on rocky shores

As in other shoreline habitats, there are a number of physical factors affecting the arrangement of organisms along the rocky shore. Many are associated with the degree of tidal inundation and exposure to the air, or immersion and emersion, that is experienced at various points along the shore's profile. On a rocky shore these zones typically include the splash zone, through the intertidal zone, to the subtidal shallows.

Through a process of natural selection, plants and animals have typically adapted to survive according to these environmental conditions, such as extended periods either in or out of water, and so occupy particular niches within the rocky shore habitat. Other important physical factors include the strength of wave action, which where great may pose problems of attachment to the rocks. The type of rock itself may affect the amount of shelter available, and according to its hardness, prevent or allow burrowing, for instance.

However, the species distribution, or patterns of zonation, that are often so clearly defined on the rocky shore, are also affected by a number of biological factors, that is, the interactions amongst the species present. With a profusion of plants accounting for the primary production, and therefore an abundance of food to support a great deal of life, levels of predation and competition between organisms, for space and other resources, are also important elements in determining where different plants and animals may thrive. For example, fast-growing sedentary species may quickly dominate the region of the shore to which they are best adapted, forcing out slower-growing species to other areas, whilst the extent of their own range may be restricted by the presence of predators.

It is a combination of physical and biological factors that affects zonation, and accounts for the distinct bands of organisms that are a common feature of the rocky shore habitat. However, it should also be noted that these bands, whilst often generally well defined, are not fixed. There may be variations within and between zones, according to intermittent physical and biological disturbances, population fluctuations and seasonal changes.

Previous page: Big Sur Coast, California.

Opposite: Pulpit Rock, Portland Bill, Dorset, England.

Right: Midshore seaweeds, seagrass and giant kelp, with Leather Stars (*Dermasterias imbricata*), exposed at low tide.

The splash zone

The splash zone refers to that part of a rocky shore that is above the high-tide mark and constantly exposed to the air, but is reached by the spray from the breaking waves, which may be extensive at exposed locations and in stormy conditions.

There are few plants or animals that are hardy enough to permanently populate the splash zone, which experiences a lack of moisture, high salinity, and extreme exposure to wind and varying temperatures. Although numerous seabirds may temporarily colonize clifftops and ledges in order to breed, they can contribute to the harsh conditions by causing erosion of what little soil may be present, and by depositing uric acid in their droppings, which corrodes vegetation.

The dominant species

Some lichens, however, appear to thrive on the nitrogen supplied by bird droppings, and these are often the dominant species present in this zone. Lichens are plants which are composed of both algae, which provide nutrients by means of photosynthesis, and fungi, which are able to retain large amounts of moisture. Thus the relationship is symbiotic or mutually beneficial. Orange lichens such as *Xanthoria* and *Caloplaca* species tend to dominate higher up, below which black encrusting lichens, such as *Verrucaria maura*, often form a distinctive belt. Lichens grow slowly, with some species living for over fifty years, and as they develop, they help to produce soil by breaking down the rock itself, eventually allowing mosses and some hardy flowering plants to become established.

With the exception of a few insect species, terrestrial scavengers and marine mammals such as seals, which may haul out on the rocks, animals are scarce in the splash zone. However, there are some periwinkles, such as the Small Periwinkle (*Littorina neritoides*), which are capable of living in crevices high above the tideline. This species is able to withstand extreme temperatures and variations in salinity, breathes with lung-like, modified gills, and feeds by grazing on lichens.

Further down, the lower limit of the splash zone and its border with the upper intertidal zone, or upper shore, may be marked by certain species of acorn barnacle belonging to the genus *Chthamalus*, which are capable of withstanding long periods of desiccation.

Above: Common Seal (*Phoca vitulina*) resting on rock.

Opposite: Common Limpets (*Patella vulgata*) on a rocky shore, Devon, England.

The upper shore

The upper shore, the landward limit of which is marked by the high-water line, is briefly submerged by the sea twice a day. It is also exposed to the air for long periods, which presents organisms with problems in terms of temperature variation, drying out, and only limited time for animals such as filter-feeders to obtain food from the water.

Lichen and Seaweed

The black lichen *Verrucaria maura*, which is common in the splash zone, is capable of withstanding brief immersion and is present here too. In addition to lichens, this zone is hospitable to many species of plants, such as certain types of macro-algae, or seaweeds, which provide food and shelter for a range of animals. Such seaweeds include brown algae such as Channeled Wrack (*Pelvetia canaliculata*), identifiable from being grooved on one side, and Spiral Wrack (*Fucus spiralis*), which often twists toward the tips of its fronds. Both occur close to the high-water mark, often in distinct bands. These seaweeds attach themselves to the rocks with a holdfast, a root-like base, which may shelter small

animals, although the growth of acorn barnacles such as *Chthamalus* and *Balanus* species may eventually cause them to detach. However, the movement of seaweed fronds at high tide will often prevent barnacle larvae from being able to settle too closely or in large numbers.

Small arthropods, including amphipod and isopod crustaceans such as sand-hoppers, and the woodlouse-like Sea-slater (*Ligia oceanica*), shelter and scavenge amongst seaweeds and debris on the upper shore, as does the Marine Bristle-tail (*Petrobius maritimus*), which is one of only a few insects to occur in a marine habitat.

Periwinkles

Amongst the slightly larger invertebrates, snail-like periwinkles, such as the Rough Periwinkle (*Littorina saxatilis*), are often the most common in this zone. As grazers of algae and lichens, their presence may be betrayed by the pathways left by their rasping tongues, even if the animals themselves have retreated into a crevice to seek moisture and shelter. However, as befitting a creature of the upper shore, the Rough Periwinkle is capable of surviving prolonged periods without submersion in water.

The middle shore

As desiccation becomes less problematic further down the shore, so a greater array of species is to be found in the mid-intertidal zone, which is exposed to the air at low tide, but may also be submerged for relatively long periods. Nevertheless, the plants and animals found here still require adaptations in order to cope with the variability of their habitat.

Common seaweeds

The middle shore is often dominated by familiar seaweeds such as Knotted Wrack (*Ascophyllum nodosum*), and Bladder Wrack (*Fucus vesiculosus*), which grow to around 39 inches in length, and may be identified respectively by the single or paired air bladders present on their fronds. These are used to float the fronds of the plant toward the surface at high tide, so as to increase the amount of light reaching them for photosynthesis to take place. Where these grow in sufficient density, they typically form distinct bands, which will limit the extent reached by encrusting acorn barnacles. Many other animals may seek refuge amongst their fronds, particularly when seeking pockets of moisture at low tide, or graze on them.

The Flat Periwinkle (*Littorina obtusata*), is often found in association with these plants, which are favored foods, and may be recognized by its rather squat shell. However, it may vary in color from olive-green to yellow-brown, and may also be patterned with bands. It has been observed that color forms appear to vary according to both the degree of wave exposure on a particular shore and with seasonal color changes in seaweeds, in order to offer the best camouflage from potential predators.

Common Mussel

Another mollusk which may be conspicuous on the middle shore is the Blue, Edible, or Common Mussel (*Mytilus edulis*). This familiar bivalve will often form dense aggregations on the rocks, to which it attaches itself with byssus threads, secretions from its muscular foot. Although adults are sedentary, the young also use these threads to drift with the tides in order to colonize new areas. The Blue Mussel is a suspension-feeder, which siphons food from the water at high tide, and in turn is preyed upon by the Dogwhelk (*Nucella lapillus*), various shorebirds, and crabs such as the Common Shore Crab (*Carcinus maenas*). Interestingly however, the Pea Crab (*Pinnotheres pisum*), a tiny species that grows to around 2 inches, often makes its home within the shell of the mussel, and whilst it does not harm its host, it will feed on particles that it collects from the water.

Opposite: Knotted Wrack (*Ascophyllum nodosum*) offers shelter to a range of animals at both high and low tide. Here a 15-spined Stickleback (*Spinachia spinachia*) swims between its fronds.

Below: Common mussel (*Mytilus edulis*) laying off byssus threads.

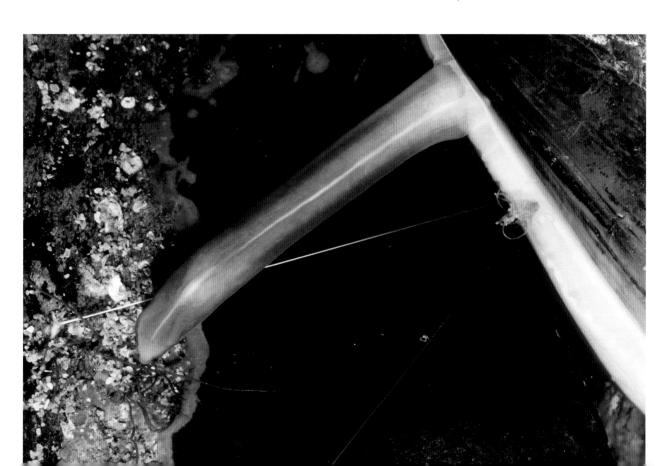

The lower shore

The lower shore, the upper limit of which is exposed to the air only briefly at low tide, and the lower limit of which is constantly submerged, provides a far more stable and productive habitat than the zones higher up the shore, and supports the greatest range of life.

The seaweeds here are predominantly those belonging to the class *Rhodophyceae*, or the red algae, their color resulting from phycoerythrin, a pigment which enables photosynthesis to occur in deeper water, where light penetration may be greatly reduced. Common examples include the symmetrically branching *Corallina officinalis* and the encrusting *Lithophyllum incrustans*, both of which are highly calcareous and hardy.

Several plant-like animals also occur on the lower shore, notably the bryozoans; minute polyp-like organisms, hydrozoans, which are related to jellyfish, and the more familiar sponges and anemones.

Encrusting sponges, such as the Bread-crumb Sponge (*Halichondria panicea*), form a low crust over rocks, particularly in crevices, whilst other types such as the Boring Sponge (*Cliona celata*), actually burrow into the rock. The Purse Sponge (*Grantia compressa*) is typically found beneath overhanging rocks, or sheltering amongst seaweeds.

Anemones

Common anemones of the lower shore include the Beadlet Anemone (*Actinia equina*) and the Opelet, or Snakelocks Anemone (*Anemonia Sulcata*). Both species adhere to rocks with a sucker-like base and use their stinging tentacles to paralyze and draw in prey, such as small crustaceans. The Beadlet Anemone is capable of withdrawing its tentacles into its body, which protects it against desiccation where it occurs higher up the shore. Unlike the Opelet, which may be found in colonies, the Beadlet Anemone is also territorial, and will gradually nudge competitors away.

The Parasitic Anemone

The Parasitic Anemone (*Calliactis parasitica*), is neither colonial nor territorial, and nor is it actually parasitic. Rather, it enjoys a symbiotic relationship with hermit crabs such as *Eupagurus bernhardus*, attaching to the shells that they inhabit in order to benefit from their feeding actions, whilst defending their host from predators such as octopi.

Aside from hermit crabs, another crab found on the lower shore and in the shallows is the Velvet Swimming Crab (*Macropipus puber*). As its name might suggest, it bears a covering of fine, velvety hair, and although it is omnivorous, consuming some seaweeds, it is also a highly aggressive predator, which has earned it the alternative name of Devil Crab.

Opposite: Parasitic Anemone (*Calliactis parasitica*) wiith Hermit crab.

Below: A Velvet Swimming Crab (*Necora puber*) in a mussel bed.

Lobsters are amongst the largest of the crustaceans found in the shallows off rocky shores, and many species, such as the Common Lobster (*Homarus gammarus*), are commercially important to man. This species may grow to about three feet in length and possesses formidable claws, which it uses to crush and cut its food. However, much of its feeding activity comprises scavenging, as opposed to active hunting.

Other large inhabitants of crevices in the subtidal zone, which are much more aggressive predators, include octopuses, which are amongst the largest and most intelligent invertebrates in the world, and conger and moray eels, which lie in wait amongst the rocks for passing prey, such as crustaceans, squid and fish, before ambushing them.

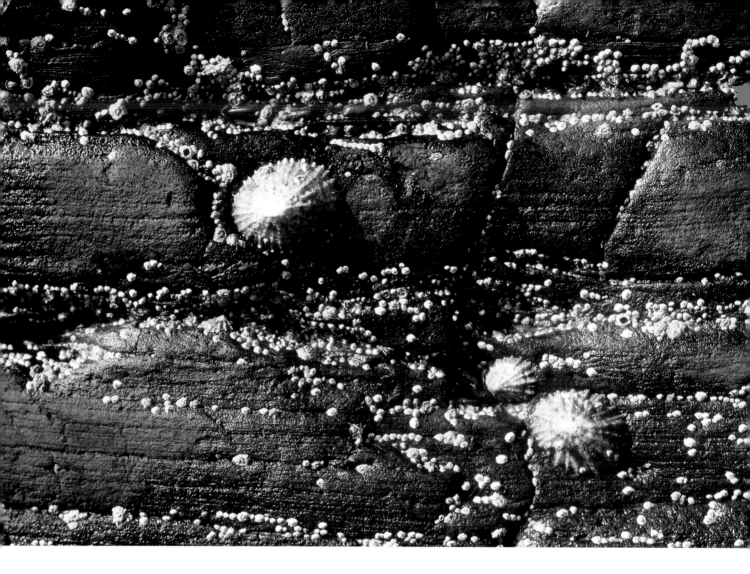

Clinging and rock-boring animals

Whilst highly mobile animals such as crabs and fish are by no means absent from the rocky shore, many of the organisms that are present are either sedentary or move very little. They cling to the substrate, or in some cases burrow into it, in order to remain in the most favorable positions, prevent themselves from being swept out to sea, or dashed against the rocks. In certain cases, a strong attachment can also protect against predation, and where an animal can form a tight seal against the rock with its shell, as in the case of limpets, it can close in moisture to prevent desiccation.

The Common Limpet

Right: The Common Limpet (*Patella vulgata*), is a familiar mollusk on many rocky shores, where it may be found clinging to rocks from the upper to the lower shore. Although it may appear sedentary at low tide, it uses its muscular foot to move around when submerged, in order to graze on algae with its rasping tongue. It then returns to a particular spot as the tide recedes, where, depending on the hardness of the substrate, the limpet's shell either gradually carves out a scar in the rock, or else the edges of the shell are worn down, both of which form an incredibly tight fit.

The barnacle zone

Acorn barnacles such as *Semibalanus balanoides* are also numerous on rocky shores, where they may establish an encrusting "barnacle zone," and like limpets, they possess a protective conical shell. In fact, barnacles were once thought to be related to limpets, but it is now known that they are not mollusks at all, but sedentary crustaceans, which are closely related to shrimps, lobsters and crabs. As larvae, these animals are initially free-floating, but they attach themselves headfirst to rocks, gradually secreting the calcareous plates that form their shells as they grow. At the apex of the shell is an opening known as the opercular aperture, which is covered by movable plates. These seal in moisture at low tide, but open when the barnacle is submerged, allowing it to extend its feathery legs into the water to trap particles of food.

Where soft substrate such as limestone and sandstone is present, some animals bore into the rock itself rather than attaching themselves, including certain types of polychaete worm, such as *Polydora ciliata*. This tiny worm, which grows to about an inch in length, is thought to burrow using a combination of mechanical and chemical action, and although it feeds on detritus, it can be damaging to oysters, mussels and other bivalves, as it will frequently make a home for itself by burrowing into their shells.

The Boring Sponge (*Cliona celata*), which is the largest sponge found on British coasts, and may be recognized by its protruding yellow lobes, also habitually burrows into the shells of mollusks as well as into rocks, and can be a serious problem where oysters or other shellfish are commercially farmed.

Burrowing mollusks

There are also burrowing mollusks, such as the Common Piddock (*Pholas dactylus*), Oval Piddock (*Zirfaea crispata*), and Wrinkled Rock-borer (*Hiatella arctica*), which use their shells like drills, rotating them in order to bore deeply into soft rocks. They then extend their siphons out of the burrow entrance in order to suspension-feed, drawing water and food particles down their feeding tubes to their mouths. Interestingly, despite its name, the Wrinkled Rock-borer does not always form a burrow, but may also attach itself to harder rocks with byssus threads, in much the same way as mussels.

Opposite above: The Common Limpet (*Patella vulgata*) gradually carves itself a niche in the rock.

Opposite below: An upturned Common Limpet, reveals its snail-like foot.

Below: An acorn barnacle (*Balanus balanoides*) feeding in Welsh waters.

The Dogwhelk: driller killer

Despite being a fairly small and innocuous-looking mollusk, the Dogwhelk (*Nucella lapillus*), which is common from the middle to lower shore, is a predatory gastropod that feeds particularly on barnacles and mussels, and is often found on mussel-beds in quite large numbers.

It moves over these areas, clinging by means of its snail-like foot, which tends to be larger in those individuals that inhabit more exposed shores, where wave action is greater, and smaller on more sheltered coastlines. Interestingly, Dogwhelks that live in more sheltered habitats, which possess a smaller foot and thus a smaller shell aperture, also tend to have a longer shell. These adaptations are thought to offer greater protection from highly motile predators such as crabs, which are more numerous in sheltered environments.

The Dogwhelk is able to prize open the calcareous plates that cover the opercular aperture of barnacles in order to feed on them. With bivalves such as mussels, it tends to bore through their shells, using a combination of its drill-like, rasping tongue, or radula, and chemical secretions, which both soften the shell of its victim and digest its body so that it can be easily consumed. These digestive enzymes are also thought to have a narcotic effect on its prey, which may help it to immobilize non-sessile animals.

However, whilst mussels are sedentary, and may appear unlikely to be able to repel such attacks, they have been known to use the byssus threads, with which they attach themselves to rocks and each other, in order to trap Dogwhelks and prevent their advance.

Dogwhelks

Adult Dogwhelks are known to exhibit cannibalism at times, and this behavior begins even before hatching. Between twenty and thirty eggs are laid in vase-like capsules, which are attached to seaweed, rocks or shells, and within which the developing Dogwhelks will consume their siblings, often until only one survivor remains.

Below: Dogwhelk (*Nucella lapillus*) with egg capsules, County Cork, Ireland

The Marine Iguana: one of a kind

The Marine Iguana (*Amblyrhyncus cristatus*), which inhabits the rocky shores of the Galapagos Islands, is unique in being the only marine lizard in the world. Although it spends much of its time on the shore and never swims far out to sea, its diet is entirely composed of a type of algae that grows on sub-tidal rocks.

It never ventures far inland, but must spend several hours basking in the sun in order to raise its body temperature sufficiently, before it can brave the cold and pounding surf. The Marine Iguana is well adapted to this existence, being black in color to absorb heat, possessing long, powerful claws with which to cling to the rocks whilst feeding, a long narrow tail, used to propel itself when swimming, and specialized nasal glands and tear ducts, which are designed to cope with salt-water exposure.

However, typically only the larger males can withstand the cold for any length of time, and are able to remain submerged for up to about ten minutes, allowing them to exploit the abundance of algae that occurs in the deeper water.

Marine Iguanas

In addition to feeding in the ocean, Marine Iguanas will also tend to take to the water for refuge if disturbed or frightened on land.

It is thought that the Marine Iguana was probably transported to the Galapagos Islands on floating rafts of driftwood from South America, where numerous iguana species occur, and subsequently gave rise to the land-dwelling species, *Conolophus sub-cristatus*.

Above: A male Marine iguana (*Amblyrhynchus cristatus*) basks on a rock.

Rockpool communities

Rockpools occur where depressions or fissures in the bedrock of the shore retain water as the tide retreats, offering an on-shore haven for a number of marine organisms at low tide, and allowing a diversity of species more commonly associated with the subtidal shallows to survive further up the shore.

In fact, rockpools may be found straddling the various zones from the upper to the lower shore, but their position does have some bearing on their form, the kinds of organisms that they contain and the problems those organisms may face. Rockpools further up the shore tend to be smaller and shallower, whilst those at lower levels are larger and deeper, offering a more stable habitat.

Salinity increase

Although most rockpools will not dry out entirely, smaller pools in particular can be subjected to extreme variations in temperature and salinity. In winter, such pools may freeze over, and in summer, temperatures may rise to levels that many organisms cannot tolerate. Additionally, as the water evaporates in high temperatures, the salt is left behind and the salinity increases. Conversely, smaller pools are also more greatly affected by rainfall and may become too inundated with freshwater for many marine animals to survive.

Larger, deeper pools are far less susceptible to the effects of air temperature, evaporation and dilution by rainwater, and are also often fully submerged by the tide for long periods. This allows the the establishment of stable micro-communities, which may contain seaweeds, a variety of invertebrates and even fish.

Chiton

Amongst the most common herbivorous grazers that feed on algae are various gastropods and other mollusks, such as chitons, which are also known as coat-of-mail shells, on account of their articulation. From above, these animals somewhat resemble woodlice or pill-bugs, and like some woodlouse species, they are capable of rolling into a ball as a form of defense. Below, however, chitons possess a muscular snail-like foot, which enables them to cling to rock and plant surfaces, and move slowly across them in order to graze on algae, using their rasp-like tongue, or radula. Although most chitons feed only on plant material, there are also omnivorous and carnivorous species, which may graze on simple encrusting organisms or attach themselves to larger animals.

Opposite: Starfish and urchins at the edge of a rockpool at low tide.

Below left: Common or pointed topshell (*Calliostoma zizyphinum*) County Cork, Ireland.

Below right: A coat-of-mail shell or chiton, (*acanthopleura sp*).

The rockpool foodchain

Although food particles may be introduced to and removed from rockpools with the tides, as elsewhere on the rocky shore seaweeds and other algae are the main producers in the rockpool food-chain, supporting the herbivorous animals, which in turn are preyed upon by carnivorous species. The seaweeds include green algae such as *Monostroma grevillei*, which, with its delicate, funnel-like fronds and bright color, may be mistaken for the Sea-lettuce (*Ulva lactuca*), although the latter is less common in rockpools, and various *Enteromorpha* species, which are also bright green, but possess long, tubular fronds. Brown algae found in rockpools includes Thong Weed (*Himanthalia elongata*), named for the long reproductive straps that emerge from its button-like base, Sea-oak (*Halidrys siliquosa*), which bears seedpod-like bladders, and Oyster Thief (*Colpomenia peregrina*), which is globular in form and often found attached to other seaweeds. *Leathesia difformis* is similar, but its brain-like growths are smaller. At greater depth, or in more

shady areas, red algae such as the calcareous *Corallina officinalis*, *Polyides rotundus*, and the bead-like *Lomentaria articulata* may also be found.

Limpets

Limpets are common in rockpools, as are the closely related topshells, such as the Gray Topshell (*Gibbula cineraria*), and Purple Topshell (*Gibbula umbilicalis*). However, the topshells are unable to graze on the harder calcareous red seaweeds and tough kelps, as they lack the iron compounds present in the radular teeth of chitons and limpets, and instead feed mainly on detritus. Predatory mollusks include the sea slugs, such as the Sea-Lemon (*Archidoris pseudoargus*), and the Common Gray Sea Slug (*Aeolidia papillosa*). The former, which is usually yellow in color, feeds on sponges, particularly the Breadcrumb Sponge (*Halichondria panicea*), whilst the latter, which may be recognized by its gray-brown or purple-gray color and the numerous cerata, or appendages on its back, preys mainly on anemones.

Predatory invertebrates

Other predatory rockpool invertebrates include crustaceans such as crabs, which may prey on a wide variety of smaller creatures and also feed on detritus, and starfish, or sun-stars, which often prey largely on mollusks, including those with protective shells. The Common Starfish (*Asterias rubens*), for example, is able to force open the shells of bivalves with the powerful tube-feet that line the underside of its arms, and evert its stomach into the shell to digest its victim. Closely related to the starfish, some species of sea urchins may feed on encrusting invertebrates, although seaweed usually constitutes a large part of their diet.

Many species of crab occur in rockpools, including various hermit crabs, so-called for their habit of occupying discarded shells, shore crabs, such as the Common Shore Crab (*Carcinus maenas*) and the Edible Crab (*Cancer pagurus*), but porcelain crabs, such as the Broad-clawed Porcelain Crab (*Porcellana platycheles*), are perhaps best adapted for rockpool life, being flattened to enable them to squeeze under stones and into crevices for shelter.

Above: The Pink Spotted Shrimp Goby (*Cryptocentrus leptocephalus*) which occurs in the Pacific.

Opposite: A Bat-star eating a sea urchin, seemingly immune to its sharp spines.

Permanent residents

Apart from birds, such as gulls and waders, which may frequent rockpools in order to feed, fish tend to occupy the top of the food chain, and although some species are transitory, some, such as the clingfish, blennies and many of the gobies, are especially well-adapted to living in rockpools, and may be permanent residents. Some are even known to return regularly to the same pools after foraging for food at high tide.

The Blenny, or Shanny (*Lipophrys pholis*), which grows to around 6 inches, is a common rockpool species in north-western Europe that feeds on various crustaceans and mollusks, particularly barnacles, which it is able to crush with its sharp teeth. It lacks scales and has a slimy coating that protects it from desiccation, and may be encountered basking out of the water at the edge of rockpools, into which it will jump if disturbed. This habit, and its rather frog-like appearance have earned it the alternative name of Sea-frog. Similarly, in tropical waters, the Frill-finned Goby (*Bathygobius soporator*), may be observed jumping from pool to pool.

Gobies and blennies are rather similar in appearance, with large heads and protruding eyes, but gobies may be distinguished by the possession of scales, the separation of the dorsal fin into two, and the presence of modified pelvic fins, which form a sucker that allows them to cling to rocks. This feature is also common to the clingfish, such as the Shore Clingfish (*Lepadogaster lepadogaster*).

Other fish that inhabit rockpools include the eel or snake-like Butterfish (*Pholis gunnellus*), so-called on account of its incredibly slippery skin. The fragile-looking, but aggressive, Marine or Fifteen-spined Stickleback (*Spinachia spinachia*), which feeds on small crustaceans and fish, but will attack fish larger than itself, and the Topknot (*Zeugopterus punctatus*). a small flatfish that may be found beneath rocks in larger pools.

Left: A Shy Albatross (*Diomedea cauta*) high on a rocky crag overlooking the sea, New Zealand.

THE SHALLOWS

Seagrasses

Unlike kelp and other seaweeds, which are algae, the seagrasses are angiosperms, or flowering plants, and belong to the same group as the familiar terrestrial grasses, shrubs and trees. Whilst there are several angiosperms that are tolerant of high salinity and intermittent immersion in sea water, such as Cord Grass (*Spartina anglica*) and Glasswort (*Salicornia europaea*), which are common salt marsh species, the fifty or so recognized species of seagrass are the only examples of flowering plants that are able to withstand constant submersion by the sea. It is thought that they are derived from terrestrial plants which have adapted to a marine existence.

Like terrestrial plants, but unlike algae, which are regarded as simple plants, seagrasses possess specialized roots, leaves, conducting tissues and reproductive parts, and are therefore regarded as higher plants.

Specifically adapted

Whilst seaweeds possess root-like holdfasts only for attachment to the substrate, and absorb both nutrients and oxygen throughout the plant, in the case of seagrasses the roots both anchor the plant within the sediment and are specially adapted for the intake of nutrients, which are then transported through the plant by a vascular system comprized of both woody and soft tissues, the xylem and phloem. Oxygen is mainly absorbed from water taken in by the leaves. The chloroplasts necessary for photosynthesis are also restricted to the leaves, as opposed to throughout the plant as in algae. Rather than releasing spores in order to reproduce, seagrasses have separate sexes and reproduce by means of pollen and flowers, or possess both male and female reproductive structures. After fertilization has taken place, seeds are distributed by fruits, which are carried away by the tide. Many seagrasses also produce rhizomes; underground runners or stems, which develop roots and shoots, giving rise to new plants.

Seagrasses inhabit both the northern and southern hemispheres, with Eelgrass (*Zostera marina*), being characteristic of temperate waters, and species such as Turtle Grass (*Thalassia testudinum*), and Manatee Grass (*Syringodium filiforme*), occurring in tropical and subtropical regions.

Seagrass meadows

Like algae, seagrasses need light in order to photosynthesize, and therefore also occur in shallow coastal habitats, but as they require soft sediments such as mud or sand in which to take root, they are most common around sheltered, sediment-depositing areas, such as salt marshes, estuaries, mangroves and coral reefs. Here, seagrasses commonly form dense beds that stabilize the sea floor with their networks of roots and rhizomes, which typically encourages further sediment deposition, and in turn enables more plants to become established, resulting in the growth of lush underwater meadows. These represent a vast and highly productive biomass, which not only contributes to the nutrient cycle significantly, but also provides a habitat for huge numbers of other organisms, which feed, shelter, reproduce and grow on and amongst the leaves, roots and rhizomes.

Life in the seagrass meadow

As seagrasses grow to a maximum of about 3 feet in height, the distribution of organisms in a seagrass meadow may appear less marked than in a kelp forest. However, certain zones and their associated flora and fauna may be identified. These include epiphytes, which live on the stems and leaves of the seagrass, the infauna, found in the sediment and amongst the roots and rhizomes, the epifauna, which dwell on the sediment, and the nekton, or free-swimming organisms that are found in the water column. However, certain organisms, such as those that spend some of their time buried in the sediment, some living on top of it or swimming above it, may not fit neatly into a specific category.

Several species of algae and many sedentary invertebrates use the seagrasses as sites of attachment, but as in kelp forests, relatively few species feed directly on the plants themselves. This is because of their high cellulose content, which most animals find indigestible. Instead, the detritus and nutrients produced by, and released from the large amounts of decaying plant material form the basis of a complex food web. This supports plankton, numerous filter-feeding and scavenging organisms, herbivores and carnivores, from tiny invertebrates to fish and larger animals such as reptiles, birds and mammals. This detritus may also be carried far from its source, into the deep oceans, where it will continue to sustain life.

Above: Common Eelgrass (*Zostera marina*) Orkney, Scotland.

Left: Garibaldi (*Hypsypops rubicundus*) swimming amongst seagrasses in California.

Previous page: A Common Eelgrass bed.

Epiphytes

Seagrass leaves and stems provide a suitable platform for a number of plants and animals, and whilst large benthic algae may be prevented from becoming well established in dense seagrass beds, it is thought that the epiphytic algae that they support, including species such as *Myrionema magnusii*, *Cladosiphon zosterae*, *Halothrix lumbricalis* and *Leblondiella densa* may sometimes account for a biomass approaching the same degree as the seagrass itself, and are therefore also important contributors to the primary production. These algae are often more palatable than seagrasses, and so provide food for a range of herbivorous animals, whilst calcareous red algae species, such as *Rhodophysema georgii*, *Melobesia membranacea* and *Fosliella farinosa* contribute to the accumulation of sediment as they decay.

Grazing on seagrasses

A variety of invertebrates may also be found living and grazing on seagrasses and their associated epiphytic algae, particularly small gastropods, such as *Rissoa membranacea*, the Edible Periwinkle (*Littorina littorea*), Needle Whelk (*Bittium reticulatum*), and the sea slug, *Akera bullata*.

Other organisms residing on Eelgrass include sedentary species such as the polychaete worms *Spirorbis spirorbis* and *Spirorbis spirillum* which dwell in coiled, calcareous tubes, as well as sponges, such as the Chicken-liver Sponge (*Chondrilla nucula*), bryozoans and hydroids.

Many mollusk and crustacean larvae use seagrasses as sites of attachment while they are developing. Highly mobile adult crustaceans such as isopods, and amphipods, and mysids, which are also known as chameleon or opossum shrimps, can be found on the leaves and stems, although they may spend much of their time swimming around and burrowing beneath the plants in search of food and shelter.

The Seagrass Sea Fir (*Laomedea angulata*) is an example of a hydroid that seems to depend entirely on Eelgrass, and it may form large colonies attached to the stems and leaves of the plant, where it will feed by filtering suspended particles from the water. Sessile, stalked jellyfish, such as the Eared Stalked Jellyfish (*Haliclystus auricula*) and (*Lucernariopsis campanulata*) are also commonly found attached to seagrasses, where they feed on a range of small invertebrates, which they capture with their tentacles.

Above: Seagrasses can form extensive beds or meadows.

Opposite: Seagrasses waving gently in the current.

Infauna

The soft sediment in which seagrasses grow enables many invertebrates to burrow easily amongst the complex networks of roots and rhizomes, where they may feed by ingesting the sediment. They extend fan-like filters or siphons to extract particles from the water above, or send out tendrils to grasp small pieces of detritus. Still others may spend much of their time sheltering in the sand or mud, before emerging to scavenge on the bottom, or swim in the water column in search of food.

Suspension feeders

Several species of worms spend much or all of their time in the sediment, from the sediment-swallowing Lugworm (*Arenicola marina*), to carnivorous nematodes, or ribbonworms, such as Oerstedia dorsalis, and sedentary tubeworms like the Sand Mason (*Lanice conchilega*), and the Slime Worm (*Myxicola infundibulum*). The former uses its long tentacles to collect detritus, whilst the latter is a suspension-feeder that possesses fan-like radioles with which to trap food. For this reason, it is also known as a fan worm.

Other suspension-feeders that make up the seagrass infauna include numerous bivalve mollusks, such as pen shells, ark shells, clams, oysters, and cockles, which usually lie buried in the surface sediment, feeding on particulate food by means of their siphons. The Common, or Edible Cockle (*Cerastoderma edule*), the Lagoon Cockle (*Cerastoderma glaucum*), and the Strawberry Cockle (*Americardia media*), are common examples. Mussels, such as the Blue, Edible, or Common Mussel (*Mytilus edulis*), and the Scorched Mussel (*Brachidontes exustus*), are also found buried in the sand, and typically establish themselves amongst the seagrass rhizomes.

Sea urchins

There are herbivorous, omnivorous and carnivorous urchins to be found in seagrass meadows. Both the Variegated Sea Urchin (*Lytechinus variegatus*) and the Long-spined Black Sea Urchin (*Diadema antillarum*) are predominantly herbivorous species, which feed on algae and seagrass, and in some areas, the destruction of large areas of seagrass has been attributed to them. However, when such food is unavailable, they will also graze on corals, which may prove equally destructive to nearby reef habitats. The distinctive Heart Urchin or Sea Potato (*Echinocardium cordatum*), which occurs in temperate Eelgrass beds, and which may be recognized by its soft, hair-like spines, is a deposit-feeder that exists largely on detritus.

Tangled network

The tangled seagrass root and rhizome networks are thought to deter many potential predators from digging for prey in the sediment. They therefore offer a relatively safe habitat for many organisms, particularly those that are capable of burrowing deeply, and that tend to remain hidden. However, more mobile animals, such as the many species of amphipod and isopod crustaceans that seek refuge there, are at risk of predation when they emerge to feed, both from highly mobile predators such as fish and crabs, and more sedentary species, like the elongated, burrowing anemone, *Peachia hastata*, which uses its stinging tendrils to catch passing prey.

Epifauna

Also known as epibenthic organisms, the epifauna or bottom-dwelling species, which live on the sea floor, are typically among the most conspicuous inhabitants of the seagrass meadow. They include a diverse range of motile and sedentary invertebrates, which may be herbivorous, feeding on algae and the seagrass itself; omnivorous; feeding on a variety of plant and animal material; or carnivorous, consuming other invertebrates.

Echinoderms such as starfish, brittle stars, sea urchins and sea cucumbers are common examples of the epifauna found in seagrass meadows, and display a range of feeding behaviors. Some starfish, for example, prey largely on small infaunal invertebrates, including mollusks, crustaceans and worms, whilst others may consume algae or detritus, sometimes ingesting sand or mud, from which tiny organisms and other organic material is then extracted.

Queen Conch

The meadow floor is also home to several mollusks, some of which, such as various conches and the Lightening Whelk (*Busycon contrarium*), may grow surprisingly large. In fact, the Lightening Whelk may attain a length of up to 16 inches, and is a carnivorous species, which feeds mainly on bivalves such as oysters and clams. The Crown Conch (*Melongena corona*), shares a similar diet to the Lightening Whelk, but grows to around half the size, whilst the Pink, or Queen Conch (*Strombus gigas*), grows to about 12 inches, in length, but is herbivorous, feeding on seagrass and algae.

Above: The Queen Conch (*Strombus gigas*).

Opposite: The Fiery Sea Urchin (*Diadema Palmeri*) feeds on submerged vegetation.

Scavenging on the bottom

Many species of crab, shrimp and lobster, including familiar species such as the Common Lobster (*Homarus gammarus*), Spiny Lobster (*Panulirus argus*), and various hermit crabs, may also be found in seagrass meadows, where they tend to scavenge on the bottom amongst detritus, or prey on small invertebrates.

In tropical waters, perhaps one of the most unusual organisms to be found residing on the bottom is the Upsidedown Jellyfish (*Cassiopea xamachana*).

Unlike most jellyfish, which tend to be found swimming in surface waters, the Upsidedown Jellyfish spends most of its time resting on the bottom, in an upsidedown position, with its tentacles extended into the water. It is capable of movement however, and can swim if disturbed. This species may absorb nutrients from the water, or catch prey with its stinging tentacles, but much of its energy is provided by microscopic algae, or zooxanthellae, that dwell within it, and benefit from the jellyfish extending its tentacles toward the sun so that they can photosynthesize.

Other large visitors include dugongs and manatees, the only herbivorous marine mammals and several species of turtle, some of which, such as the Hawksbill Turtle (*Eretmochelys imbricata*) and Green Turtle (*Chelonia mydas*) feed directly on seagrasses.

Nekton

The nekton may be defined as those animals which spend most of their time swimming in the water column, and includes invertebrates, fish, reptiles and mammals. In seagrass meadows, fish tend to dominate, whilst invertebrates are usually restricted to shrimp, jellyfish, squid and cuttlefish species.

Shrimps associated with seagrass include some of the aptly named grass shrimps, such as *Palaemonetes pugio*, and also commercially important species such as the Common Shrimp (*Crangon crangon*), and Pink Shrimp (*Pandalus montagui*), although, whilst their larvae commonly hide amongst vegetation, as adults these last two species tend to be found in more exposed locations, such as over the sandy substrate adjacent to seagrass beds.

The Common, or Big-clawed Snapping Shrimp (*Alpheus heterochaelis*) is often numerous in seagrass habitats. It was formerly confined to tropical and subtropical waters, but is currently increasing in its range and is now present off European coasts. This remarkable animal stuns its prey, which includes other small crustaceans, by snapping shut its oversized claw, which somewhat resembles a boxing glove. The snapping motion shoots a jet of water and an air bubble out of the claw, and as the bubble collapses, it produces not only sound, but light, and an estimated temperature of over 8490F.

The Common Cuttlefish (*Sepia officinalis*), is also capable of the rapid expulsion of water, and may do so both to stun its prey, and to move swiftly in order to avoid predation. It is also able to confuse a potential predator by squirting a cloud of ink, or sepia, into the water, and by changing color. Common Cuttlefish feed on mollusks, crustaceans and small fish, and may also prey on other cuttlefish species such as the Small Cuttlefish (*Sepiola atlantica*).

Opposite above: A Horn Shark (*Heterodontus francisci*) searches for prey in a seagrass bed.

Opposite below: Most sea turtles are herbivorous, feeding on seagrasses and algae.

Below: The Leafy Seadragon (*Phycodurus eques*) is excellently camouflaged by its frond-like fins. This male is carrying eggs beneath its tail.

Fish in the seagrass

Many fish inhabit seagrass meadows, particularly juveniles that may use them as nurseries before entering the open ocean. However there are also numerous resident species, and transient predators that come in search of food.

Seahorses, and the closely related pipefish, may spend almost all of their lives in seagrass beds, and the latter are particularly well adapted to doing so, being camouflaged by closely resembling the leaves and stalks of the plants that they live amongst. Both seahorses and pipefish exhibit unusual breeding behavior, in that the females deposit eggs into a brood pouch in the male, where fertilization takes place. The young then develop in the male's pouch, and it is the male that effectively gives birth to them. Examples include the Short-snouted Seahorse, (*Hippocampus hippocampus*), and the Snake Pipefish (*Entelurus aequoreus*).

Other fish found in seagrass habitats include small species such as gobies, blennies and wrasse that are also found in kelp forests, commercially important species such as flatfish and juvenile Atlantic Cod (*Gadus morhua*), and in tropical waters, countless reef fish, that may visit the seagrass in search of food or refuge. These in turn may attract predators such as sharks and Barracuda (*Sphyraena barracuda*).

Eelgrass disaster

Prior to the 1930s, meadows of Eelgrass (*Zostera marina*) were highly abundant in coastal waters on both sides of the North Atlantic. However, during that decade, vast quantities were devastated by a fungal wasting disease, commonly referred to as "slime mould," which was to have a severe effect on many associated organisms, and lasting implications for those habitats that were affected. In fact, in some areas, the coastline itself, which had formerly been protected by the wave-dampening and sediment-stabilizing effects of the Eelgrass, was permanently changed by increased erosion.

Many species of invertebrates and other animals that relied directly on the Eelgrass for food were drastically reduced in these areas, and some are even thought to have become extinct. Many more organisms that depended on these animals, or upon the meadows as nursing grounds for their young, or as refuge from predators, also suffered. Mollusks, crustaceans and other invertebrates disappeared, and the numbers and diversity of fish species present declined. The overall result was that the entire ecosystem was thrown into turmoil.

As on land, life in the sea is sustained by photosynthesis, whereby chlorophyll-containing plants use the sun's energy to convert water and carbon dioxide into the carbohydrates, or simple sugars that feed the cells of all living organisms. However, as sunlight is required for photosynthesis to take place, and water rapidly absorbs light with depth, this process can only occur in the photic zone; the surface waters of the open oceans or in shallow coastal waters where light can penetrate.

In the open ocean, the vast majority of this primary production is carried out by the microscopic, single-celled algae or diatoms that constitute the free-floating phytoplankton. In coastal waters, the larger algal forms, or macro-algae, which are more commonly known as seaweeds, and the only marine angiosperms, or flowering plants, the seagrasses, may contribute significantly to the primary production.

Moreover, these plants not only provide food, but also sites for attachment and shelter, and where they form vast forests and expansive meadows they typically support a huge wealth of life. Large and well-established beds of vegetation stabilize the sediment beneath them and may also help to protect coastlines and their habitats by reducing the power of the waves as they approach the shore.

Devastation of the Eelgrass

One of the most notable effects, seen on both sides of the Atlantic, was amongst populations of the Brent Goose (*Branta bernicla*) which relied extensively upon Eelgrass for food whilst overwintering on the coast. It has since been estimated that following the outbreak of the slime mould, its numbers may have decreased by as much as 90 percent, as a direct result of the scarcity of its preferred food. Despite this, Brent Geese appeared to adapt over time, by feeding on other Zostera species, such as Dwarf Eelgrass (*Z. noltii*), and Narrow-leaved Eelgrass (*Z. angustifolia*) and also on algae such as Enteromorpha species. However, the decline of the Eelgrass can be seen as akin to an ecological disaster, emphasising both the importance of the plant and the delicate balance of nature.

Opposite above: Brant, or Brent Geese (*Branta bernicla*) flying over a salt marsh. The loss of seagrass beds once dramatically threatened their numbers.

Below: Bladder Wrack seaweed (*Fucus vesiculosus*) The gas-filled bladders help to maintain buoyancy, raising the fronds into sunlit water when submerged.

Green, brown and red algae

Algae are grouped into three main Classes; *Chlorophyceae*, or green algae, *Phaeophyceae*, or brown algae, and *Rhodophyceae*, or red algae. Almost all contain the green pigment chlorophyll, but the brown and red algae contain additional pigments, phycoerythrin and fucoxanthin respectively, which enable them to absorb different wavelengths of light, according to the depth of water that they inhabit. Generally, green algae are found in shallower water, whilst brown and red algae may be found at greater depths, particularly in clear waters.

Whilst the class *Chlorophyceae* contains the largest number of species, most of these are restricted to freshwater, and so green algae are comparatively scarce in marine habitats; however, some such as the Sea-lettuce (*Ulva lactuca*), and related species are a common and familiar sight on rocky shores.

The red algae meanwhile, is a large group that consists mainly of fairly small marine species, and although they may occur at depth, some such as Irish Moss (*Chondrus crispus*) also thrive in rockpools or in shaded areas on the shore. This group also contains calcareous or coralline examples, which contribute to reef formation, and individuals that do not photosynthesize, but which are parasitic, or epiphytic on larger algal forms.

Whilst the brown algae are represented by the fewest number of species, they thrive mainly in cold and temperate waters, and contain some of the most well known of the seaweeds, the wracks, or fucoids, and those which attain the greatest size, the laminarians or kelps.

Kelp forests

The kelps are amongst the most complex of all algae, and some species, notably the giant kelps of the genus *Macrocystis*, can reach remarkable lengths and display phenomenal rates of growth. These, and somewhat smaller species, such as Oarweed, or Sea-belt (*Laminaria digitata*), Cuvie (*Laminaria hyperborea*) and Sugar Kelp (*Laminaria saccharina*), often form dense aggregations in coastal areas that may stretch along vast expanses of coastline, forming underwater beds and forests. These are home to a multitude of organisms, from tiny algal forms to predatory fish and mammals. In shallower water, on the lower shore for example, or where the algae remains submerged, it is usually referred to as a kelp bed, but where these stands reach to the surface, particularly from greater depths, they become known as kelp forests.

Kelp distribution

Significant kelp forests occur around the coasts of Western Europe, South Africa, Southern Australia, in the Americas from Alaska to southern California and along the west coast of South America. They flourish in nutrient-rich colder waters, at depths of about 6 to 100 feet, where they are protected from the most severe wave action, and typically off rocky shores, where the firm substrate offers the best chance of attachment for their well-developed, branching holdfasts.

Although these may be root-like in appearance, the holdfasts do not function like the roots of more complex plants, which draw in water and nutrients, but are simply a means of anchorage. However, they can be seen as habitats in their own right, which often support micro-communities of organisms. From the holdfast extends a prominent stipe, or stalk, which is flexible and strong enough to withstand buffeting currents, and to support the large, leaf-like fronds. These may be tall and slender or very broad, and extend toward the surface and the light in order to maximize the potential for photosynthesis. In many cases, the stipes and fronds are also buoyed by gas-filled bladders, known as pneumatocysts.

As in terrestrial forests, there are typically distinct vertical zones in the kelp forest, from the canopy formed by the fronds, to the seabed, the equivalent of the forest floor, and each of these zones is home to a diverse assembly of plant and animal species.

Right: An urchin-grazed forest of the kelp Cuvie (*Laminaria hyperborea*).

Life in the kelp forest

Despite the high plant biomass in a kelp forest, there are relatively few animals that feed directly upon the living vegetation, which is protected by being tough, rubbery, and in some cases unpalatable, due to the production of acids and other chemicals such as polyphenols. Instead, much of the available food matter is contributed by dead and decaying material that is shed from the plant as it grows or by the rotting down of fronds that are severed by strong currents and waves. This organic detritus forms a rich soup of nutrients in the surrounding water, which provides sustenance at a range of levels for bacteria, microscopic animals, larger filter-feeders and plankton-feeding fish, as it gradually descends to the seabed below, where a host of scavengers lie in wait. In turn, these animals are consumed by numerous predatory species, including carnivorous invertebrates, fish, diving birds and mammals. Some animals are transitory, visiting the kelp forest in search of food and shelter, or in order to breed, establishing nurseries in the relative safety provided by the dense fronds. Other organisms are kelp specialists that make the forest their permanent home.

The canopy

In the forest canopy, those animals that feed directly on the kelp fronds and other vegetation include the Blue-rayed Limpet (*Helcion pellucidum*), which may be recognized by its translucent, blue-spotted shell, sea slugs, such as the Sea-hare (*Aplysia punctata*), and various marine snails, including topshells, pheasant shells and the Black Turban Snail (*Tegula funebralis*). Kelp-eating crustaceans include the amphipod Kelp-curler (*Ampithoe humeralis*), so-called because it dwells in a small chamber that it creates by rolling up kelp fronds and sticking them together with a kind of silk, and crabs such as the Southern Kelp Crab (*Taliepus nuttallii*), which is common in the kelp forests of the US Pacific coast.

In addition to feeding on the kelp itself, this distinctive red species also feeds on bryozoans, tiny, colonial plant-like animals, which form encrustations on the kelp fronds. Also known as moss-animals or sea mats, common examples found on kelp include the Lacy-crust Bryozoans *Membranipora membranacea* and *Membranipora tuberculata*. These sessile organisms do not feed on the kelp, being suspension feeders, which use their tentacles to trap food particles from the water, but they are capable of damaging the seaweed by weighing down the fronds and blocking sunlight from them. However, these bryozoan colonies are rarely able to grow large enough to cause serious damage, as in addition to being eaten by kelp crabs, they are grazed upon by several species of mollusk, and fish such as wrasse. There are also fish, such as the Opal Eye (*Girella simplicidens*), which feed on the kelp itself, as well as small invertebrates that may be attached to it.

Left: A Yellow-crested Weedfish (*Cristiceps aurantiacus*) in a New Zealand kelp bed.

Opposite: Long Handed Spiny Lobster (*Justitia longimanus*).

The understory

Beneath the uppermost canopy, amongst the lower fronds and stipes, younger, smaller kelp plants, which are restricted in their growth by a lack of light, and dense growths of red algae, such as the red Sea Oak (*Phycodrys rubens*), Sea-beech (*Delesseria sanguinea*) and Dulse (*Palmaria palmata*), which often grow as epiphytes on the stipes of kelp, form a distinct understory. Bryozoans are present here too, as are other simple animals such as sponges, sea squirts and hydrozoans that use the stipes as sites of attachment.

Left: Kelp growing attached to boulders, Islay, Scotland.

Predators in the kelp

Additionally, many fish seek refuge from predators amongst the vegetation in this zone, where they thrive by feeding on the wealth of plankton, crustaceans and other small invertebrates that are present.

The vast kelp forests off the Californian coast are particularly species-rich, and common midwater fish include the Senorita (*Oxyjulis californica*), Sheephead (*Semicossyphus pulcher*), Surfperch (*Brachyistius frenatus*), Blacksmith (*Chromus punctipinnis*), Garibaldi (*Hypsypops rubicundus*), Kelp Rockfish (*Sebastes atrovirens*), and Kelp Rockfish (*Paralabrax clathratus*). In addition to fish, swimming invertebrates such as squid and cuttlefish may also be found in the water column.

Despite the relative security offered by the dense vegetation, larger predators also frequent the kelp forests in search of food. Sharks generally prefer to feed in open water, but the Blue Shark (*Prionace glauca*), found in inshore waters throughout much of the Pacific and Atlantic, will often patrol the fringes of kelp forests in search of unsuspecting prey. Other large visitors attracted by the abundance of food include marine mammals such as sea lions, seals, and even whales.

The Gray Whale (*Eschrichtius robustus*) passes through Californian waters during its long migrations, and will enter kelp forests both in order to feed, and to shelter from predatory Killer Whales (*Orcinus orca*), whilst the California Sea Lion (*Zalophus californianus*), may be a familiar sight throughout the year. The Common, or Harbor Seal (*Phoca vitulina*), is widespread in both northern Pacific and Atlantic waters, and may be observed feeding amongst kelp along the coasts of Europe and the US.

In parts of Europe, notably along stretches of the Scottish coast, the Otter (*Lutra lutra*), which is more commonly associated with freshwater habitats, has adapted to a coastal existence, feeding around kelp beds on small fish and crabs. The Sea Otter (*Enhydra lutris*), is a truly marine species that is found along the US Pacific coast, from Alaska to southern California, where it is a resident of the kelp forests, and important in protecting them from overgrazing by bottom-dwelling invertebrates such as sea urchins and abalone.

Below: California Sea Lion (*Zalophus californianus*) in kelp forest, California.

Opposite above: The Gray Whale will enter kelp forests both in order to feed and to shelter from predatory Killer Whales.

Opposite below: Common cuttlefish, (*Sepia officinalis*) near the ocean floor.

The Sea Otter: A keystone species

The Sea Otter (*Enhydra lutris*), which inhabits the kelp forests of the North Pacific, is regarded as a "keystone species," meaning that the role that it plays within its ecosystem is of crucial importance, and that if it was to be removed from its ecosystem, then that system would be drastically altered.

The reason for this is that the Sea Otter needs to consume approximately a quarter of its bodyweight in food each day, and that its preferred diet consists largely of herbivorous invertebrates such as sea urchins and abalone, which can have a devastating effect on kelp if their populations are able to grow unchecked. Whilst other factors, such as climatic conditions, have played a role in the decline of kelp forests over the years, it is widely acknowledged that kelp forests flourish best where urchin populations are low and otter populations are high.

Man and the otter

In fact, the depletion and disappearance of vast swathes of kelp forest throughout the Sea Otter's range, which encompasses northern Japan, the Aleutian Islands and the west coast of North America, has been largely attributed to man's persecution of the otter for its fur. During the eighteenth and nineteenth centuries this almost led to the extinction of this beautiful and highly important species. Before an international treaty was agreed in 1911 to protect the Sea Otter from hunting, it is estimated that the otter population was reduced by as much as 90 percent, from some 20,000, to around 2,000 or fewer. At that time, it was presumed that the Sea Otter would not survive, but owing to continued protection and reintroduction programmes, the current world population is estimated to be in the region of some 100,000 to 150,000. However, the Californian subspecies, *Enhydra lutris nereis*, remains threatened to this day.

The reason that Sea Otters were hunted so extensively, is that their fur is more dense and luxurious than that of any other mammal, with around 500,000 hairs per square inch. Because the otter lacks an insulating layer of blubber, or fat, and may spend its entire life in the ocean, this incredibly dense coat is required to keep the animal warm; trapping a layer of air between the otter's skin and the cold water that it inhabits.

Breeding

Sea Otters tend to be solitary, although males will sometimes associate in groups known as "rafts," however when breeding, they will become territorial. This may occur throughout the year, and is polygynous, meaning that males will mate with several females. Following mating, gestation lasts for around seven months, after which a single pup is most commonly born, although pregnancy occasionally results in twins. The female cares for her young alone, for some six months or more, during which time they learn to dive, hunt and groom themselves. Adults grow to between 31 – 99 pounds in weight, and attain a length of between 40 and 60inches, with females being smaller than males, and may live for up to twenty-three years in the wild.

Left: The Sea Otter (*Enhydra lutris*) dwells in rocky coastal shallows where its food is most abundant. It is rarely found more than a mile from the coast but hardly ever comes ashore – feeding, sleeping and even giving birth at sea, usually taking to land only when threatened by severe storms.

Above: Sea Otter (*Enhydra llutris*) mother and baby resting in kelp bed.

The Sea Otter is found in shallow coastal waters, particularly around rocky coastlines where there are extensive kelp beds or forests, which offer some protection from storms and predators such as sharks and Killer Whales (*Orcinus orca*), and which support large populations of its prey.

In addition to sea urchins and abalone, the Sea Otter will consume other invertebrates such as crabs, squid and octopuses, but it is when feeding on urchins and hard-shelled animals that it demonstrates its most remarkable feeding behavior. Following a short dive, usually of less than two minutes, the otter will surface and turn onto its back to consume its meal, and if it has caught an urchin, abalone or similar creature, it will either strike its prey against a rock placed on its chest, or place the prey animal on its chest and strike it with a rock. This behavior is passed from mothers to their offspring, and is thought to be the only example of tool use by a mammal other than amongst primates.

Foraging is crepuscular, that is, performed mainly at dawn and dusk, and the rest of the otter's time is preoccupied with grooming, in order to maintain the condition of the coat, and resting or sleeping. When at rest, the Sea Otter will often wrap itself in a strand of kelp to prevent it from drifting

Holdfast communities and the kelp forest floor

At the base of large kelps, the knotted holdfasts, which secure the plants to the sea floor, act as microhabitats for a large number of different invertebrates, providing shelter. They also help to trap the falling kelp detritus and other organic matter that provides much of the food in this zone. Many of the motile animals found higher up the kelp, on the stipes and fronds, occur amongst the holdfasts, but a diverse range of bottom-dwelling residents, including bristle worms, anemones, urchins, starfish, mollusks, small amphipods and other crustaceans, also establish their homes here, as well as on the surrounding forest floor.

Opposite: The egg case of the Spotted Ratfish (*Hydrolagus colliei*)

Below: Red algae growing up through a kelp holdfast.

Filter feeders

There are numerous sedentary filter-feeders, such as sponges, sea squirts, bryozoans, hydrozoans and sea-fans that colonize the holdfasts and adjacent rocks, as well as tubeworms and bivalves, all of which siphon or strain food particles from the water.

Where conditions are favorable, soft corals, relatives of the sea anemones, may form fleshy colonies, with their tentacled polyps extended into the current to trap food. A common example is Dead Man's Fingers (*Alcyonium digitatum*), so-called because the feathery nature of the finger-like polyps give the appearance of decomposition.

Colonial sea squirts, such as the Star Ascidian (*Botryllus schlosseri*), may be superficially similar, being composed of individual animals or zooids, which form encrusting or lobed colonies. However these are actually chordates, belonging to the same group that contains the vertebrates, as their free-swimming, tadpole-like larvae possess a supporting notochord and a nerve chord. Like the soft corals, the sea squirts filter food particles from the surrounding water, drawing the water in by beating their tiny, hair-like cilia. In the Star Ascidian, the individuals are arranged around a common exhalant opening through which the filtered water is passed out, which provides the colony's star-like shape.

Other sessile filter-feeders include polychaete worms such as the Keel Worm (*Pomatoceros triqueter*), which dwell in calcareous tubes attached to the substrate, whilst more mobile suspension-feeding animals include anemones, feather-stars and brittle-stars.

Dahlia anemone

The Dahlia Anemone (*Urtica felina*), is amongst the largest of the anemones found in European waters, and is often abundant beneath kelp where it may form large beds. It attaches firmly to the substrate with its adhesive base, but is capable of movement, and will position itself where food is most plentiful.

Similarly, feather-stars, such as *Antedon bifida*, attach themselves to rocks with cirri that protrude from beneath their central discs, but they also traverse the sea floor, and some species are even able to swim by beating their arms. As their name might suggest, the arms of feather-stars are lined with feathery protrusions, which are used to collect falling detritus and small organisms. Closely related brittle-stars, such as the Common Brittle-star (*Ophiothrix fragilis*), and Black Brittle-star (*Ophiocomina nigra*), are also common around kelp, and may occur in very high

densities. They feed in much the same way as feather-stars, collecting particles from the water with their tube feet, but will also scavenge deposited material from the sea floor. The Black Brittle-star has also been observed to feed on carrion and to graze on living plants. Other animals that may feed on the lower parts of the kelp include large, herbivorous mollusks, such as the Pink or Corrugated Abalone (*Haliotis corrugata*), and Red Abalone (*Haliotis rufescens*), which are found in the Pacific. However, their diet is largely comprised of red algae and detached fronds that sink to the bottom, known as drift kelp.

Sea urchins

Under normal circumstances, the diet of sea urchins is also comprised largely of drift kelp, other deposited plant material and smaller invertebrates which they scavenge from the sea bed. When there is a lack of such food, urchins may develop a roving habit, emerging from the crevices where they spend much of their time to feed on the living kelp. They may climb the stipes to feed on the fronds, but more damaging is their habit of eating away at the holdfasts, setting the kelp adrift. Where urchins are able to establish themselves in

significantly large numbers, for example if predators such as fish and mammals are relatively scarce, entire kelp forests may be decimated, resulting in an "urchin barren." In the Pacific, urchin species responsible for such devastation include the Red Sea Urchin (*Strongylocentrotus franciscanus*), and Purple Sea Urchin (*Strongylocentrotus purpuratus*). In European waters, the Common or Edible Urchin (*Echinus esculentus*), may also be potentially damaging to kelp. However, urchin densities are usually kept in check by a number of predators, including other echinoderms, such as starfish and sun-stars.

Arthropods

Arthropods account for some of the more highly mobile animals that hunt and scavenge on the kelp forest floor, from tiny sea spiders, like *Nymphon Gracile* and *Pycnogonum littorale*, which feed on hydroids, bryozoans and anemones, to the more familiar crabs and lobsters. Some, such as many of the spider crabs, are also tiny, but the Common Lobster (*Homarus gammarus*), and Californian Spiny Lobster (*Panulirus interruptus*), which can be remarkably long-lived, may grow to around 40 inches in length.

The Common Starfish

The Common Starfish (*Asterias rubens*), and Common Sun-star (*Crossaster papposus*), are both carnivorous species that feed on a range of invertebrates. They use their powerful arms and tube feet to grasp their prey, and are capable of prising open the shells of bivalves. Both may include urchins in their diet, but the Common Sun-star is also known to prey upon the Common Starfish. Larger species, such as the Spiny Starfish (*Marthasterias glacialis*), and Giant Sea Star (*Pisaster giganteus*), which both attain spans of around 23inches, may face attack from the marine mammals that also feed on urchins, but like all starfish, they display amazing abilities of regeneration, and are quite capable of losing and re-growing limbs.

Above: A Common Starfish (*Asterias rubens*) attacks a Common Cockle (*Cerastoderma edule*).

Kelp reproduction and growth

Kelp fall into two major catergories; lamarians, which occur mainly in the northern hemisphere, which typically possess fairly short stipes and elongate fronds, and bladder kelps, which are generally found in the southern Atlantic, Indian and Pacific Oceans, and may be characterized by the possession of very long stipes that are buoyed up by pneumatocysts, or bladders, at the base of the fronds.

These bladder kelps include the giant kelp such as *Macrocystis pyrifera*, the world's largest algae and marine plant, and large bull kelps such as *Nereocystis luetkeana* and *Durvillaea pottatorum*, all of which exhibit some of the fastest growth rates of any plants. Amazingly, *Macrocystis pyrifera*, which forms dense beds off the coasts of California, South America, Australia and New Zealand can grow up to 300feet in length in favorable conditions, and may grow at an optimal rate of between 20 inches and 40 inches, in a single day.

Giant kelps

Where giant kelps and bull kelps occur in close association, *Macrocystis* species will usually dominate, out-competing bull kelps for available light, particularly in calmer waters, but the hardier bull kelps will thrive in more exposed conditions, being able to withstand higher wave activity.

Some kelp species are annuals, living for just one year, but others are perennial, and may live for up to seven. Regardless of this however, the reproductive cycle is generally similar, with generations alternating between sexual and asexual stages. The visible kelp plants are sporophytes, which produce and release microscopic spores, usually in early spring, which then germinate to give rise to microscopic male and female plants, known as gametophytes. In turn, these develop male and female gametes, or reproductive cells. The male gametes then fertilize the female gametes, giving rise to new sporophytes, which, where the female gametes are not released into the water, may begin their lives as growths upon the female gametophyte. These settle on the sea floor, where they grow rapidly into the large and conspicuous kelp plants.

Surviving the winter

As with many terrestrial plants, in the northern hemisphere, most of the kelp's growth occurs in spring and summer, and by fall they have released their spores and begin to die. In the case of annuals, the sporophyte dies completely, but perennials merely die back over the winter months to grow anew the following spring. During the winter, storms may also have a significant effect on kelp forests, as the increased wave action tears away fronds, and in severe weather, whole plants may be ripped from the substrate. However, as in terrestrial forests, this creates spaces where new plants can become established, and allows light to penetrate to the forest floor, which will encorage growth. Relatively little is known of the microscopic stages of kelp, but it is thought that the spores and gametophytes are probably highly susceptible to pollution, suffocation by sediment and consumption by numerous animals.

Below: This Spiny Dog Fish (*Squalus acanthias*) lurks amongst large kelp fronds.

Sirenians

The order Sirenia is divided into two families: Dugongidae, which today contains only the Dugong (*Dugong dugon*), and Trichechidae, which comprises the three species of manatee: the West African Manatee (*Trichechus senegalensis*), the Amazonian Manatee (*Trichechus inunguis*), and the West Indian Manatee (*Trichechus manatus*). However, the latter occurs in two races or subspecies: the Florida Manatee (*T.m. latirostris*) and the Antillean Manatee (*T.m. manatus*).

Today, sirenians are found only in tropical or subtropical waters, with the manatees being found along Atlantic coasts and adjacent rivers, and the Dugong inhabiting the Indo-Pacific region. However, the order,

which is believed to have originated in Africa some 50 to 55 million years ago during the Eocene Period, is thought to have once contained many more species, which were at one time, much more widely distributed around the globe. In fact, a huge species of Dugong, known as Steller's Sea Cow (*Hydrodamalis gigas*), was discovered by Georg Wilhelm Steller in the cold waters of the northern Pacific Ocean in 1741, but it had been hunted to extinction for its flesh within less than thirty years.

The sirenians are also known collectively as sea cows, no doubt on account of their grazing behavior, and they are in fact the only herbivorous marine mammals, although some would suggest that only the Dugong is truly marine, as the Manatees also inhabit

freshwater. Both feed on seagrasses and other aquatic vegetation, and are the largest animals that graze in seagrass meadows, growing to between 10 – 13 feet in length, with the Dugong weighing up to about 2,000 pounds, and manatees weighing up to around 3,500 pounds. It is also estimated that they may consume between 10 and 15% of their bodyweight in vegetation per day. Most feeding is performed underwater, with vegetation being rooted out with the prehensile, bristled muzzle, although manatees have been observed partially hauling themselves on to river banks in order to reach vegetation.

The Dugong and manatees are similar in appearance, being large, gray-brown, almost hairless animals, with flipper-like forelimbs, and massive, walrus-like heads. Unlike walruses however, sirenians lack hindlimbs, and instead possess either a notched, fish-like tail, as in the Dugong, or a rounded, un-notched paddle, as in the manatees. The manatees also differ from the Dugong in lacking incisors, and with the exception of the Amazonian Manatee, in possessing nails on their front flippers.

Both however are regarded as sub-ungulates and are thought to share a common ancestry with the hoofed mammals. Perhaps somewhat surprisingly however, their closest living relatives are thought to include elephants and hyraxes.

Above: Florida Manatees (*Trichechus manatus latirostris*) resting on the sea bed in shallow water.

Opposite: The Dugong or Sea Cow (*Dugong dugong*).

Reproduction

Neither manatees nor the Dugong ever haul out of the water completely, and like the cetaceans, or whales and dolphins, they give birth to, and nurse their young, in the water. The reproductive rate for sirenians is low however, with female manatees reaching sexual maturity at about five years of age, and males at around nine years of age, whilst female Dugongs may not be sexually mature until they are ten years old. Gestation lasts for about a year, and once a calf is born, it may remain dependent upon its mother for up to two years. As a result, it is thought that a female will produce on average just one calf every two to five years.

Although the Dugong and manatees generally suckle their young underwater, it has been suggested that they may sometimes nurse them in an upright position, which, although somewhat difficult to believe, is thought to have given credence to the ancient legends of mermaids, or sirens, resulting in the order to which they belong becoming known as Sirenia.

Left: Florida Manatees (*Trichechus manatus latinostris*) swimming in the Crystal River, Florida.

MANGROVES

Tropical shores

Like the salt marshes and tidal flats of temperate regions, mangrove forests, swamps, or mangals, as they are also sometimes known, straddle the border between the terrestrial and the marine. They are common features of estuaries and river deltas, where the accumulation of deposited sediment provides a rich, muddy substrate in which the mangrove trees can become established.

However, mangroves not only colonize the brackish waters of estuaries and their adjacent coastlines, but also occur along shores that are sheltered from wave action by coral reefs, and in fact it is in locations such as these that mangrove forests tend to be most extensive. Yet mangroves not only require shelter if they are to thrive, but also warmth, which accounts for them being characteristic of tropical and subtropical shores.

The largest and most diverse mangrove forests are found throughout the Indo-Pacific, where reefs are most numerous and extensive, climatic conditions are most favorable, and warm water currents dominate. Mangroves are also found along stretches of Atlantic coasts, perhaps most notably in West Africa, and in the Americas from the Florida Everglades, across the Caribbean to Brazil.

The particular species inhabiting these forests, and their relative diversities may vary. For example, there are just three principal species of mangrove tree occurring together in parts of North America, in comparison to around forty in parts of the Indo-Pacific. Mangrove habitats are broadly similar in their form and function, being highly productive intertidal forests, which provide a unique habitat for numerous species of terrestrial and aquatic organisms, particularly birds, fish and invertebrates. Additionally, mangroves help to accrue sediment and stabilize coastlines, and act as a filter for both organic matter and potentially harmful runoff from terrestrial habitats such as farmland.

Previous page: Mangrove lagoon.

Left: The branching roots of plants such as the Small-stilted Mangrove *(Rhizophora stylosa)* help to trap soft sediments.

Mangrove trees

The term "mangrove" is not restricted to a particular species, genus or even family of trees, but instead is applied to a diverse group of trees and shrubs. In fact, there are around seventy species in total that are commonly designated as mangrove trees, which are often broadly divided into Old World and New World species, with around sixty belonging to the former group and ten placed in the latter. These vary from fairly short shrubs, of perhaps 3-6 feet tall, to huge trees of up to about 100feet in height, and a small number of palms, ferns, climbers and vines also regarded as mangroves.

However, they share a distinct preference for the intertidal habitat of shallow, muddy, tropical and subtropical estuaries and shores, and demonstrate an extraordinary tolerance of high salinities. They not only have to cope with some degree of tidal inundation, but also with the brackish conditions of estuaries or sheltered lagoons, and the varying input of freshwater provided by rainfall.

Dealing with variable salinities

Overall, what links these plants are certain characteristic adaptations to the habitat in which they occur, such as modified and specialized roots and leaves to deal with high and variable salinities, and particular strategies for dealing with reproduction for example, many of which display evidence of convergent evolution. Despite this, the various mangrove plants also exhibit marked preferences for particular parts of their mangrove habitat, resulting in patterns of zonation, whereby different plants thrive in different areas according to the degree of tidal inundation and salinity experienced, the depth and consistency of the substrate, and the availability of nutrients.

Opposite: Small-stilted Mangrove (*Rhizophora stylosa*) Great Barrier Reef, Australia.

Below: An Estuarine Crocodile (*Crocodylus porosus*) lurks amongst submerged vegetation.

Adaptations

Along with needing to cope with euryhaline conditions, another major problem for mangrove plants is a lack of available oxygen in the sediment. Just as in salt marshes, the high levels of organic matter produced and deposited in mangrove forests, which makes them highly productive and nutrient-rich habitats, also leads to a depletion of oxygen in the soil. Below the surface layer of sediment, conditions may be completely anaerobic, as the oxygen is expended by the extremely high levels of bacteria that are breaking down the organic material. This problem is compounded by the dense mud being waterlogged, and resistant to gaseous exchange. Therefore, the two main problems experienced by mangrove plants are high or variable salinity, and lack of oxygen, and they display various adaptations in order to solve both.

The roots of mangroves vary in form, but all tend to spread horizontally through the upper layer of sediment where oxygen is most readily available, and to have portions exposed to the air, which contain lenticels, or areas of porous tissue through which oxygen may be obtained. In many mangroves the roots are buttress-like, spreading out from the trunk high above the water, whilst the submerged, spreading roots may send up snorkel-like projections. These are known as pneumatophores, or a series of bends, which are usually referred to as knee-roots.

Mangrove roots are typically also responsible for some degree of salt regulation, and often use a process known as ultrafiltration, which reduces salt uptake, but the salt that is absorbed is then usually dealt with by specialized leaves. The leaves often accumulate salt, which may be secreted through salt glands, or simply shed, and are also modified to retain water in order to dilute the salt content of the plant. Such modifications include having thick waxy leaves and layers of hairs to reduce water evaporation, and large areas for storing water, as in cacti and other succulent plants.

Reproduction

Many mangrove plants demonstrate an unusual method of reproduction, known as vivipary, whereby new seedlings, known as propagules, grow from their seed pods whilst still attached to the parent plant. Quite what advantages this presents remains a subject for discussion, but it is known that the parent plants are able to regulate the salt intake of the seedlings as they develop, and by the time that they are ready to detach, they already possess well developed roots and leaves. The propagules are then able to root themselves and begin growing extremely quickly, either having dropped directly into the mud below, or having been dispersed to a suitable location by floating.

Opposite: Brown Pelican (*Pelecanus occidentalis*) nesting in mangroves, Galapagos.

Right: Young mangrove with stilts, Solomon Islands.

Below: Nurse Shark (*Ginglymostoma cirratum*) with school of juvenile jacks.

Mangrove fauna

Mangrove forests provide a unique combination of habitats in which terrestrial and marine animals coexist; from the forest canopy and well established forest floor, which may be home to numerous birds, insects, reptiles and mammals, to the tangled root systems, shifting mud and shallow waters of the intertidal zone. This region is dominated by marine invertebrates and frequented at high tide by various species of fish.

One of the main sources of primary production in the mangrove forest comes through the breaking-down of large quantities of leaf litter produced by the mangrove trees, which sustains a vast assemblage of herbivorous and detritivorous organisms below, particularly invertebrates. These may obtain their food in a variety of ways, such as by extracting particles from the water, ingesting the sediment, or by scavenging on its surface. In turn these creatures provide food for larger predatory animals.

The mangrove roots serve as sites of attachment for many animals, including encrusting barnacles such as the Striped Barnacle (*Balanus amphitrite*) various sponges, anemones, hydroids and sea squirts, bryozoans, such as the Mangrove Lace Coral (*Sundanella sibogae*) and bivalves such as the Leaf Oyster (*Isognomon ephippium*) and Enigma Oyster (*Enigmonia aenigmatica*). The roots are also burrowed into by animals such as the Wedge Piddock (*Martesia cuneiformis*) and shipworms, which are actually mollusks with reduced shells. Grazing mollusks, such as the Mangrove Periwinkle (*Littorina angulifera*), Common Nerite (*Nerita lineata*) and Mud Creeper (*Cerithidea obtusa*) also traverse the roots, and can often be found well out of the water on tree trunks at low tide, probably to avoid scavenging predators below. At high tide, the roots provide shelter for shoals of small fish.

Opposite: A Mangrove Viper (*Boiga dendrophila*) prepares to strike.

Below: A cleaner goby attends to a large grouper in the Caribbean.

Beneath the roots

Beneath the roots, the mud may be oxygen-poor, but it is nutrient-rich, and provides a home for the burrowing invertebrates that constitute the infauna, offering them a degree of protection from desiccation and from predators. There are large burrowing anemones such as the Giant Mangrove Anemone (*Anthenopleura africana*), and numerous worms, including sediment-swallowers, carnivorous flatworms and ribbonworms, and also many detritus feeders, like the tubeworms and keelworms that dwell in tubes of debris-coated mucus or calcareous material and extend tentacle-like appendages into the water to trap food. The Peanut Worm (*Phascolosoma arcuatum*) is an unusual species, which lies buried deeply in the mud and extends its elongated feeding apparatus to the surface.

Burrowing animals

Similarly, numerous bivalves feed from beneath the mud through their siphons, including species such as the Lantern Clam (*Laternula truncata*), Sunshet Shell (*Gari elongata*), and the Nest Mussel (*Musculista senhausii*). Some bivalves, such as the Toothless Clam (*Anodontia edentula*), have greatly reduced or absent siphons, and instead derive much of their nutrition from the sulfur-oxidizing bacteria that live in their gills. All these burrowing animals help to introduce oxygen into the sediment, as do the numerous species of crabs which may form conspicuous hordes at low tide as they move around above the sediment in search of food.

Left: Mangrove roots often act as a nursery for young fish and also provide feeding and resting places for adults.

Mangrove crabs

The fiddler crabs, such as the Mangrove Fiddler (*Uca thayeri*), and Orange Fiddler (*Uca vocans*), are perhaps amongst the most familiar, and are best known for the outsized claw of the males, which is used both for attracting females and warding off rivals. The other claw is used for feeding, spooning sediment into the mouth, from which organic material is extracted.

Other common mangrove crabs include grapsid crabs, such as the Orange Signaller Crab (*Metaplax elegans*), the males of which possess vivid orange claws, ghost crabs, soldier crabs and mud crabs, many of which feed directly on the decomposing leaves of mangrove trees.

Other mangrove crustaceans include mud lobsters, such as *Thalassina anomala* and *Thalassina gracilis*, which make extensive mounds and burrows, and several species of prawn, which play important roles as both consumers of detritus, and as food for larger species. The Hairy-handed Prawn (*Caridina propinqua*) is notable for the hairs on its pincers, which help it to trap particles of food.

Above: Feather duster worms extend their tentacles into the water to trap passing food.

Opposite: A male fiddler crab gestures with its outsized claw.

Fresh water and marine species

Despite the brackish conditions typical of mangroves, the food-rich waters typically support large numbers of fish, and where the mangroves line estuaries, these may include freshwater as well as marine species. Some fish are well adapted to euryhaline conditions, and may be found in mangrove habitats throughout their lives, whilst others use them as nursery habitats in which to shelter when young.

Common mangrove fish include jacks, mullets, tarpons, basses and groupers, as well as many species commonly associated with seagrass beds and coral reefs, which may venture into mangroves in order to feed, breed or shelter.

Amphibians and reptiles
Amphibians themselves are uncommon in mangroves, preferring fresh to brackish water. However, parts of the Indo-Pacific are home to the Crab-eating Frog (*Rana cancrivora*), which unusually, is able to tolerate saline conditions.

Reptiles such as snakes and lizards may be common in the trees, whilst watersnakes, seasnakes, crocodilians and turtles may be found in the shallows below.

Left: An Archerfish (*Toxotes jaculator*) spits water at an insect to dislodge it from its resting place.

Mudskippers

Perhaps the most unusual and striking of mangrove fish are the mudskippers. These fish are closely related to gobies, and somewhat resemble them, with their bulbous eyes and modified pectoral fins, which allow them to traverse the mud as if walking. Perhaps most remarkable of all are species such as the Gold-spotted Mudskipper (*Periophthalmus chrysospilos*), which not only crawl across the mud with their modified fins, but actually use them to haul themselves up the roots and trunks of trees. Mudskippers are able to breathe out of water by retaining water in their gill cavities and refreshing it as necessary; it is also thought that like amphibians, some species are able to absorb oxygen through their skin.

Above: Mudskippers (*Periophthalmus sp.*) rest on a branch out of the water. Ujong Kulon, Java.

Right: A Green Iguana (*Iguana iguana*) basks in the branches of a mangrove tree, Costa Rica.

Mammals and birds

Mammals are relatively scarce, but may include raccoons, otters, squirrels, rats, wild pigs, cats and dogs, and also monkeys, such as the Long-tailed Macaque (*Macaca fascicularis*), Silver Leaf Monkey (*Presbytis cristata*), and the Proboscis Monkey (*Nasalis larvatus*). This species, which takes its name from the enlarged nose of the males, is found in Borneo and Sumatra, where it feeds almost exclusively on mangrove vegetation. Bats, such as the Lesser Dog-Faced Fruit Bat (*Cynopterus brachyotis*), are also common roosting in mangroves, as are many species of birds, several of which make mangroves their permanent home, whilst others may visit them in order to breed, or during migrations.

Kingfishers, darters, cormorants and large waders such as herons, egrets and ibises may be observed feeding on fish in the shallows. Smaller waders such as plovers, redshanks and sandpipers may patrol the mud at low tide in search of invertebrates, and the forest canopy may be home to a myriad of small tree-dwelling birds.

Above: Ibises, such as this Scarlet Ibis (*Eudocimus ruber*) frequent mangroves to roost and feed on fish.

Opposite above: Proboscis Monkey (*Nasalis larvatus*) Borneo.

Opposite below: Chimpanzee (*Pan troglodytes*) young, swinging on mangroves, West Africa.

THE FROZEN
POLAR COASTS

Freezing Arctic and Southern Oceans

In the barren, windswept polar interiors, where temperatures are at their lowest, there may be little visible life, and in fact, with the exception of bacteria and other microscopic organisms, almost no life at all. However, at the polar coasts, where rock and ice meet the freezing Arctic and Southern Oceans, a variety of animals are able to thrive, sustained by the nutrient-rich waters.

Yet these coasts are unlike any others on earth, seasonally shrinking and growing by hundreds of miles each year as the loose pack ice freezes to the permanently frozen ice that forms the Arctic ice cap or the fast-ice which surrounds the Antarctic continent, before thawing and breaking apart once more.

Permanently frozen water

The two polar regions differ greatly in this respect; the Arctic comprises a mass of permanently frozen water that sits at the heart of an almost fully enclosed ocean, fringed by the landmasses of North America, Greenland and Eurasia, whilst Antarctica is a rocky landmass, isolated by hundreds of miles of ocean from any other.

With the exception of the polar cap, the Arctic coasts are contiguous with areas of temperate mainland, which has enabled plant and animal species to adapt more easily to changing conditions. Antarctica's isolation ensures that it is both colder, lacking the warmth that would otherwise be supplied by close proximity to other landmasses, and resistant to colonization by terrestrial species from elsewhere. In the Arctic summer, the retreating ice reveals rocky coasts and vegetated tundra where a diverse array of terrestrial animals flourish, but in Antarctica, where perhaps only four percent of the land is ever free of ice, the largest organism that does not rely directly on the sea for its food is a species of midge. However, the ice itself forms an extension of the land, upon which terrestrial and marine animals can feed and reproduce, and the waters around both poles literally teem with life, from tiny planktonic forms, to mighty whales.

Right: A juvenile Harp Seal (*Phoca groenlandica*) swims beneath the Arctic ice.

Arctic flora and fauna

Despite the seemingly inhospitable conditions of polar seas, their coldness actually ensures that they are oxygen-rich, whilst glaciers and the run-off from rivers add nutrients, phosphates and nitrates that together sustain the diatoms and other single-celled plants that comprise the phytoplankton which forms the base of the Arctic marine food web. In summer, when the ice breaks up and light is available, these microscopic algal forms bloom at an astonishing rate, staining the underside of the ice yellow-brown, and providing food for a community of herbivorous, sympagic, or ice-associated organisms, some of which make up part of the zooplankton. These are mainly copepod crustaceans, which may crawl along beneath the ice and through the channels of brine that flow between the ice crystals, but they may also spend time swimming or drifting in the surrounding water. Other members of the zooplankton include the larvae of benthic (bottom-dwelling) invertebrates, carnivorous jellyfish and ctenophores, or comb jellies, as they are also known, and pteropods, or winged snails, which swim by beating their modified mollusk foot as if it were a pair of wings.

The zooplankton in turn provides food for larger, predatory invertebrates, including cephalopods, such as squid and octopus, like the Arctic Lesser Octopus (*Eledone cirrhosa*), numerous fish, including species such as the Arctic Cod (*Boreogadus saida*), Herring (*Clupea harengus*),Grayling (*Thymallus thymallus*), Arctic Char (*Salvelinus alpinus*), and several species of salmon. These in turn provide food for many seabirds and large mammals such as seals and whales, many of which may also feed directly on plankton. The largest Arctic fish, the Greenland Shark (*Somniosus microcephalus*), however, has few, if any predators. It may grow to over 20 feet in length and weigh up to 2000 pounds, and feeds on fish, including other sharks, seals and even small whales.

Close to the shore, the formation and movement of ice in winter may crush bottom-dwelling invertebrates, but in summer, and below the ice on the continental shelves, a wide range of benthic organisms may be found. These include anemones and sea cucumbers, such as the Red Sea Cucumber (*Stichopus tremulus*), brittle-stars, starfish, urchins, barnacles, limpets, periwinkles, bivalve mollusks and crabs, including the Witch Crab (*Paromola cuvieri*). These animals may feed dissolved organic matter or scavenge amongst the adaptations to living in water that is close to freezing, including having slow metabolisms, dehydrating themselves to prevent internal freezing, and possessing enzymes that are efficient at extremely low temperatures.

Marine mammals: whales, seals and the walrus

Several cetaceans, or whales and dolphins, may be found in Arctic waters, but two species are endemic, the Narwhal (*Monodon monoceros*), and the Beluga, or White Whale (*Delphinapterus leucas*), whilst a third, the Bowhead, or Greenland Right Whale (*Balaena mysticetus*), is restricted to the Arctic Ocean and neighboring seas. In summer, both the Narwhal and the Beluga may be found in shallow coastal waters, whilst the Bowhead is often encountered close to the edges of the ice, and tends to calve in shallow waters in spring.

Both the Narwhal and Beluga feed mainly on fish, although squid, mollusks, crustaceans and other invertebrates are also consumed. Regarded as primitive whales, they are closely related species, and are of a similar size, growing to a length of around 13 – 16 feet, and a weight of about 1.6 tons. However, they differ in various ways, perhaps most notably in that the male Narwhal possesses a spiralled tusk that extends from the head, which may be up to 10 feet long. This is actually a modified tooth, and is used in breeding displays.

The Bowhead whale

The Bowhead whale grows to around 60 feet in length, and may weigh as much as 100 tons. During the eighteenth and nineteenth centuries, it was hunted almost to extinction. Ssince that time stocks have recovered somewhat and it is now protected, although the native Inuit people are allowed to hunt it on a limited basis. The Bowhead is a baleen whale, which means that it possesses huge plates of baleen rather than teeth, which are used to filter vast quantities of plankton from the water.

Left: A male and female Narwhal (*Monodon monoceros*). Only the males possess the distinctive tusk.

Below: A Bowhead Whale (*Balaena mysticetus*) surfaces close to floating ice, near Baffin Island, Canada.

Seals in the Arctic

Five species of seal occur in the Arctic: the Ringed Seal (*Phoca hispida*), Harp Seal (*Phoca groenlandica*), Hooded Seal (*Cystophora cristata*), Bearded Seal (*Erignathus barbatus*), and the Banded, or Ribbon Seal (*Phoca fasciata*), which are all classed as true, or earless seals, belonging to the family Phocidae. The Hooded Seal and Harp Seal are generally pelagic, and are rarely found close to land, but the others are often seen in coastal waters or on inshore ice, particularly when breeding. The Ringed Seal is the most common and widespread species, and also the smallest, growing to about 5 feet in length and weighing around 286 pounds. It feeds on small fish and crustaceans, and the females typically give birth to their pups in snow caverns, in order to minimize predation by Polar Bears. The Ribbon and Bearded Seals tend to give birth on the shifting pack ice or drifting floes, for the same reason. The Ribbon Seal breeds near land in spring, but is thought to be largely pelagic for much of the year, dispersing with the broken pack ice in summer. It too feeds on fish and crustaceans and is a

small species, attaining a length of about 6 feet, and a weight of around 200 pounds.

The Bearded Seal however, is up to 10 feet long and 880 pounds in weight. Its name is derived from its prominent whiskers, or vibrissae, which it uses in sensing hard-shelled, bottom-dwelling prey such as crustaceans and mollusks. These seals are all well adapted to their marine existence, being powerful, streamlined swimmers, and also to the extreme cold of their habitat, with a thick layer of insulating blubber. A further adaptation amongst females is that of delayed implantation, whereby following mating, implantation of the fertilized egg into the womb can be delayed by several months until conditions are more favorable.

Opposite: Beluga Whales (*Delphinapterus leucas*) in the shallows of Cunningham Inlet, Somerset Island, Central Arctic.

Below: Bearded Seal (*Erignathus barbatus*) Svalbard, Norway.

Walrus

Like the true seals, the Walrus (*Odobenus rosmarus*), lacks external ears, but like the sea lions and fur seals it has the ability to rotate its rear flippers forward, and to use them like feet on land. However, it belongs to its own family, Odobenidae, meaning "tooth walkers," in reference to its habit of using its tusks to pull itself onto the ice.

There are two races or subspecies, the Pacific, *Odobenus rosmarus divergens*, and the Atlantic, *Odobenus rosmarus rosmarus*, with the Pacific being slightly larger, growing to a maximum length of about 12 feet, and a weight of around 4,000 pounds, whilst the Atlantic race reaches around 10feet in length, with a weight of about 2,000 pounds. They are sociable animals, and frequently gather on beaches or ice floes in large numbers, but males become territorial when breeding, at which time the tusks may be used in fighting. Walruses feed on some fish and squid, but are typically bottom-feeding, and their diet consists largely of clams and other benthic mollusks. However, large males in particular may also kill and eat seals.

Above: Walruses
(*Odobenus rosmarus*)
often haul out in groups
following diving.

The Polar Bear

The Polar Bear (*Ursus maritimus*), is the largest and most powerful predator of the Arctic shores and sea ice, and in fact the largest of all terrestrial carnivores, growing to an average of about 9 feet in length and 1,000 pounds in weight. It is also the most carnivorous of all bear species, feeding mainly on seals such as the Ringed Seal and Bearded Seal, but it is an opportunist hunter and will also kill and eat small mammals such as rodents, birds, fish and invertebrates, small whales, Walruses and sometimes even Musk Oxen (*Ovibos moschatus*). Additionally, it will supplement its diet with carrion and vegetation. When hunting for Ringed Seals in spring, the Polar Bear will often pounce on the females and pups as they hide in their snow caverns. Female Polar Bears also give birth to their young in snow caves, usually in early winter, where they will remain until spring, when conditions are more favorable, and the cubs, usually two in number, are capable of following their mother as she begins to hunt after a long period of fasting. The cubs will also be ready to begin eating solid food, but they may continue to suckle for over two years. As the cubs grow, they rapidly develop their thick fur and a layer of insulating blubber, which will protect them from the cold winds and icy water.

Polar Bears are powerful swimmers, and are able to close their nostrils in order to remain submerged for up to two minutes. With their extreme bulk they are no match for a streamlined seal, Beluga or Walrus in the water. They tend to stalk their prey across land and ice, or otherwise surprise it at the water's edge or at breathing holes in the ice.

Below: Polar Bears (*Ursus maritimus*) sparring.

Birds of the Arctic

With the exception of the Snowy Owl (*Bubo scandiacus*), Gyrfalcon (*Falco rusticolus*), Ptarmigan (*Lagopus mutus*), Raven (*Corvus corax*), and Ross's Gull (*Rhodostethia rosea*), few birds are well adapted enough to survive throughout the unforgiving Arctic winter, when temperatures may plummet to -58°F. Even these species may be forced to move to more southerly latitudes or adopt nomadic behavior in order to find food. However, many birds, including waders, ducks and geese, breed on the Arctic tundra and shores in summer, when temperatures are less harsh and food more plentiful, before migrating south to warmer lands. Seabirds, including numerous gulls, auks and terns, may also establish large colonies near the coast in summer, taking advantage of the abundance of fish that are sustained by the blooming plankton, before heading out to open waters following the breeding season. Some, such as the Arctic Tern (*Sterna paradisaea*), and Arctic Skua (*Stercorarius parasiticus*), which is also known as the Parasitic Jaeger, for its habit of preying on other birds' eggs, and for harrying smaller birds into giving up their food, even migrate as far south as Antarctica, a distance of some 12,000 miles.

Above: Arctic Tern (*Sterna paradisaea*)
An adult returns to its breeding colony in late evening light, Iceland.

Opposite: The Thick-billed Murre (*Uria lomvia*) nests on vertical cliff faces to avoid potential predators.

Antarctic flora and fauna

With no terrestrial animals larger than a tiny, wingless midge, Belgica antarctica, which may grow to only a fraction of an inch in length, and only two flowering plants, Antarctic Hair Grass (*Deschampsia antarctica*), and Antarctic Pearlwort (*Colobanthus quitensis*), the terrestrial ecosystem in Antarctica is based around microscopic invertebrates, algae, mosses, lichens and liverworts, many of which thrive best around exposed, ice-free, rocky outcrops along parts of the coast. Further inland, the soils are so impoverished and there is such a lack of precipitation that large areas are effectively desert, and not only desert, but one of the least diverse habitats anywhere on Earth. In fact, Antarctica is the coldest, driest and least hospitable of all the continents, and yet in remarkable contrast, the waters of the Southern Ocean are amongst the most complex and productive of any marine habitats on the planet.

The waters here are undeniably cold, but they are rich in oxygen and nutrients, and fed by a unique system of currents, such as the Antarctic Circumpolar Current, and Antarctic Convergence, which results in upwellings, whereby the meeting of cold and warm waters gives rise to a constant flow of nutrient-rich water to the surface from the deep ocean. In the summer, with periods of prolonged light, this promotes the growth of phytoplankton, which sustains the key component in the Antarctic food web: krill.

Krill

Krill are small, shrimp-like crustaceans, with a worldwide distribution, but in Antarctic waters, one in particular, the Antarctic Krill (*Euphausia superba*), is of chief importance. Like the Arctic copepods, the Antarctic Krill may spend time living amongst the ice, but in summer, when diatoms and other microscopic plant life flourish, they become the main component of the free-floating zooplankton, accounting for an estimated biomass of perhaps 100 to 700 million tons each year, with their swarms frequently exceeding densities of over 15,000 individuals per cubic yard of water. These swarms are effectively at the mercy of the currents and waves, although the krill are able to make vertical migrations through the water column; typically surfacing at night to minimize predation.

A huge range of creatures relyies on them either directly or indirectly for food, including other marine invertebrates such as squid, fish, seals, penguins, seabirds and whales, and they are consumed in vast quantities. At the top of the food chain are the Leopard Seal (*Hydrurga leptonyx*), which feeds on large amounts of krill, but also small seals and penguins, and the Killer Whale (*Orcinus orca*), which will feed on penguins, seals and even other whales.

Above: Chinstrap Penguins (*Pygoscelis antarctica*) clamber onto a massive iceberg in the Southern Ocean.

Right: Freshly-caught Krill (*Euphausia superba*) This vast resource is exploited by man for consumption and fish bait, and also for processing into animal feeds.

Seals and whales

Six seal species are found in Antarctic waters, the Crabeater Seal (*Lobodon carcinophaga*), Weddell Seal (*Leptonychotes weddellii*), Ross Seal (*Ommatophoca Rossii*), Leopard Seal (*Hydrurga leptonyx*), Antarctic Fur Seal (*Arctocephalus gazella*), and the massive Southern Elephant Seal (*Mirounga leonina*). However, only the first four are commonly regarded as true Antarctic seals, as the other two are generally found on and around more northerly sub-Antarctic islands.

The Crabeater Seal is by far the most numerous seal in the Antarctic, and one of the most abundant of all large mammals on Earth. It grows to around 10 feet in length and may weigh up to 660 pounds, and despite its name, it feeds almost entirely on krill.

Right: Crabeater Seals (*Lobodon carcinophaga*) haul out onto an ice floe.

Below right: Southern Elephant Seals (*Mirounga leonina*) and King penguins (*Aptenodytes patagonica*) on South Georgia Island.

Below left: The Southern Fur Seal (*Arctocephalus gazella*).

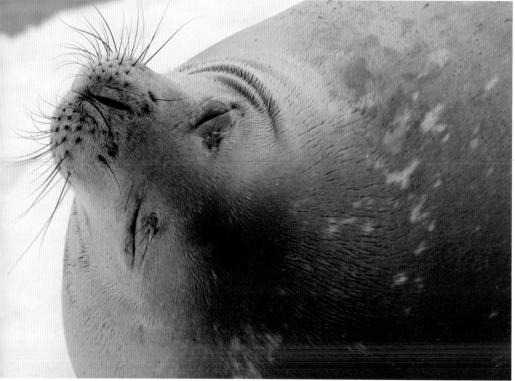

The Weddell Seal feeds mainly on fish and squid, has large eyes for improved underwater vision, and can remain submerged for over an hour. It grows to around the same length as the Crabeater Seal, but may be slightly heavier, and is mostly associated with coastal areas and the fast-ice attached to the Antarctic continent. The Ross Seal however, is smaller, at about 6 feet long and 440 pounds, and is more elusive, spending its time on the floating pack ice.

Opposite: Antarctic Fur Seal (*Arctocephalus gazella*).

Left: The Weddell Seal (*Leptonychotes weddellii*).

Above: A female Southern Elephant Seal (*Mirounga leonina*) with pup, South Georgia Island.

Fearsome hunters

Opposite above: The Leopard Seal (*Hydrurga leptonyx*) is found mainly around the pack ice, but it can be common in coastal areas where it will lie in wait for penguins. It is a large species, often exceeding 10 feet in length, and weighing up to about 660 pounds.

Opposite below: Sei whale (*Balaenoptera borealis*) near Pico Island in the Azores,

Above: Only the Killer Whale, or Orca (*Orcinus orca*) is a more fearsome, powerful and efficient predator in these waters, attaining a length of up to 30 feet, and weighing in at some 7 tons. These highly intelligent and sociable mammals often hunt cooperatively in packs, killing and eating anything from fish and squid to penguins, seals and even young Blue Whales (*Balaenoptera musculus*).

The Blue Whale

Right: The Blue Whale (*Balaenoptera musculus*) is
one of six species of baleen whale that come
to Antarctic waters in summer to feed on krill,
which they filter from the water through plates
of keratin, suspended from their upper jaw.
As an adult, the Blue Whale can reach
a length of 100 feet and weigh up to 150 tons,
making it the largest mammal on Earth.
The other baleen whales found in the Antarctic
are the Fin Whale (*Balaenoptera physalus*), Minke
Whale (*B. acutorostrata*), Sei Whale (*B. borealis*),
Southern Right Whale (*Eubalaena Australis*), and
the Humpback Whale (*Megaptera novaeangliae*).

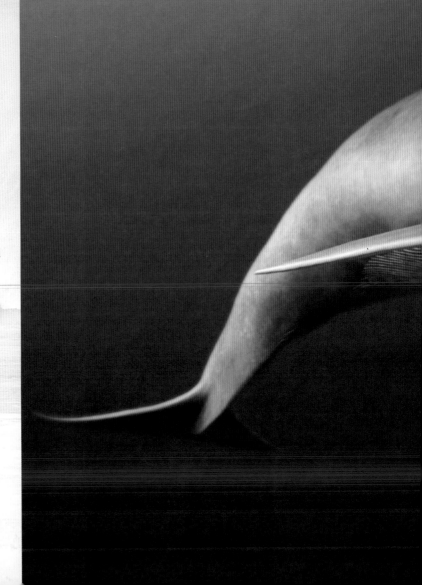

Above: The Humpback Whale may be observed
feeding quite close to the shore, and has an unusual
method of catching krill. A pair of Humpbacks will
often work cooperatively to produce a "bubble net"
by releasing air from their blowholes beneath a
swarm of krill, which compacts the swarm and
forces it toward the surface, where it may then be
swallowed.

Penguins

All of the world's seventeen penguin species are restricted to the southern hemisphere, with the exception of the Galapagos Penguin (*Spheniscus mendiculus*), whose island homes straddle the equator, but only four breed on the Antarctic continent; the closely related Chinstrap Penguin (*Pygoscelis antarctica*), Gentoo Penguin (*Pygoscelis papua*), and Adélie Penguin (*Pygoscelis adeliae*), and the Emperor Penguin (*Aptenodytes forsteri*), and of these, only the Emperor is restricted in doing so, with the others also breeding on islands further north.

The Chinstrap, Gentoo and Adélie all tend to nest on rocky coasts, but the Emperor Penguin breeds on the pack ice, and remarkably, does so in winter, when conditions are at their harshest, probably in order to ensure that conditions are most favorable when the young are approaching independence. The females produce a single egg, which is incubated by the male for around nine weeks, during which time the females go to sea in order to feed. The males are left huddled in huge colonies, with the eggs resting on their feet. The eggs are thus prevented from touching the freezing ice, and are also protected by a roll of skin known as the brood pouch. When the females return to feed the young, the males then trek across the ice for several miles in order to enter the sea to feed, having lost a considerable amount of bodyweight during the winter.

Opposite: Adult King Penguins (*Aptenodytes patagonica*) with young, South Georgia.

Below left: Macaroni Penguins (*Eudyptes chrysolophus*).

Below: Chinstrap Penguin (*Pygocelis antarctica*) with chicks, Deception Island.

Arctic ice

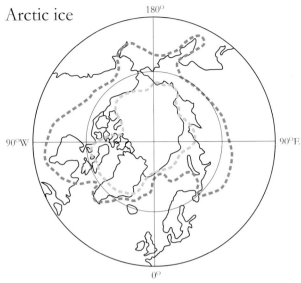

Antarctic ice

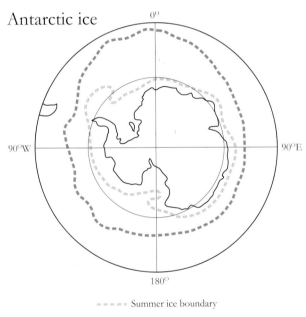

- - - - Summer ice boundary

- - - - Winter ice boundary

Above: The extent of the ice in winter and summer months in the Arctic and Antarctic. The polar coasts are unlike any others on earth, seasonally shrinking and growing by hundreds of miles each year as the loose pack ice freezes to the permanently frozen ice that forms the Arctic ice cap or the fast-ice which surrounds the Antarctic continent, before thawing and breaking apart once more. The two polar regions differ greatly; the Arctic comprises a mass of permanently frozen water that sits at the heart of an almost fully enclosed ocean, fringed by the landmasses of North America, Greenland and Eurasia, whilst Antarctica is a rocky landmass, isolated by hundreds of miles of ocean from any other.

All Antarctic penguins are well adapted to swimming in the cold seas, being highly streamlined, protected by insulating blubber, and with wings that have become modified flippers, which preclude flight, but make them highly agile in the water. Most penguins tend to feed on krill and small fish taken in surface waters, but the Emperor, which is the largest of all penguins, at about 45 inches long, tends to dive deeply in search of larger fish and squid.

Opposite: A lone Gentoo Penguin (*Pygocelis papua*).

Above: A group of Gentoo Penguins prepare to dive in search of food. Their diet consists largely of krill.

Right: Two Gentoo Penguins on a rocky coast, with glacial ice meeting the sea beyond.

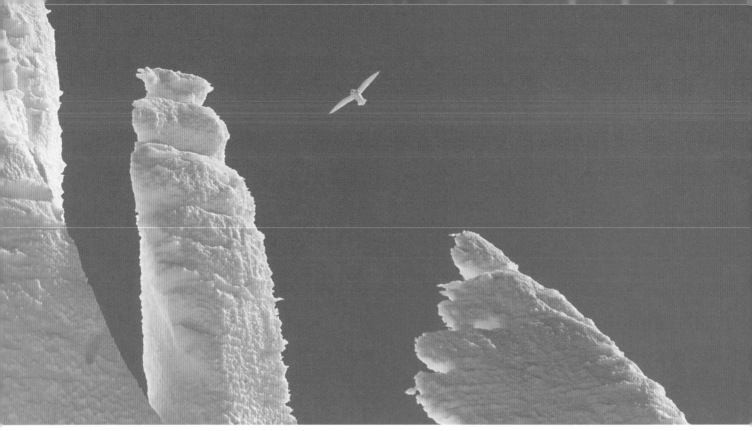

Other Antarctic seabirds

Whilst penguins may be the most familiar and recognizable of Antarctic birds, over thirty species of seabirds live south of the Antarctic Convergence, and around twenty breed on the continent itself, typically in vast densities, forming huge colonies along the small areas of coast that are free of ice.

Most Antarctic seabirds belong to the order Procellariiformes, or the "tubenoses," which comprises of the albatrosses, shearwaters, prions, petrels and fulmars, whilst others include skuas, gulls, terns, sheathbills and cormorants.

The Antarctic Petrel (*Thalassoica antarctica*), and the Snow Petrel (*Pagodroma nivea*), are the most southerly occurring of all birds, often nesting well inland on the Antarctic continent, in incredibly harsh conditions. They rely on the coastal waters and their abundant supply of crustaceans in order to survive and feed their young. Other closely related species, which are more common along the coast, include the Cape Pigeon, or Petrel (*Daption capense*), Southern Fulmar (*Fulmarus glacialoides*), Antarctic, or Dove Prion (*Pachyptila desolata*), Wilson's Storm Petrel (*Oceanites oceanicus*), and the Giant Petrel (*Macronectes giganteus*). The Dominican Gull (*Larus dominicanus*), Arctic Tern (*Sterna paradisaea*), and the related Snowy Sheathbill (*Chionis alba*), all breed on Antarctica, and the latter is unusual in having only partially webbed feet. It is essentially a scavenger which feeds on carrion around penguin colonies, but it will also take food from penguins at times. More confrontational are the skuas however, such as the South Polar Skua (*Catharacta maccormicki*), and Brown Skua (*Stercorarius antarctica*), which will take both penguin eggs and chicks.

Opposite above: The Antarctic Petrel (*Thalassoica antarctica*) and the Snow Petrel (*Pagrodoma nivea*) The Snow Petrel is one of the most southerly occurring of all birds.

Opposite below: A Brown Skua (*Catharacta antarctica*) perches on a mossy outcrop, Marion Island.

Right: Blue-eyed Shag (*Phalacrocorax atriceps*) New Island, Falkland Islands.

CORAL REEF

The garden of the sea

Built up over hundreds or even thousands of years, the seemingly rocky coral reef is actually composed of the calcareous skeletons of millions of plants and animals, generation after generation of which have contributed to its structure. This process brings the reef close to the ocean's surface often forming wide platforms and lagoons, perhaps dotted with patch reefs, with large piles and columns interspersed with numerous channels, which may stretch along huge expanses of coastline. Yet, atop the reef's limestone necropolis, the living reef is home to a huge range of fish and invertebrates. These occur in a dazzling array of colors, shapes and sizes, and it is perhaps not surprising that coral reefs are sometimes known as the rainforests or gardens of the sea, for like the rainforests, they are amongst the most biologically diverse and productive of all habitats on Earth.

A unique ecosystem

Coral reefs occur in the warm, shallow, clear waters of tropical seas and oceans, mainly between the latitudes of 30°N and 30°S, particularly throughout the Indo-Pacific region, including the Arabian and Red Seas. They may also be found in the Atlantic, notably around the Caribbean. Coral reefs are, however, much more scarce along the western coasts of the Americas and Africa, where water temperatures are greatly reduced by cold currents. Other limiting factors include low salinities and the deposition of excessive sediments, such as where large river systems drain into the oceans, depth, and the excessive turbidity caused by an abundance of phytoplankton.

For whilst corals require nutrients in order to survive, those that are considered as reef-builders also require light, without which, photosynthesis could not occur and the corals could not survive in these nutrient-poor waters. However, no matter how plant-like the animals, or colonies of animals, which populate these underwater gardens may appear, they are incapable of photosynthesis. Instead many of them contain an abundance of living microscopic plants within their bodies; an example of just one of the many symbiotic relationships that take place within this unique ecosystem.

Structure and feeding

Corals are simple, multi-cellular organisms that belong to the phylum, which also contains the jellyfish and sea anemones, with which they share their basic form and radial symmetry. They have a hollow body cavity, with a central mouth surrounded by tentacles. In fact, with the exception of some of the large, solitary corals, such as mushroom corals, each individual animal, or polyp, closely resembles a miniature anemone.

However, there are several types of coral, occurring in a wide range of forms: the millepore, or fire corals, are closely related to jellyfish; the gorgonians or horny corals, such as the sea fans, form flexible plant-like colonies. The black or thorny, deepwater corals, and the true reefbuilders or hermatypic corals, the madrepores, are also known as stony corals.

These are the most diverse and numerous of the corals, and differ from the soft corals, anemones and other closely related species, in producing a large, external limestone skeleton. They have a base plate attached to the substrate, and a cup, or theca, which protects the soft polyp, and into which the tentacles can be withdrawn.

The vast majority of the stony corals are colonial animals, which grow together, sharing their skeletons and connective tissue, or coenosarc, which may be interconnected by a series of gastrovascular canals, enabling the sharing of nutrients so that the colony essentially functions as a single organism. Such a colony may consist of thousands of polyps, each of which is typically only an $^1/_8$ of an inch in diameter, which grow, layer upon layer, on the skeletons of former generations in a staggering variety of shapes. These include encrusting sheets, plates, pillars, leaves, antlers, spheres and brains. These forms may not only vary from species to species, but also according to where they happen to occur on the reef. For example, the shape of a colony may be affected by a host of local environmental conditions, such as depth, currents, availability of food, competition with other species and the actions of storms, as well as by animals that bore into or feed upon coral.

Feeding

Like all Cnidarians, corals are carnivorous and possess stinging cells, or nematocysts, on their tentacles, with which to kill or immobilize their prey. This typically consists of the tiny free-floating animals that constitute the zooplankton. However, large corals may also consume larger invertebrates or even fish. Once caught, the food is then passed to the mouth by the tentacles, to be digested in the gastrovascular cavity, and the waste products are discharged back through the single opening. The fire corals take their name from the strong toxins that they possess, which can be harmful to humans. In addition to stinging cells, some corals use mucous to ensnare their prey and transport it to the mouth with tiny cilia, or hairs, which line the tentacles.

Opposite: Corals are simple, multi-cellular organisms and have a hollow body cavity, with a central mouth surrounded by tentacles.

Below: A white Christmas tree worm amongst the Orange Cup Coral (*Tubastraea coccinea*).

Right: Large shoals of fish swim close to the reef to find food and shelter.

Reef-building

As well as feeding on zooplankton, the reefbuilding corals derive much of their nutrition from their symbiotic, or mutually beneficial, relationship with a type of single-celled yellow-brown algae known as dinoflagellates, or zooxanthellae. Millions of these microscopic plants are harbored within the tentacles and body tissues of the polyps, where, like other plants, they photosynthesize, producing oxygen and carbohydrates which feed their host. In return, the plants benefit from a steady supply of carbon dioxide and other nutrients, and also a relatively safe and stable environment in which to live. As all plants require sunlight for photosynthesis to take place, reefbuilding corals are typically only found in depths of up to about 200 feet, where there is sufficient light to drive the proces. The most well-developed corals are usually found closest to the surface. In deeper waters, slow-growing forms such as the black corals, may be found which lack symbiotic algae, but these are not considered as significant contributors to reef development. In fact, it is the presence of zooxanthellae that enables the reef-building corals to grow quickly enough to establish reefs. For they not only provide the energy required for the rapid growth of their calcareous skeletons, they use up large amounts of carbon dioxide, which would otherwise combine with the water to create carbonic acid, which is capable of dissolving the limestone of coral skeletons.

Coral bleaching

In certain circumstances, polyps eject much of their symbiotic algae, or it may be killed off by a lack of light, by pollution, disease or changes in salinity or temperature, which leads to a phenomenon known as "coral bleaching." This term is derived from the fact that it is the algae that give the polyps their pigmentation, and without it the coral appears white. If the algae do not recover quickly or significantly enough, the coral itself will die, and in extreme circumstances, this can lead to the devastation of entire reefs.

It was once thought that there was just one species of zooxanthellae (*Symbiodinium adriaticum*) but there are now known to be several algal species which form symbiotic relationships with corals, which may not even be closely related.

Opposite above: Orange tunicates dwelling amongst pillar coral, which has its polyps extended to feed.

Opposite below: Large-grooved Brain Coral (*Diploria labyrinthiformis*) This species of coral gains its name from its similarity to the appearance of the human brain.

Below: Clownfish (*Amphiprion ocellaris*) at home with a sea anenome.

Reproduction

Corals reproduce using both sexual and asexual methods, but there can be considerable variation between species in the precise mechanics of these. Asexual reproduction typically occurs through a process of division or budding, which takes two principle forms; intratentacular and extratentacular growth. In the first process, the oral disc of the polyp becomes increasingly constricted to form a figure of eight, eventually giving rise to two separate mouths, sets of tentacles and other organs, resulting in the development of two identical polyps, side by side. These separate, but remain connected by calcareous material and a layer of jelly-like tissue. In the second process, part of the external wall of the original polyp is evaginated or distended to form a small bud. This then develops a mouth, tentacles and other organs, until a new, smaller polyp is produced. This separates from the "mother" polyp and begins to produce its own calcareous secretions, binding it to the colony. A further means of asexual reproduction exhibited by some corals is that of fragmentation, whereby a fragment of broken coral that has become detached from a colony may survive and, if it is carried to a suitable site for attachment, will be able to establish a new colony.

Apart from this method, all colonies originally become established as the result of sexual reproduction, and a colony several yards across, which has grown in size through asexual division, may have originated from a single polyp.

Fertilization

In the sexual reproduction of corals, male and female gametes, or eggs and spermatozoa, fuse through a process of fertilization, resulting in the production of a zygote, which then develops into a free-floating larva, known as a planula. This disc-like, planktonic organism eventually settles somewhere on the reef or sea bed. It begins to attach itself with calcareous secretions, eventually growing into a single polyp with its own corallite cup.

Most stony corals are hermaphroditic, producing both male and female gametes within the same colonies and even polyps, but some species form gonochoristic, or single-sex, colonies. Both however typically reproduce by spawning, releasing their gametes into the water, often in a sac, which floats to the surface, where fertilization will take place. In many cases, these spawning events are synchronous, not only between corals of the same species, but sometimes with hundreds of different species spawning almost simultaneously on a reef, usually at night. This is thought to be as the result of environmental triggers such as temperature and the lunar cycle.

Some corals, particularly non-stony species, do not release female gametes at all, and instead rely on a process of brooding, or internal fertilization, whereby the egg is fertilized within the mature polyp, and the larval planula is released. In stony corals which exhibit this trait, the planulae may be well developed and already contain zooxanthellae at the time of their release, enabling them to be carried over vast distances before they find a suitable substrate for attachment.

Opposite: The coral reef at Rock Island in Palau.

Below: A school of Goldman's Sweetlips (*Plectorhinchus lineatus*) which are characterized by their oblique black banding,

Reef types and formation

As many as seven different types of coral reef are sometimes described, including apron, patch, table and ribbon reefs, but there are three principle formations that are widely recognized. These are based on initial observations and descriptions by Charles Darwin during the 1830s and '40s. These are fringing reefs, platform, or barrier reefs and atolls, or atoll reefs.

Most coastal coral reefs take the form of fringing reefs, which occur in the shallow waters close to a coastal or island shore. They comprise a band of corals which runs parallel to the coast, typically with a narrow, inner lagoon, which may show signs of coral remnants as the reef grows progressively further out to sea. As in other reefs, corals may also grow along the reef crest or flat, where the waves break, particularly those capable of coping with some degree of emersion, or where the flat remains substantially submerged, but their growth is most prolific along the sloping, seaward profile of the reef.

Platform or barrier reefs are large, continuous, well-developed reefs, which also run parallel to the shore. Characteristically they are separated from the coast by an expansive lagoon, which may contain areas of patch reef. They may often represent a further development in the growth of a fringing reef, which may have reached its limit at the edge of the continental shelf and begun to expand into a wide platform. They can also begin forming in shallow offshore waters. Such reefs can be very extensive and present a series of smaller ribbons and coral islets, punctuated by channels and small

lagoons. The largest and most famous example is the Great Barrier Reef in northern Australia, which is actually composed of numerous individual reefs, which stretch for over 1,250 miles. The submerged, seaward parts of barrier reefs may be divided into broad, sandy terraces which are interspersed with corals. Both fringing and barrier reefs can play an important part in protecting shorelines from coastal erosion, by slowing waves and currents as they approach the shore.

Atoll reefs

Atoll reefs are generally circular, and encompass a central lagoon. They may occur close to the continental shelf, but are more commonly isolated in much deeper waters. They are formed initially by the development of a fringing reef, or series of these reefs, around an emergent volcanic island, which over time will eventually subside and vanish into the sea, leaving behind a well-developed, circular, barrier reef and inner lagoon. The lagoon may be almost fully enclosed, or connected to the ocean by a number of channels, and the inner lagoon is typically sandy, on account of the erosion of coral debris behind the fringing reef as it grew outward

from the island. As a result of prevailing winds, sand may build up on one side of the lagoon, forming a bank above sea level. If it continues to accrue it can lead to the formation of an island, which may eventually be colonized by vegetation, birds and man.

Whilst hermatypic, or stony corals are the principal originators and contributors to the building of reefs, there are numerous other organisms that play a part in their construction, particularly hardshelled mollusks and tubeworms, whose calcareous skeletons may also help to build the reef. The same can also be said of coralline algae, particularly encrusting forms, which additionally help to stabilize and cement the reef as they grow.

Opposite: Sea fans amongst the coral in the Virgin Islands. They are attached in mud or sand with each of the polyps having eight tentacles, used to catch plankton.

Above: A variety of sea life swims over the diverse coral forms.

Life on the reef

Despite the lack of nutrients in the warm, clear waters in which coral reefs occur, the reef as a whole is extremely efficient at recycling those nutrients that are available. As an ecosystem, the coral reef is almost self-sufficient, and able to survive on far less nutrients than other systems of a comparable size or biomass. In addition to the corals themselves, and the zooxanthellae contained within reefbuilding corals, blue-green algae, or cyanobacteria, play an important part in the productivity of the reef and the recycling of nutrients. In particular they provide the corals with readily absorbable nitrates. Other highly productive algal forms include coralline algae, and other seaweeds, such as low-growing turf algae. Phytoplankton, whilst not greatly abundant, also contributes to the reef's productivity. These various plants form the base of a complex web, providing food and nutrients to a host of organisms, including herbivorous grazers, and also the tiny larval forms and other minute animals that constitute the zooplankton, upon which corals and numerous other invertebrates feed. In turn, these small invertebrates, and the coral polyps themselves, are consumed by larger invertebrates and a huge variety of fish, which may attract large predators such as sharks to the reef's edge.

Other visitors include dolphins, and reptiles such as turtles and sea snakes, whilst there is also an ever-present horde of detritivores. These constantly feed upon and break down any dead organic matter, recycling it back into the food chain.

Intense competition

It is not just an abundance of food that makes the reef so inhabitable to so many organisms: the reef structure, the complex growths of coral colonies and coralline algae, with their varied shapes and spaces, contours and caves, provide a wealth of sites for attachment and shelter. Even empty corallite cups are utilised as homes, and living corals and anemones offer refuge amongst their protective, stinging tentacles.

In such a crowded habitat, competition for the available resources, such as light, food, space and shelter can be extreme. This has led to a number of specialisations amongst species, and to a number of complex relationships between them, including symbiosis or mutualism.

Above: The Ocellaris Clownfish (*Amphiprion ocellaris*) tends to live amongst sea anemones, which it uses for protection and shelter. In return the clownfish will feed the anemone, increase the oxygen supply and remove waste material.

Opposite: As with all seahorses the male Longsnout Seahorse (*Hippocampus reidi*) gives birth to the young. This particular species does so in vast numbers, and over fifteen hundred young have been recorded from a single male.

Reef invertebrates

Like the madrepores or stony corals, sea anemones are anthozoans, meaning "flower-animals." They also belong to the subclass Hexacorallia, as each polyp bears six,
or multiples of six, tentacles, as opposed to the eight-tentacled octocorals, which includes soft corals and gorgonians. Although they may be found in close proximity to each other, anemones are solitary rather than colonial animals. Whilst they tend to adhere to the substrate, they are capable of moving along on their basal disc. Like corals, they are carnivorous and possess stinging cells, or nematocysts, at the tips of their tentacles, which are used to immobilize and even kill their prey.

This varies from the small crustaceans and larva that make up the zooplankton, to fish, depending on the size of the anemone. Many sea anemones are found in association with coral reefs, but by far the most impressive are the giant anemones, which include species such as *Condilactys gigantea*, which can grow to around 12 inches in diameter, and Mertens' Sea Anemone (*Stichodactyla mertensii*), which can exceed 3 feet across. Like the stony corals, some of these anemones contains zooxanthellae, which supply them with nutrients. Perhaps more remarkable, considering that many of them also feed voraciously on small fish, is the relationship between various large anemones and clownfish. These small orange and white fish, which

belong to the genus *Amphiprion*, typically shelter amongst the tentacles of large anemones, rarely venturing far from the protection that their stinging cells offer against potential predators. It was once thought that only the clownfish benefited from this relationship, but it is now understood that the clownfish also protect the anemone, by driving away predators such as butterflyfish, which feed on them and are apparently immune to their stings. The clownfish themselves, are protected by a layer of mucus, which prevents the anemone from sensing them as prey.

Many anemones position themselves in rocky crevices, into which they can withdraw if threatened, but there are also species such as the Banded Tube Anemone (*Pachycerianthus maua*), which secrete and dwell within protective tubes of mucus.

Tube-dwellers

Similarly, there are several species of tube-dwelling, sedentary, polychaete worms to be found on coral reefs, which may secrete either mucous or calcareous tubes, and of these, the Christmas Tree Worm (*Spirobranchus giganteus*), is amongst the most striking. This species bores into stony corals, where it secretes its own calcareous tube, from which it extends its feathery tentacles, or radioles, into the water to breathe and to feed on suspended particles. It is particularly notable for the spiralling arrangement of these radioles, which provides its common name, and also for its vivid pigmentation.

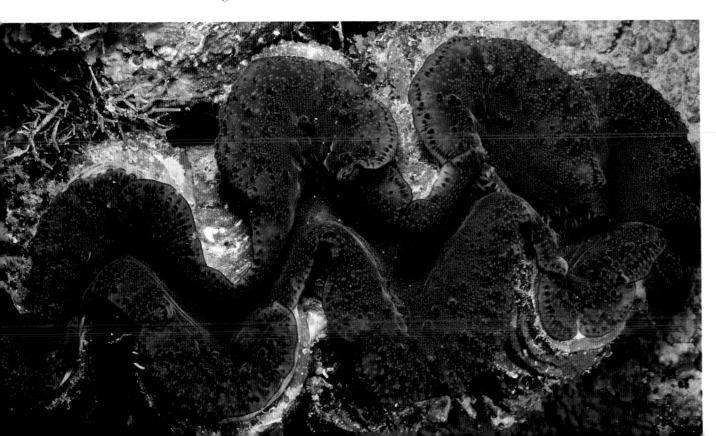

the world's largest bivalve, *Tridacna gigas*, which may grow to a length of over 3 feet. However, most species such as *Tridacna maxima* and *Tridacna crocea* grow to between about 12 – 20 inches. Like other bivalves these clams are filter feeders, which siphon suspended food such as plankton from the surrounding water. Like stony corals, they also contain zooxanthellae within their tissues, and it is the presence of these microscopic plants that enables giant clams to reach such large sizes. The Fluted, or Zig-zag Oyster (*Pycnodonta hyotis*), is another large specimen, which may be identified by its corrugated shell, which provides an excellent site of attachment for corals and encrusting sponges, which are also prevalent on reefs. It may not be conspicuous unless its highly patterned mantle is exposed.

Far more mobile is the Rough Fileclam, or Flame Scallop (*Lima scabra*), of the Caribbean. This colorful bivalve, which possesses a brilliant red mantle and protruding tentacles, tends to remain hidden by day, but at night it is able to propel itself through the water by opening and closing its shell in a clapping motion.

Reef-dwelling flatworms

Equally vibrant are many of the reef-dwelling flatworms, particularly those of the genus *Pseudoceros*, which move over the surface of corals in order to feed on tiny invertebrates, or may be seen swimming with undulating movements. They are sometimes mistaken for nudibranchs, or sea slugs, but lack the feathery external gills visible on most of those species. Other common worms include errant bristleworms, such as the Bearded Fireworm (*Hermodice carunculata*), whose common name is derived from the fact that it will readily deliver a painful toxin from its long bristles when touched. This species is predatory, feeding on coral polyps, anemones and other small invertebrates, and it can cause extensive damage to coral colonies in a relatively short period of time. In turn, it is thought to fall prey to predatory mollusks such as cone shells, amongst others.

A huge variety of mollusks occurs on coral reefs, from gastropod snails and sea slugs, to sedentary bivalves, and the highly intelligent, free-swimming cephalopods, such as octopuses, cuttlefish and squid. The genus *Tridacna*, or the giant clams, contains some of the largest mollusks to be found on the coral reef, and

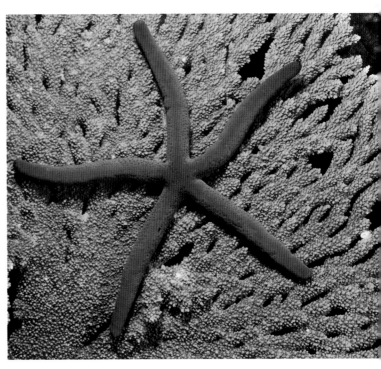

Above left: The Flamingo Tongue Cowrie (*Cyphoma gibbosum*) dwells amongst the soft corals and sea fans upon which it feeds.

Above right: The Blue Starfish (*Linckia laevigata*).

Opposite: The Giant Clam (*Tridacna gigas*) is the largest living bivalve mollusk, sustained mainly by minute symbiotic algae.

World of vibrant color

Some of the most attractive mollusks that inhabit the coral reef are the brightly colored sea slugs, such as *Chromodoris quadricolor* and the Spanish Dancer (*Hexabranchus sanguineus*), and also numerous hard-shelled species, many of which possess beautifully shaped, patterned and colored shells. The Pheasant Trochid (*Phasianotrochus eximius*), has an iridescent, conical shell, and is a herbivorous grazer that feeds on algae, which it rasps from the surface of the reef with its tongue, or radula. Perhaps better-known however, are the cowries, such as the Tiger Cowrie (*Cypraea tigris*) and the Flamingo Tongue Cowrie (*Cyphoma gibbosum*), both of which posses a large mantle that is capable of enveloping much of the shell. Cowries are typically omnivorous, and will graze on algae, sponges and corals, but the Flamingo Tongue Cowrie tends to be mainly carnivorous, feeding on sea fans and other gorgonians, such as *Gorgonia ventalina* and *Plexaura homomalla*.

The cone shells, such as the Geographic Cone (*Conus geographus*), Tulip Cone (*Conus tulipas*), and Textile Cone (*Conus textile*) are more active predators. They feed on fish, worms and other snails, and deliver a powerful neurotoxin into their prey by means of an extended proboscis and radula. Several species of cone shell can be dangerous, and even fatal to humans.

Whilst not a danger to man, the Sea Triton (*Charonia tritonis*), is a large mollusk that can grow to around 16 inches, in length, and is also carnivorous. Its main prey consists of echinoderms such as starfish, and includes the Crown of Thorns Starfish (*Acanthaster planci*), which has been known to devastate coral reefs with its own feeding habits. This large starfish may attain a diameter of up to 20 inches, and as its name might suggest, is covered in long spines. It feeds on reefbuilding corals, which it digests by evaginating its stomach. An individual is capable of consuming a square yard of coral polyps in a single day, and so when populations are large, damage to the reef can be extensive.

Starfish

Somewhat more benign are smaller species such as the Blue Starfish (*Linckia laevigata*), and the closely related Comet Starfish (*Linckia guildingii*), which possess thick, tubular arms. Like other starfish, they are capable of regenerating lost limbs, but they are also able to regenerate a complete starfish from a single arm, and can reproduce asexually in this way; shedding an arm that will develop into a new individual.

Crinoids or feather stars, such as *Cenometra bella* are also common reef inhabitants, as are brittlestars, such as the Green-banded Brittlestar (*Ophiarachnella gorgonia*), and the Ruby Brittlestar (*Ophioderma rubicundum*), and sea urchins, which are often found on the back reef and reef flat, where they graze on algae. They occur in a variety of forms, from the long-spined, such as the Black Long-spined Sea Urchin (*Diadema setosum*), to the short-spined, such as the Pincushion Urchin (*Asthenosoma varium*), and the thick-spined, such as the Pencil Urchin (*Heterocentrotus mammillatus*). The closely related sea cucumbers, or holothurians are usually found on the sea floor at the base of the reef, where most feed by ingesting sediment and scavenging on detritus.

Crustaceans

Crustaceans may be found throughout the reef, and many types of crabs and shrimps, such as the Anemone Shrimp (*Periclimenes holthuisi*), and the Atlantic White-Striped Cleaner Shrimp (*Lysmata grabhami*), are to be found living in association with corals, anemones and sponges. Like clownfish, they benefit from being protected by their host, whilst ridding it of small parasites and detritus. Others, such as the Banded Coral Shrimp (*Stenopus hispidus*), remove parasites and dead skin from fish, including large, predatory species such as moray eels, and certain prawns actually share their burrows with gobies. The prawn maintains the burrow, whilst the goby keeps watch for potential predators. The prawn maintains contact with the fish with its antennae, and is alerted to the presence of a predator as the goby begins to retreat into their shared home.

Opposite: The Crown of Thorns Starfish (*Aacanthaster planci*) can be both harmful to man and devestating to coral reefs.

Below: Found living amongst sea anemones the Spotted Cleaner Shrimp (*Periclimenes yucatanicus*) waves its body and antennae in the water to attract food.

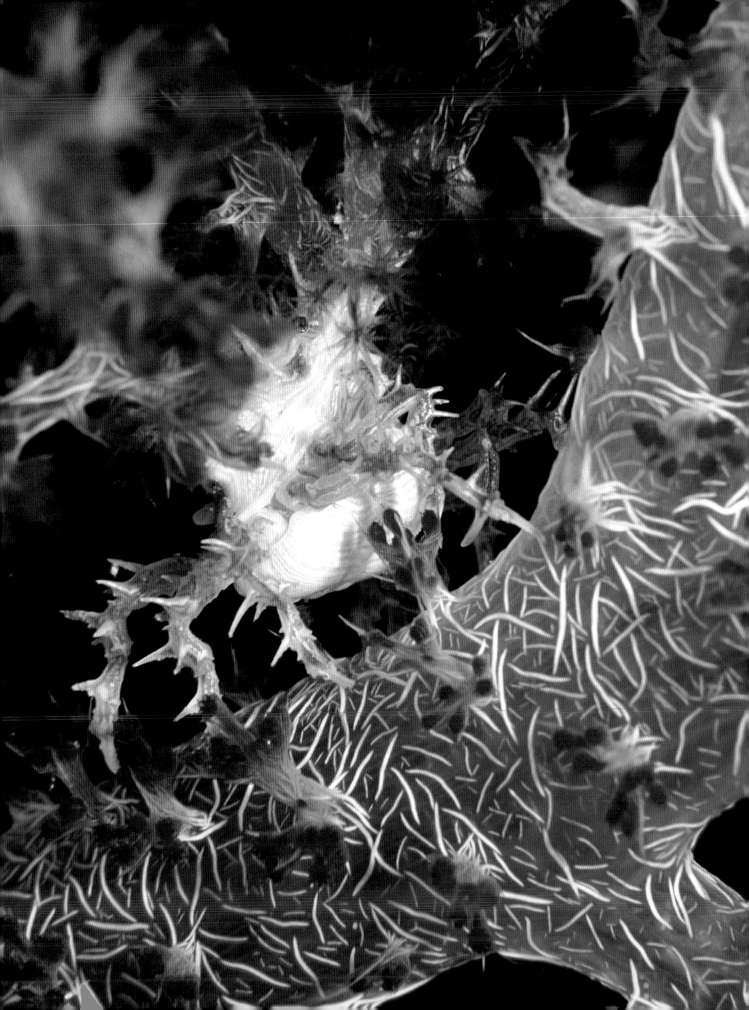

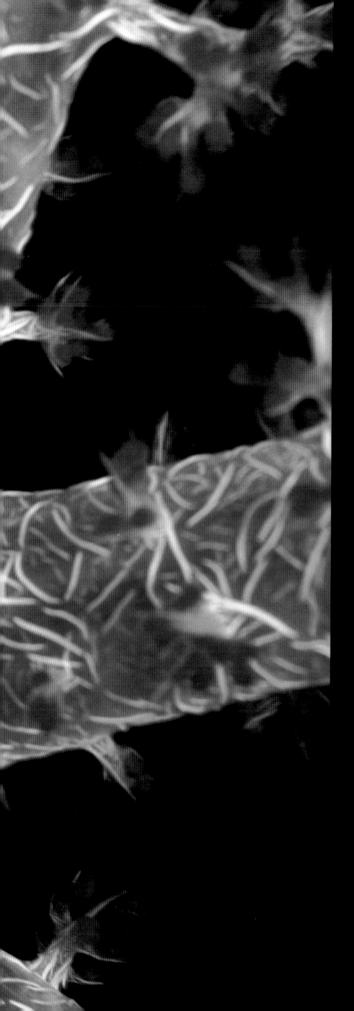

Above: Crinoids are also known as feather stars or sea lilies. Most are free swimming and have a mouth on the top that is surrounded by feeding arms.

Left: The Decorator Crab (*Oregonia gracilis*) seen here on soft coral has gained its name from a habit of decorating itself with pieces of seaweed and sponges to provide camouflage.

Crustaceans are heavily preyed upon by fish, and also large cephalopod mollusks such as the Broad Club Cuttlefish (*Sepia latimanus*), and the small, but highly venomous Blue-Ringed Octopus (*Hapalochlaena lunulata*). However, some species such as the sponge crabs of the genus *Dromia*, reduce the risk of predation by clasping living sponges to their backs. The sponges do not attach permanently, but continue to grow, providing the crab with an excellent form of camouflage. Some crustaceans, such as the Mantis Shrimp (*Odontodactylus scyllarus*), however, are more active in their defense. This species possesses hugely powerful claws, with which it smashes the shells of its prey, but which it will also employ in order to repel and injure an aggressor.

Reef fishes

Coral reefs are home to some of the largest, and undoubtedly the most diverse assemblages of fish of any ocean habitat, with over 4,000 different species, or almost a third of all marine fish, known to occur in their waters. Some of these fish are transient, typically visiting the reef in search of food, or perhaps seasonally as they enter shallower water in order to breed, and additionally, most of the fish found on reefs belong to groups that are well represented in other oceanic habitats. However, there are also families such as the butterflyfish and damselfish that are reef specialists and are rarely to be found elsewhere. Regardless of this however, all of the fish that are resident on reefs tend to demonstrate particular adaptations to living there, and moreover, a huge range of different physical forms and behaviors are exhibited as a direct result of such an abundance of fish living in a relatively small habitat, where competition for food and space is intense, and predators are often to be found living side by side with their prey.

Butterflyfish

The butterflyfish are amongst the most common and colorful of reef fishes, and their common name is derived from a combination of their flitting movements, vivid colors and symmetrical patterns. Like butterflies, many species also possess large eyespots to the rear of their bodies, an adaptation that is thought to confuse potential predators; making the fish seem larger than it is, or disguising in which direction it might flee from attack. The real eye meanwhile is often masked by a

Above: Masked Butterflyfish (*Chaetodon semilarvatus*) shelter under a coral ledge.

Opposite: The Banded Butterflyfish (*Chaetodon striatus*) with its distinctive black, chevron-shaped bands.

Left: The Foureye Butterflyfish (*Chaetodon capistratus*) has a prominent eyespot to confuse predators as to which way it is facing.

dark band. Their bodies are laterally compressed, enabling them to pass easily between the branching corals toward the top of the reef, where most species are found. Some occur in small shoals, but most tend to occur in pairs, which will often defend a small territory, often a particular coral colony, where they may feed on the coral polyps, algae or small invertebrates. Butterflyfish belong to the family *Chaetodontidae*, meaning "hair-toothed," as their small mouths contain brush-like teeth, which are used for grazing or eating small, soft-bodied invertebrates. Some species may be generalists, whilst others, such as Meyer's Butterflyfish (*Chaetodon meyeri*), and the Baronessa Butterflyfish (*Chaetodon baronessa*), tend to feed on particular corals, and the Copperband Butterflyfish (*Chelmon rostratus*), and the Long-nosed Butterflyfish (*Forcipiger flavissimus*), have particularly elongated snouts, which are used to reach invertebrate prey in tiny cracks and crevices. Despite their bright colors, these fish are often well camouflaged against the reef during the day, when they are active, but at night, when they retreat into crevices and caves to rest, their pigments often fade.

Angelfish

The marine angelfish, which belong to the family *Pomacanthidae*, are also diurnal, and are closely related to the butterflyfish. They are also similar in appearance but they tend to be larger at between 8 – 24 inches and are often even more vividly colored, particularly in yellows and blues. They may also be distinguished by the possession of strong spines projecting from their gill covers. Angelfish may be found throughout the reef at various depths, but most larger species, such as the Emperor Angelfish (*Pomacanthus imperator*), are found in the deeper waters of the lower reef, where they feed on sessile organisms such as large sponges and sea squirts. Smaller species such as the Bicolor Angelfish (*Centropyge bicolor*), tend to be found higher up the reef and also in the back reef and lagoons, where they feed mainly on algae, whilst some, such as the Blackspot Angelfish (*Genicanthus melanospilos*), are plankton feeders. Many angelfish tend to change color as they grow, but perhaps more remarkably, it is also known that they are protogynous hermaphrodites, with females being able to change sex in the absence of male fish.

Below: The Blueface Angelfish (*Pomacanthus xanthometopon*) is solitary and territorial and can be found on coral slopes.

Opposite above: Preferring to hide in rocky reefs the Clarion Angelfish (*Holocanthus clarionensis*) feeds mainly on sponges and small invertebrates.

Opposite below: The elegant Queen Angelfish (*Holacanthus ciliaris*) has a black spot surrounded by a blue ring, situated above the eye, which is referred to as its "crown."

Right: The Regal Angelfish (*Pygoplites diacanthus*) is highly solitary and often found near crevices and caves.

Opposite above: With its distinctive spotted face, the Golden Damsel (*Amblyglyphidolon aureus*) tends to be a solitary fish, living mainly amongst sea fans and black corals.

Opposite below: The Yellow Tailed Surgeon Fish (*Prionurus laticlavius*) normally seen swimming in schools, has three horizontal black polka-dots in front of the yellow tail.

Life in the shoal

The damselfish, which belong to the family *Pomacentride*, are another common, colorful, and perhaps even more conspicuous group, as many of them tend to live in large shoals. However, the damselfish are a large and diverse group, and there are notable differences between the various species. Those that live in large shoals, such as the Green Chromis (*Chromis viridis*), Sergeant Major (*Abudefduf vaigiensis*), and Atlantic Sergeant Major (*Abudefduf saxatilis*), feed on plankton in the water column, but remain close to the reef for protection, whilst many other species, such as the Black Vent Damsel (*Dischistodus melanotus*), and Honey Head Damsel (*Dischistodus prosopotaenia*), are territorial herbivores, which graze on algae and can be very aggressive to other fish and even divers. Other damselfish may be omnivorous and more opportunistic in their feeding habits, but most species are renowned for their aggression when breeding, regardless of their size. This family of fish also includes the clownfish or anemonefish, which live in pairs in association with anemones, such as the Western Clownfish (*Amphiprion ocellaris*), which often dwells with the Magnificent Anemone (*Heteractis magnifica*).

Parrotfish

Generally larger, but also brilliantly colored, are the Parrotfish, which belong to the family *Scaridae*. Their common name is derived from the fact that their teeth are fused into a beak, which is particularly well adapted for rasping algae from corals. However, whilst these fish are generally regarded as herbivorous, their beaks are often also powerful enough to break off fragments of hard coral that contain polyps, which are then ground up with the molar-like pharyngeal teeth, to be expelled as sand. When young, parrotfish may be found in small shoals, but as they grow they tend to become more solitary. As adults, they vary in size from around 12 inches to over 40 inches in the case of the largest species, the Double-headed Parrotfish (*Bolbometopon muricatum*), which has a large, distinctive hump on its head.

Above: Parrotfish are characterized by their beak-like mouths. They feed on algae and corals, and will wedge themselves into crevices to sleep.

Right: The carnivorous Coral Grouper (*Dephalopholis Niniata*) is both territorial and solitary, feeding mainly on other fish.

Opposite: Reef view with clownfish amongst sea anemones.

The Humphead

The Humphead, or Napoleon Wrasse (*Cheilinus undulatus*) is similar in appearance, and as its name suggests, it also possesses a prominent hump on its head. However, this species may grow even larger, attaining a length of over 6feet. The wrasses belong to the family *Labridae*, and are closely related to the parrotfish, but they are one of the largest and most diverse groups of fish, and the various species fulfil many roles on the coral reef, from herbivorous grazers and consumers of plankton, to predators of large invertebrates and other fish. Perhaps one of the most interesting functions however, is that performed by the cleaner wrasses, such as the Blue, or Striped Cleaner Wrasse (*Labroides dimidiatus*), which will remove parasites from the bodies, mouths and gill cavities of other, often much larger fish. They are even known to establish permanent "cleaning stations," which other fish will regularly frequent in order to be attended to. The False Cleanerfish (*Aspidontus taeniatus*), meanwhile, closely resembles the Blue Cleaner Wrasse, but it will often bite at the bodies and fins of larger fish, rather than attempt to remove them of parasites, a trait which has earned it the alternative, if somewhat exaggerated name, the Sabre-toothed Blenny. However, there are more fearsome fish on the coral reef than this diminutive species.

Fearsome fish

Although most triggerfish are small to medium-sized fish that feed on corals and other invertebrates, they possess very strong, sharp teeth, and some species, such as the Picasso Triggerfish (*Rhinecanthus aculeatus*), which grows to around 12 inches in length, can be highly territorial and aggressive, particularly when breeding. Similarly, the Titan Triggerfish (*Balistoides viridescens*), which can reach 30 inches in length, may be regarded as a potential threat to divers. The triggerfish take their name from their ability to raise and lower spines on their dorsal fins, which enables them to wedge themselves in crevices or prevent them from being swallowed by predators, and they are closely related to the boxfish, cowfish, pufferfish and porcupinefish, many of which use defensive measures such as inflating their bodies to prevent them from being consumed. Several of these fish, which belong to the order Tetraodontiformes are also highly toxic, but nonetheless, the often fall prey to larger fish.

Above: Red Hind seabass (Grouper) in the Caribbean.

Opposite above: The Common Lionfish (*Pterois volitans*).

Right: The Yellow-Margined Moray Eel hiding in soft corals in the Red Sea, and the Reef Lizardfish (*Synodus variegatus*) far right, are a sit-and-wait predators.

Ambush predators

Some of the most common large, predatory fish which inhabit reefs are the groupers, such as the Coral Grouper (*Cephalopholis miniata*), and the Giant Grouper (*Epinephelus tauvina*). These fish, which grow to about 18 and 30 inches) respectively, are primarily ambush predators, which lurk motionlessly in caves or beneath overhangs, before rapidly darting forward to seize and swallow their prey with their very large mouths. The Queensland Grouper (*Epinephelus lanceolatus*), can exceed 9 feet in length, and has been known to attack humans. Other sit-and-wait predators include moray eels, the largest of which, *Thyrsoidea macrurus*, may exceed 11 feet, the Reef Lizardfish (*Synodus variegatus*), the Crocodilefish (*Cymbacephalus beauforti*), scorpionfish, and stonefish. Whilst morays lurk in caves, the others are cryptically colored and may also bury themselves amongst sediment and debris in sandy parts of the reef and lagoon in order to hide. The scorpionfish and stonefish are particularly feared by divers as they possesses numerous spines, which are capable of delivering potentially fatal venom, and the Reef Stonefish (*Synanceia verrucosa*), is thought to be the most venomous fish in the world. The closely related Common Lionfish (*Pterois volitans*), is also venomous, but is regarded by many as incredibly beautiful, particularly when swimming, with its spines and plume-like fins expanded.

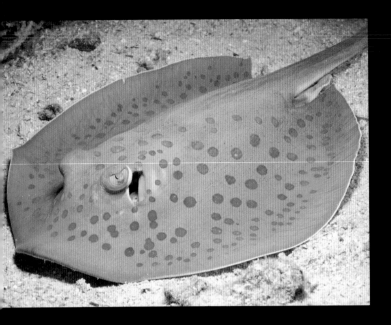

Above: The Blue Spotted Lagoon Ray (*Taeniura lymma*).

Below: The White-tip Reef Shark (*Triaenodon obesus*).

Sharks and rays

At the edge of reefs, typically where there is a drop-off into deeper water, barracudas and large sharks, such as the Hammerhead Shark (*Sphyrna lewini*), and Tiger Shark (*Galeocerdo cuvieri*), may be found patrolling for prey, but many sharks that are found on the reef itself, such as the White-tip Reef Shark (*Triaenodon obesus*), and the Blacktip Reef Shark (*Carcharinus melanopterus*), tend to be relatively small, at under 6 feet long, and are not regarded as dangerous to man. The Ornate Wobbegong (*Orectolobus ornatus*), however, grows to a length of almost 10feet, and is potentially aggressive if disturbed. This unusual shark, with its flattened head and barbels, is active at night and tends to lie on the sea bed during the day, hidden by its cryptic coloration. Similarly, several of the closely related rays, such as the Blue Spotted Lagoon Ray (*Taeniura lymma*), Honeycomb Stingray (*Himantura uarnak*), and Southern Stingray (*Dasyatis americana*), which are also common on and around reefs, tend to lie concealed on the reef floor for much of the time, and some can inflict severe and even fatal wounds with the venomous barbs on their tails.

Sea snakes

There are around 50 species of sea snake, which belong to two families, the true sea snakes of the Family *Hydrophiidae*, and the amphibious sea snakes of the Family *Laticaudidae*. Only one species, the Yellow-bellied Sea Snake (*Pelamis platurus*) is truly pelagic, occurring in offshore waters hundreds, or even thousands of miles from land, with most others being found in relatively shallow, tropical waters, and several occurring on or close to coral reefs.

All sea snakes are known to have evolved from land-dwelling ancestors, but share particular adaptations to life in the sea, such as laterally compressed tails, which are used for swimming, nostril valves and enlarged lungs, which enable them to remain submerged for long periods, and salt glands in the mouth, with which remove excess salt from the body. The true sea snakes are also viviparous, that is capable of producing live young, which they do in the water, but the amphibious sea snakes are oviparous, and must return to land to lay eggs in order to reproduce. All sea snakes feed on fish, their eggs, and invertebrates, and are venomous, with some possessing extremely powerful neurotoxins, which can cause paralysis and death. However, their mouths and fangs are often too small to effect bites on humans.

The Banded Sea Krait (*Laticauda colubrina*), is an amphibious species, which is fairly common around reefs, and may also be found on the shore. It grows to around 5 feet in length, and may be identified by its alternating light blue and black bands. The face is also yellowish, which has earned this species the alternative name, the Yellow-lipped Sea Krait.

The Olive Sea Snake (*Aipysurus laevis*), is also common on reefs and in lagoons, but this species is a true sea snake and is not encountered out of the water. It generally grows to a length of around 4 feet, but has been known to exceed 6 feet in length. This species is generally brown in color, becoming paler below, with a white tail, and often white scales speckling its body. It is known to be highly inquisitive, and will often approach divers, but like other sea snakes, it is rarely aggressive in such situations.

Above: The Banded Sea Krait (*Laticauda colubrina*) with its paddle-like tail.

THE OPEN OCEAN

Layered water

The waters of our temperate seas and open oceans are not homogenous. Within the water column there are distinctive layers with differing properties of light, temperature and oxygen which all have an enormous influence on the density and types of marine life to be found there. As the earth spins on a slightly tilted axis, the strength of the Sun's rays on different parts of the planet varies according to the time of the year. The effect is most profound in the temperate and polar regions and gives rise to the seasons. Thus, the temperate zones will receive more or less of the Sun's light and warmth depending on the season of the year, ranging from as little as four hours in winter to twenty hours in the summer months.

Temperate seas

The temperate seas in summer will absorb this energy and heat the uppermost layer (50 yards or thereabouts), creating a boundary between it and the cooler waters underneath. This boundary is called a thermocline and can act as a physical barrier for plankton, small creatures and nutrients, trapping them above or below it. In temperate waters it exists as a seasonal thermoclineduring the summer – when the Sun's rays are at their most powerful and the waters of the ocean are generally calm. The thermocline can be so marked as to produce a difference of up to 64°F between the surface waters and those beneath it.

In the winter the nutrients in the two layers will mix again for a number of reasons: the thermocline tends to break down during winter storms as the waters swirl and mix; secondly, rivers will swell and pour nutrients into the sea, thus adding to the turbulence and the mix; thirdly, as the temperature drops the surface water will cool, become dense and sink, displacing the deeper cooler waters. This process is known as overturn.

The nutrient-rich sea is warmed again the following spring and increased sunlight allows for a huge explosion of primary growth – phytoplankton. These are the plankton blooms which attract small and large feeders alike and which sustain life in the oceans.

Tropical waters

Tropical and subtropical waters of the open ocean are not as rich in nutrients as the cooler temperate seas; they are also much more stable – overturn does not occur as the surface waters are never cool enough to sink and mix with the underlying water. Thermoclines are therefore much less likely to break down and so nutrients and plankton will become trapped in the different layers, being unable to break through the barrier the thermocline represents.

Neuston layer

Light will also have an influence on the layers. The top three feet of the open ocean is called the neuston layer. The Sun can warm this section in tropical seas to 77°F. Despite this, the density of nutrients is comparatively high; this is because the waste chemicals excreted by plankton and the oils and chemicals from larger dead organisms will float up through the water column from the deeper waters.

Sunlit zone

Beneath the neuston layer, down to a depth of about 656 feet, the sunlit zone or surface layer of the ocean is still shallow enough to receive light from the sun. This allows the nutrients to be synthesized by the phytoplankton and produces a rich source of food.

Intermediate layer

Deeper still is the intermediate layer, stretching down to a depth of about 3,280 feet. The water becomes increasingly gloomy as the Sun's rays fail to penetrate very far, and temperatures at the top of the intermediate zone may be as low as 52°F, falling to just 41°F as it meets the colder waters of the deep ocean. Here, the difference in the temperatures creates a permanent thermocline, forming a barrier that most forms of marine life will be unable to breach. Those that do will have adapted in some way to cope with the starkly differing conditions.

Oxygen depletion

Oxygen levels will also act as a boundary within the intermediate zone. The oxygen minimum level denotes the level at which the amount of oxygen dissolved in the water is at its minimum. Although life does exist below this in the deep waters, these organisms have adapted to the oxygen-depleted conditions. However, animals that normally live in the surface waters where oxygen levels are optimal, will not beable to penetrate beyond this point

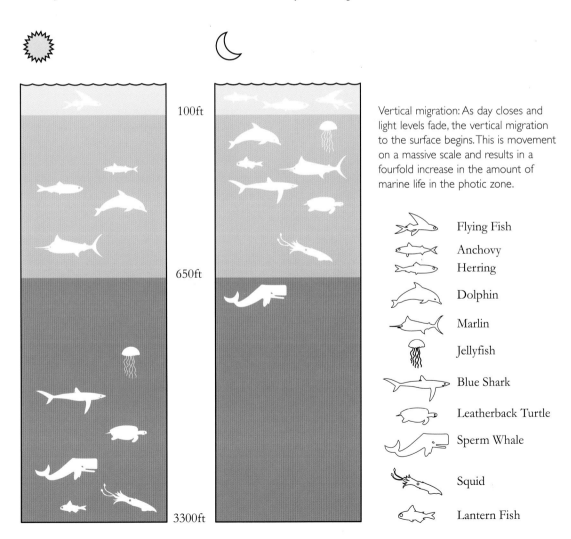

Vertical migration: As day closes and light levels fade, the vertical migration to the surface begins. This is movement on a massive scale and results in a fourfold increase in the amount of marine life in the photic zone.

Flying Fish

Anchovy

Herring

Dolphin

Marlin

Jellyfish

Blue Shark

Leatherback Turtle

Sperm Whale

Squid

Lantern Fish

100ft

650ft

3300ft

Vertical migration in the photic zone

All marine life is on the constant search for food. Throughout the oceans there are areas where optimal conditions exist for supporting life and it is to these that many species are attracted. Winds and currents will dictate the location of these concentrations of food. Warm water currents have a low nutritional and plankton content but where they push up into temperate seas, they give tropical species the opportunity to swim into the surrounding food-rich cooler waters.

Camouflage

Cold water currents, by contrast, are rich in nutrients and plankton; those that flow into subtropical regions will bring this abundance with them and attract masses of tropical and subtropical marine life to their margins to feed.

The lack of cover in the surface waters of the open ocean, where plankton are most abundant, means the potential to be preyed upon is high. Some species have adopted camouflage to reduce the risk of being seen: mackerel, for instance, are dark coloured on their top sides to blend in with the dark sea when viewed from above, but their undersides are silvery bright so that predators approaching from beneath will find it difficult to distinguish them from the brightness of the sky. This is known as counter shading.

Nightfeeding

The vast majority of marine organisms feeding on phytoplankton and zooplankton will use the darkness as a means of escaping attention. During the day, they will swim deeper in the twilight zone where predators find it tricky to detect them in the gloom. As day closes and light levels fade, the vertical migration to the surface begins. This is movement on a massive scale and results in a fourfold increase – literally overnight – in the amount of marine life in the photic zone.

Lantern fish

The lantern fish are a superb example of adaptation to these conditions, making an upward journey of 5,600 feet every evening to feed at the surface before returning to the depths each morning.

Vertical migration on such a scale was discovered only about sixty years ago by scientists using sonar to measure ocean depths. In some areas, readings varied according to the time of day they were taken, being deeper at night than during the day. It was eventually discovered that the migration of life back to the twilight zone at the end of the night resulted in a deep scattering layer which was large enough and dense enough for the sonar not to penetrate.

Predators on the move

The distances traveled will vary between species, with the smallest plankton rising perhaps 30 or 60 feet and the larger zooplankton up to 100 feet. Shoaling fish, such as mackerel, herring and anchovy, will follow the plankton on their upward migration. Larger animals, like the Blue Shark (*Prionace glauca*), Atlantic Blue Marlin (*Makaira nigricans*) and Sperm Whale (*Physeter macrocephalus*), will also leave the deeper waters and head for the surface and the rich pickings to be found there.

Left: Yellowtail Snappers schooling, Galapago.

Opposite: Unusually, the Day Octopus (*Octopus Cyanea*) is a diurnal, rather than nocturnal species.

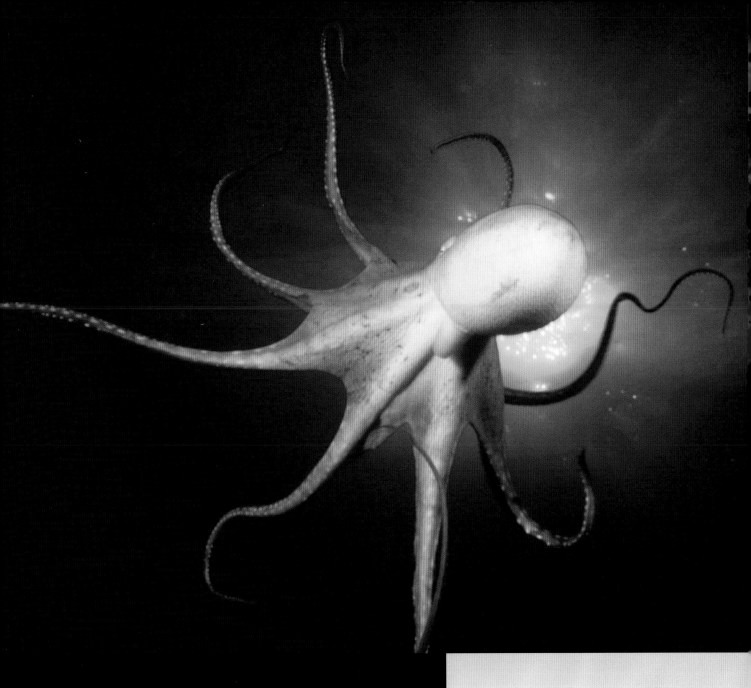

Octopus

The octopus is a shell-less mollusk, belonging to the group known as
Cephalopods (Greek: head and foot), and can be found in many
ocean habitats, but more commonly among the reefs.

Characterized by eight suction-bearing tentacles which emerge
from its head, it can range in size from as little as 2 inches to 29 feet.
The octopus has highly developed eyes and is extremely intelligent;
these attributes, together with its superior colour-changing camouflage
techniques make it a superbly efficient predator.

A shy and solitary creature, it will hide in rocky crevices during
the day, leaving its den at night to hunt its usual prey of fish, crabs
and other mollusks. Having initially moved slowly and stealthily, it will
pounce extremely quickly injecting the victim with a paralyzing poison
before pulling it in to be crushed by a powerful bird-like beak on its
underside.

Venomous

Most octopuses will avoid humans and
will only attack if provoked. The toxicity
of their poison varies greatly from an ability
to numb for a few minutes to the lethal
venom of the Blue-ringed Octopus
(genus: *Hapalochlaena*). This small
creature is a rock dweller, measuring less
than 10cm in length, but has the ability to
kill a human adult in just a few minutes
through paralysis and ultimately
respiratory failure. Octopuses are
themselves preyed upon by sperm
whales, sharks and the savage moray eel;
they are also widely caught and eaten by
humans.

Plankton

The surface waters of some parts of the open ocean team with life at different times of the year. The cooler waters of the temperate seas are more nutrient-rich than those in the tropics, and in the spring, when sunlight increases in duration and intensity and winter storms have mixed the nutrients with the surface waters, blooms of plankton appear.

Phytoplankton

Phytoplankton are tiny, often single-celled plants which belong to the plankton community. They are quite simply the stuff of life, being the first "link" in the marine food chain. These tiny plant organisms are eaten by zooplankton, which in turn are consumed by fish, which are prey to larger fish and so on. The chain ends with the great hunters of the oceans.

Phytoplankton live in the surface waters, up to about 300 feet deep, where they use the Sun's light energy to synthesize the nutrients necessary for tissue formation; this process is called photosynthesis. Their design, size and shape vary enormously.

Cyanoplankton, the smallest, are single-celled organisms which have the ability to convert nitrogen gas into nitrates, important for other life forms. They are most abundant (hundreds of millions per cubic yard of water) in the early spring at the start of the bloom. Diatoms, beautiful single-celled forms, float and drift passively in the surface waters. These are capable of making oxygen and are relatively fast growers; as spring progresses their numbers increase and outstrip those of the picoplankton. In turn, the diatoms give way to free-swimming dinoflagellates.

Zooplankton

Planktonic animals are known as zooplankton. They are free-swimming, able to break through the thermocline and are therefore found at all depths, not just the surface waters. They may be herbivorous, feeding on phytoplankton, or carnivorous, feeding on each other. To avoid being eaten themselves, they will migrate to the surface waters to feed at night when detection and therefore capture is less likely. Being slower to develop than phytoplankton, the zooplankton bloom occurs later. Individual organisms can be as tiny as a few microns, or as large as 6 feet across.

There are two main types of zooplankton: holoplankton which live and remain in the open water; and meroplankton – eggs and larvae which spend some time amongst the plankton before developing into adult forms of larger animals. Crab, lobster and shrimp larvae, fish eggs, young mollusks and sea urchins are examples of these.

Some zooplankton, such as the salps, will feed on picoplankton which they catch in mucous "nets" within their bodies. But the chief consumers of phytoplankton are the copepods – tiny crustaceans that use their appendages to form and sweep currents of plankton-rich water through their bodies. Copepods, in their turn, are eaten by larger zooplankton.

Opposite above: A variety of marine zooplankton at various larval stages.

Opposite below: Jellyfish are one of the largest animals that make up the zooplankton and often swarm in large numbers.

Below: Plankton bloom, Great Barrier Reef, Australia. Such blooms can be large enough to be detected by satellites from space.

Jellies

Toward the end of the spring, jelly-like zooplankton begin to appear in large numbers. These include the comb jellies and true jellyfish. The latter develops from a polyp phase into a planktonic stage at which time it becomes free-swimming. The tentacles of jellyfish are covered in poisonous cells known as nematocysts and can give painful and sometimes paralyzing stings to any passing animals, including humans. The severity of the sting will depend upon the species, box jellyfish, for example, can kill a human in minutes.

The importance of plankton as a source of food cannot be over-estimated. Planktivores, that is, animals that feed on plankton, are numerous and wide-ranging; from herring and sardines, through seabirds, turtles, sunfish and the Basking Shark (*Cetorhinus maximus*), to baleen whales. Many will migrate long distances to coincide with the spring bloom.

Above: Moon Jellyfish (*Aurelia aurita*) may measure up to 18 inches in diameter. The threadlike tentacles of the Moon Jellyfish contain the stinging cells used to immobilize its prey.

Left above: Propulsion is achieved by pulsing movements of the bell-like body.

Opposite: Root mouthed jellyfish.

Left below: Conical warts cover the dome.

The importance of currents

Phytoplankton represent the start of the marine food chain, and their importance cannot be over-emphasised. For phytoplankton to thrive they need to feed on nutrients and minerals present in the water. Certain properties of water will affect its nutritional content: in general it is in the colder, denser, deeper waters of the oceans where such content is highest; but the plankton also need sunlight to grow and this is in short supply or absent altogether in the depths.

How the two meet – the nutrients and the sunlight – to produce the plankton blooms the rest of the food web directly or indirectly relies on, is left to the oceanic and localized currents around the world.

Winds – the Coriolis effect

It is the constant winds that form currents, by pushing the water along, so at the surface the water will move in the same direction as the wind. However once below the surface and out of the air moving across it, the Coriolis effect will come into play with the water now moving in a direction of 45° to the wind. In the northern hemisphere the water moves 45° to the right and in the southern hemisphere, 45° to the left; at the equator it flows in parallel. The Coriolis effect describes the way winds are blown slightly westward due to the rotation of the Earth. The deeper the water, the greater the effect so that by the time the wind's influence is zero – around 300 feet – the water will be moving at 90° to the prevailing wind.

Upwellings

In this way, upwellings occur; if the wind is blowing parallel to the coast, then under the Coriolis effect, the warm top layers of water move offshore at 90° to the wind and the cooler deeper waters rise up to replace them. These are nutrient-rich and are sunlit; ideal conditions for phytoplankton to multiply.

Below: The surface temperatures of the world's oceans have a significant effect on the distribution of different organisms.

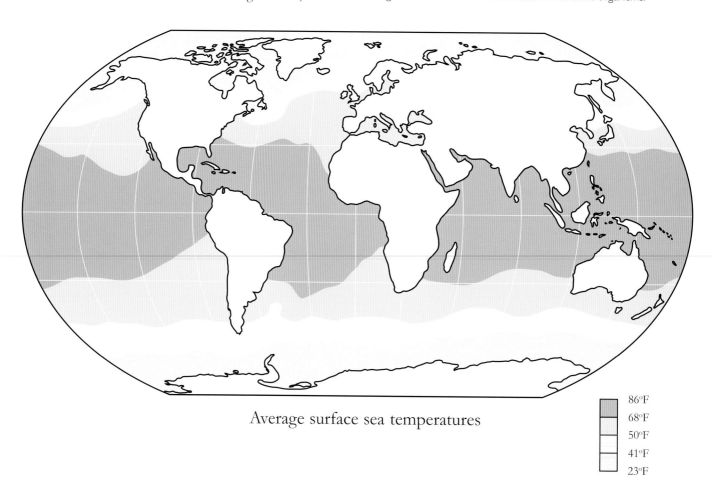

Average surface sea temperatures

	86°F
	68°F
	50°F
	41°F
	23°F

Seamounts

Upwellings occur around islands in the middle of oceans. Submerged islands are called seamounts and may be the remains of extinct volcanoes. In either case, cold, nutrient-laden water will be forced upward to form a circular current around the promontory. The conditions are perfect for plankton to thrive and many pelagic species will migrate across the oceans to these localized fertile feeding grounds.

Away from the coasts in the open oceans, the global winds and the Coriolis effect together give rise to gyres. These are large bodies of water which move in a circular fashion due to different currents meeting. Rotating clockwise in the northern hemisphere and anti-clockwise in the south, the effect of gyres is to produce massive currents which sweep across the oceans in both hemispheres. An example of this is the Gulf Stream in the northern Atlantic which moves up the eastern coast of North America and peels eastward across the ocean to northern Europe. It is strong and fast moving but slows as it heads out to sea.

A peculiarity of gyres is that the water at the center of the spiral is higher, by about 3 feet, than the rest of the ocean. This effect can be seen in the Sargasso Sea in the North Atlantic.

A distinction is made between warm and cold water currents and the effect they have on the migration of life in the search for food. They are formed from the equatorial prevailing winds pushing the top layers of water toward the poles.

Gulf Stream

The warm waters of the Gulf Stream, for example, are up to 52°F warmer than the surrounding sea. Warm water currents have poor nutritional content and thus a relatively sparse plankton population, but they do allow species that inhabit them to follow the currents into the cooler temperate seas where food is more plentiful. Feeding areas around the borders of such currents are particularly rich, and surface hunters, such as tuna, will make raids into the colder waters to feed.

By contrast, cold water currents are high in nutrients, allow plankton to proliferate and thus attract the predators that feed on them. They move slowly and are usually found where gyres flow from the poles toward the Equator. The Humboldt Current moves north from Antarctica along the coast of Chile, carrying its nutrients with it. Once in the tropics, the strong sunlight brings about a plankton bloom which first attracts small tropical fish to the outer edges of the current to feed, and then the larger fish, which are further up the food chain.

Fish of the open oceans

Living in the neuston layer (the top yard) of the ocean has distinct advantages in terms of a plentiful supply of nutrients and food, but it is fraught with danger, particularly during the day: the powerful sunlight allows all things to be seen and therefore predators abound, above and below the water-line.

Flying fish

Many marine animals have developed strategies to avoid capture, and perhaps none is more flamboyant than that of the flying fish. Feeding on plankton very close to the surface, both day and night, they attempt to avoid detection by means of perfect body camouflage: their white undersides are almost invisible against the bright sky when viewed from below. Looking down into the sea, their gray backs merge with the dark waters below. Despite this, they are regularly spotted by tuna, sailfish, sharks and other predators, and it is at this point that they attempt to make good their escape.

Two-winged flying fish have highly developed and enlarged pectoral fins which can be fanned out to form wings. Four-winged species additionally use their pelvic fins in a similar way. Once pursued, the fish will swim fast toward the surface, opening out its fins as it breaks into the air and rapidly beating its tail to gain and maintain height and speed.

In this way, it can remain airborne for more than 30 seconds, gliding for a distance of up to 300 feet, beyond the reach of its predator. Sadly for the flying fish, this strategy is not always effective; boobies will dive out of the sky from heights of 60-100 feet and catch them as they fall back into the sea, whilst tuna are capable of following and capturing flying fish at the start of their flight and frigate birds will take them mid-flight.

Herring

Atlantic Herring (*Clupea harengus*), are small planktivores that are renowned for their huge schools which often reach hundreds of thousands. Drawn to the surface waters of temperate seas to feed on the plankton bloom, they are highly vulnerable to attack from larger predators such as dolphins, killer whales and tuna. During the day they are easily seen in the sunlit waters, and stay down in the deep water until darkness falls. They will then come to the surface to feed on the zooplankton, their daily diet. Whilst feeding they will swim in loosely formed groups with mouths wide open to receive and sieve the plankton through their gill-

rakers. As dawn approaches, they reform into tighter, perfectly synchronized schools to return to their hiding places in the deep water.

Other schooling fish have similar habits to the herring; feeding at either end of the day and avoiding the brightly-lit hours. Some, however, will find oxygen levels too poor in the deeper water and are forced to remain near the surface. Others will be unable to see the plankton they feed on in the darkness, and again, have no option but to risk the sun-lit surface waters.

Lantern fish

Lantern fish have developed an effective method of feeding as their eyes are sensitive enough to detect plankton at night. Yhey follow them up through the water as darkness falls to take their fill.

Baitballs

Even in the gloomy depths, however, schools of fish may be spotted. Predators such as dolphins, tuna and some whales and seabirds, will dive beneath a herring school, forcing it to panic and head upward. At the same time, the fish will tighten their formation until they become one huge swirling mass near the surface. These baitballs, as they are called, attract more and more predators from above and below with the herring devoured as easy prey.

Billfish

Billfish are large predatory fish and include marlin, sailfish and swordfish. There are eleven species, the largest of which is the Atlantic Blue Marlin (*Makaira nigricans*) measuring over 16 feet and weighing more than 990 pounds. All have the ability to swim at high speed; marlin have been recorded traveling at 47 mph and sailfish at an incredible 80 mph.

Marlin have rounded spear-like bills which they use to hit and stun their prey of squid, fish and planktonic crustaceans. Patrolling the surface waters of tropical oceans, Blue Marlin can be found in the western Pacific, Atlantic and Indian Oceans. They rely on their acutevision to locate prey, and therefore, prefer the daylight hours for hunting.

Striped Marlin (*Tetrapturus audax*), are smaller than their cousin, the Blue. They also hunt the surface waters of tropical and sub-temperate seas. Unusually for billfish, which tend to be solitary hunters, Striped Marlin will work in groups of up to thirty if it is to their advantage, and the size of the catch demands it. They will work as a team, maneuvering a school of fish into a baitball at the surface before moving in for the kill. A favourite of sporting anglers, their numbers have dwindled in some areas where they were once abundant, but it is hoped that the introduction of catch and release schemes will help to maintain or increase the stock once again.

The Portuguese Man-of-war

Not a true jellyfish

So named because of its visual similarity above the water to the sails of 15th century Portuguese caravels, the Portuguese Man-of-war is a close relative of the jellyfish. It belongs to the order of siphonophores and can be found in the surface waters of both temperate and tropical seas, often in groups of up to several thousand.

Colonies of "people"

Its distinction from the true jellyfish lies in the fact that it is not a single animal, but a collection of many organisms. The whole colony consists of four types of polyps, which are known as "persons," each with different functions.

One type is responsible for movement, another for paralyzing and catching prey, a third for digestion and the final one for reproduction. Each colony can contain up to 1,000 persons, co-existing as a single entity, but unable to live independently of each other.

Poisonous

From above the water line, the Portuguese Man-of-war is seen as a floating blue and lilac gas-filled bag topped with a comb-like fringe or sail. The bag measures up to 12 inches in length. Beneath the float, a mass of tentacles extends for up to 50 feet into the water. Coated in millions of highly poisonous nematocysts, they are capable of capturing and paralysing fish as large as mackerel.

Stings to humans are excruciatingly painful, but rarely fatal. The Nomeus, or Man-of-war fish (*Nomeus gronovii*) shelters in the tentacles unharmed. Some turtles, sea slugs and sea snails are also immune to the poison.

Opposite above: Barracuda (*Sphyraena sp.*)

Opposite below: The Striped Marlin (*Tetrapturus audax*) is one of the fastest swimmers in the sea.

Below: Portuguese Man-of-war (*Physalia physalis*).

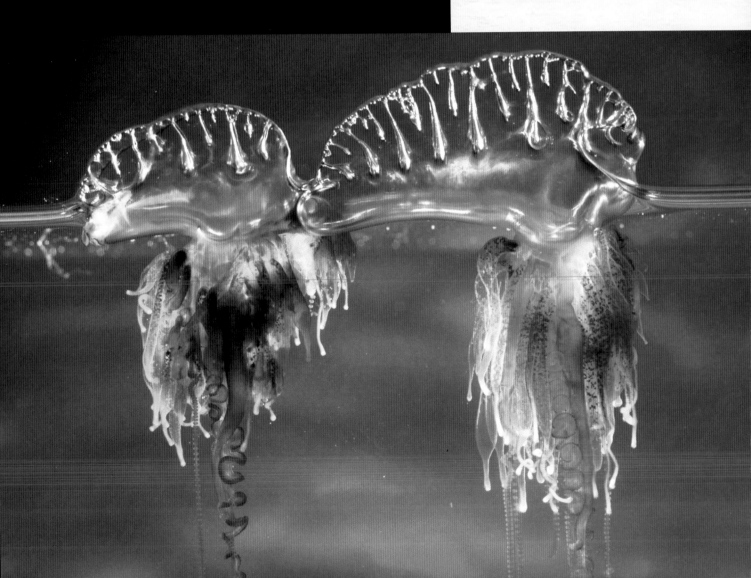

Swordfish

The broad flat bill of the Swordfish (*Xiphias gladius*), or Broadbill as it is also known, is undoubtedly for defence, but will also be used to attack and stun its prey before swallowing it whole. This toothless, and ruthless predator of the ocean likes to feed on smaller pelagic fish such as tuna, mackerel, dorado, and squid, but is known to attack almost all possible sources of food, including whales.

The huge eyes are sensitive to light, and this, together with high body fat levels and a counter-current circulatory system, allows this fish to hunt in deep water below the thermocline. Specially adapted organs behind the eyes and close to the brain maintains their temperature even in the cold depths, thus improving vision even further. Diving is limited by the oxygen minimum level. At night they may follow the vertical migration to the surface to feed. Swordfish have few predators; their fearsome bill acting as an effective deterrent. However, mako sharks, with their swiftness and razor sharp sets of teeth are their main adversary.

Barracuda

Barracudas are ray-finned fish, some species of which can grow up to 6 feet in length. Found in tropical and sub-tropical waters around the world's oceans, their powerful jaws full of strong, needle-sharp, uneven teeth have earned them the reputation of voracious and vicious predators.

They can be found in schools around reefs and in the open ocean, or roaming singly, lying in wait for their prey before outrunning them in short bursts of speed.

Whilst they are certainly efficient and successful hunters, their notoriety for attacks on humans is ill-founded: unprovoked attacks are extremely rare, although barracudas will sometimes follow divers among the reefs.

Tuna

Tuna, are large, pelagic hunters with few predators, but they also swim in schools. Their system of hunting allows them to cover wide areas of the sea to substantial depths. They are heavy and keep afloat by swimming constantly, which they must do at speed to ensure oxygen-rich water flows through their gills.

Schools of tuna are the fastest fish in the ocean, and once food is located, they will accelerate at great speed to reach it. They possess a counter-current blood system whereby cold venous blood returning to the heart is warmed by lying close to arterial blood vessels running the other way. This means the tuna can keep its body temperature up and is thus able to hunt in cooler deeper waters as well as those of the sunlit zone.

Sharks

No animal seems to invoke more fear in people than the shark. Its sinister appearance, speed in the water and ferocious teeth give the impression of a merciless and voracious predator. Whilst it is true that sharks do eat a huge variety of life found in the oceans, are adept at hunting out and killing their prey, and som species have been known to attack people, they are by no means mindless killers of men; shark attacks on humans are relatively uncommon.

All sharks are cartilaginous, that is there skeleton is made of cartilage, a hard gristle-like substance, as opposed to bone. They are thought to have evolved into their present form about 100 million years ago, although the lack of fossil records makes this figure an estimate.

There are thought to be 415 species, many of which are carnivorous, but there are also plankton-eating sharks – the biggest fish in the world, the Whale Shark (*Rhincodon typus*), eats only plankton as it swims the surface waters of the warm oceans. Measuring in at 39 feet, and weighing fourteen tons, it is a supreme example of the energy efficiency of primary feeding.

The Basking Shark is another large plankton eater. Weighing up to five tons and measuring 30 feet long, it patrols the thermoclines of the surface waters, devouring large quantities of the tiny organisms by ploughing open-mouthed through the water and using its gill-rakers to trap the plankton.

The meat-eaters

The large carnivorous sharks, such as the Great White (*Carcharodon carcharias*), Tiger (*Galeocerdo cuvier*), and Great Hammerhead (*Sphyrna mokarran*), can grow to considerable lengths of about 20 feet, whilst at the other end of the spectrum, the dogfish is only 8 inches long.

Most sharks are found in the warm shallow coastal waters of the tropics where food is in abundance, though there are some species, such as mako and hammerhead sharks, which work the open oceans, and others that are deep sea dwellers, such as the Greenland Shark (*Somniosus microcephalus*).

The Blue Shark (*Prionace glauca*) inhabits temperate and tropical oceans. During the day it dives to depths of up to 2000 feet, traveling below the thermocline to cold waters hunting for its preferred meal of squid and octopus. It cannot remain here indefinitely, however, and must return to the warmer surface waters every hour or so to heat up again. At night, feeding gets slightly easier as its prey follows the vertical migration to within 300 feet of the surface.

Opposite above: The Great White Shark (*Caracharodon carcharias*) is amongst the most feared animals in the ocean, but attacks on humans are quite rare.

Opposite below: Scalloped Hammerhead Sharks (*Sphyrna lewini*) swimming amongst small fish.

Below: Caribbean Reef Shark (*Carcharhinus Perezi*).

Sensing their prey

Superb hunters and locators of their prey, sharks have an army of sensory tools at their disposal; their amazing sense of smell allows them to pick up the scent of one part blood to 100 million parts water; they can feel minute vibrations from the movement of other marine life up to 300 feet away. Originally thought to have poor vision, sharks do use their sight when homing in on their catch, and some species will lie in wait in deep water until they spy the outline of their prey silhouetted against the light from the sky at the surface, before they move in for a swift attack. All animals, through muscle movements, give out weak electrical signals, and sharks use specially adapted organs called ampullae of Lorenzini to detect these.

Carnivorous sharks' diets will be mostly fish, although they also eat sea turtles, seals, birds and other sharks. Their stomachs can expand to many times normal size to accommodate large prey, and many strange objects have been found inside captured sharks, including cans of food, plastic bags, clothes, broken clocks and even a reindeer!

Teeth

The shape and size of their teeth will vary depending on the species. Those of the larger predatory sharks will be triangular and serrated in some way, and exceedingly sharp. The mako sharks for example, have long, sharp, pointed teeth, reminiscent of daggers, and these together with its swiftness make it a very effective pelagic hunter of large species. Sharks' teeth grow in rows so that lost or blunt ones are immediately replaced by those from the row behind. The bite of a shark is characterized by its crescent shape and jagged edges so different species can be identified by the indent of their bite on an animal or human.

Above: Caribbean Reef Shark (*Carcharhinus Perezi*).

Opposite: Despite its imposing size, the Whale Shark (*Rhincodon typus*) is a harmless planktivore.

Reproduction

In contrast to bony fish, all sharks mate directly and internal fertilization occurs. Gestation can take two forms; some sharks including the Whale, Cat and Greenland sharks, lay eggs in small tough sacs, sometimes called mermaid's purse. Each one contains a single embryo and floats in the sea attached by tendrils to seaweed or rock crevices. The young are born between 7-10 months later.

In most open-ocean sharks, such as the Blue and the hammerheads, eggs will hatch within the mother's body where the embryo will feed on the yolk sac, or in some species nutrients and oxygen are given through a placenta. In both cases the female will subsequently give birth to live young.

Whales

Descendants of land mammals that took to the sea some 70 million years ago, whales are the biggest of all marine mammals. Indeed, one of their number, the Blue Whale (*Balaenoptera musculus*), is the largest animal that has ever lived on Earth.

All whales are marine and have evolved over many millions of years to become perfectly adapted to life in the water. Their hairless bodies are torpedo-shaped to allow smooth and sometimes swift movement through the water; they have flipper-like forelimbs and a large horizontally fluked tail which can be moved up and down to drive themselves forward; their single breathing – or blow hole lies on top of their heads. As mammals, they need to surface to breathe and will exhale stale air through the blow-hole intermittently, but all are capable of diving to substantial depths for considerable periods of time. The Humpback Whale (*Megaptera novaeangliae*), for example, can dive to 656 feet for up to 45 minutes, and Sperm Whales may reach depths of 3280 feet and remain underwater for over an hour.

Whales fall into two distinct groups; the baleen or filter feeders and the toothed whales.

Giant filter-feeders

Species of baleen whales include the Blue, Fin (*Balaenoptera physalus*), Common Minke (*Balaenoptera acutorostrata*), Sei (*Balaenoptera borealis*), and Gray Whales (*Eschrichtius robustus*). Despite their huge size, they feed only on tiny plankton, mostly krill, which is sieved from the sea water through massive hairy plates (baleen) hanging down from the roof of the mouth. They take in large amounts of sea water is pushed it out through the plates using their tongues whilst swallowing the krill and other plankton left behind.

The Blue Whale

The Blue Whale is the giant of all whales, measuring up to 100 ft tip to tail and weighing in at almost 200 tons, an adult blue is a staggeringly impressive sight in the water. Usually found swimming alone or with a calf, the blue whale feeds only on zooplankton, and like other baleens, will migrate great distances from warm-water breeding grounds to the colder seas of the temperate and polar regions to find rich sources of food.

Hunting to extinction

The creature's size and the amount of blubber it carries have, in the past, seen it hunted almost to extinction by its only predator, man. For several decades from the beginning of the 20th century the hunting of blue whales became an aggressive and lucrative business. By 1965, their numbers had dwindled to such an extent that the International Whaling Commission gave them protection. As a result, in the last few decades, the numbers off the coast of California have been increasing; but those in the Southern Ocean have shown no signs of repopulating, and it is feared that the Alaskan Blue Whales have completely disappeared.

Since the Blue Whale has been afforded protection, other baleen species have been targeted. There used to be three different populations of Gray Whale around the world, but hunting has reduced this to just one. This group feeds on the food-rich waters of the northern Pacific around the coasts of eastern Siberia and Alaska. It travels south during the winter months to breeding grounds in the warm coastal seas off California. Since the middle of the twentieth century, protection laws have been enacted for the gray whale and numbers are once again increasing.

Communication

Both baleen and toothed whales make low-pitched sounds, sometimes called singing, to communicate. Humpbacks, which breed in warm tropical waters, can be heard singing as they migrate north in the spring. It is thought that this helps keep the herd together.

Whales have no vocal chords; it appears that the sound is produced by forcing air through sacs below the blow hole.

Like dolphins, whales use echolocation to navigate and find sources of food. Baleens use a low-pitched sound which bends around objects, whilst toothed whales use sonar at a higher frequency that bounces back off the object.

The toothed hunters

There are seventy-five species of toothed whale, which include dolphins and porpoises. The Sperm Whale is the largest; it weighs 50 tons and measures over 65 feet and feeds on giant squid and cuttlefish. It has been hunted in large numbers in the past, for its oil – used as a machine lubricant, and for ambergris – a highly prized substance which forms the basis of many perfumes, but now protected.

Most toothed whales do not make the seasonal migrations common to the giant baleens. As they feed on animals further up the food chain their diet is less energy efficient than that of the filter feeders; they therefore need to remain near to their food supply throughout the year. They have not been as ruthlessly hunted as the baleen whales – being smaller and generally swifter, they are not such easy targets for whalers, and their relatively thin layers of blubber are not as lucrative.

All whales are born tail first and will swim or be helped to the surface to take their first breath. Gestation in the blue whale last 11-12 months and at birth the calf will measure 23 feet in length and weigh three tons. By the time it is weaned at around seven months it will have grown at a rate of 1½ inches and put on 200 pounds a day!

Left: Humpback Whale (*Megaptera novaeangliae*) mother and calf. As with other mammals, whales will nurse their young until they can fend for themselves.

Opposite: A Humpback Whale leaps from the sea.

Previous page: The planktivorous Basking Shark (*Cetorhinus maximus*).

Dolphins

Ruthless predators

Sociable, intelligent, sometimes playful and good-natured, dolphins are everybody's favorite marine mammal. But this view of them belies their true nature; they are in fact highly efficient and ruthless predators of the oceans.

All dolphins belong to the order of mammals called cetaceans, and to the suborder of toothed whales (*odontoceti*). Their teeth serve a purpose: they are carnivorous, and the pelagic hunters among them prey upon a wide range of marine life.

There are some freshwater species, but the majority of dolphins are marine and found throughout the oceans of the world. These include the Bottlenose Dolphin (*Tursiops truncatus*), which is found in the seas of the coast of the eastern Unites States, the Mediterranean Sea and the warm and temperate waters of the Pacific; the Common Dolphin (*Delphinus delphis*), renowned for its graceful arching flight and for following in the wake of ocean-going ships, which lives in warm and temperate seas; spotted dolphins and the Spinner Dolphin (*Stenella longirostris*), which are found in deep, tropical oceans; and the Orca, or Killer Whale, which inhabits all the world's oceans from the polar regions to the tropics. The latter, despite its name, is a true dolphin and the only one that preys on warm-blooded animals, such as other dolphins and pinnipeds, as well as the usual fare of fish, seabirds and turtles.

Swift and adaptable

Comparatively little is known about dolphins' migration habits as they are hard to track in the open ocean, but it is clear that they can travel at speed and great distances to find plentiful supplies of food. They are superbly adapted to life in the sea, reaching speeds of more than 15mph and diving to depths exceeding 1000 feet. A Killer Whale has even been recorded reaching a staggering 3000 feet down. They are able to remain underwater for six or seven minutes before needing to take a breath. When they do surface for air they can exchange up to 80% of the air in their lungs for oxygen, in a single breath.

Young

Being mammals, dolphins give birth to live young; calves are born underwater after a gestation that can last from eight to sixteen months, depending on the species. At birth, the mother immediately assists the calf to the surface so that it can take its first lungful of air. The offspring will suckle for up to twenty months, gradually being introduced to a mixed diet of fish and squid.

Above: Atlantic Spotted Dolphins (*Stenella Frontalis*). Dolphins are highly sociable and may live in groups of just a few individuals, or in some cases, several thousand.

Below: A calf swims alongside its mother.

Echolocation

Through a range of clicks and whistles, many of which are inaudible to humans, dolphins are able to communicate with each other. They also use an extremely sophisticated system of echolocation to find sources of food. The dolphin will generate a click which is forced out as a sound wave into the water ahead. When the sound hits an object, some of it is reflected back toward the dolphin as an echo. The echo is received by the dolphin and transmitted to the brain. Further clicks and echoes will allow it to judge the distance between itself and the object, its direction and size in terms of volume and surface area.

Dolphins' echolocation systems are complex and ultra-sensitive; they are able to whistle and echolocate simultaneously and to echolocate two different objects at the same time. They are such experts at finding their prey that other predators will often simply follow them to the food source and share in the spoils.

Working as a team, dolphins will seek out food, and continue this co-operation when co-ordinating their attack. As they pen in their prey and force schooling fish to the surface, their clicks and whistles will often disorientate and panic the school into a tight baitball, at which point the dolphins will move in for the kill.

Predators

Predators of dolphins include sharks, which will usually attack the young, the sick, nursing mothers and the elderly, and Killer Whales. Man, through pollution of the seas, depletion of fish stocks and the use of dolphin meat as bait for the hunting of sharks, contributes to the reduction in their numbers.

Dolphin pods

Dolphins live in groups, which are known as pods, herds or schools, which can range in size from just a few individuals in coastal waters to the extremely large pods of the pelagic species, which can be several thousand strong. The size of the school is dependent upon the type of prey they seek. The Risso's Dolphin (*Grampus griseus*), for example, feeds mainly on squid, which is found in relatively small amounts and has a fairly low nutritional value. Therefore, the hunting group is small.

Dolphins that chase shoaling fish in the open ocean are able to support much bigger pods because the supply is plentiful and fish are highly nutritious. As such, the herds of the Common, Spotted and Spinner dolphins are huge.

Opposite and Below: Coastal Spotted Dolphins (*Stenella Attenuata*). Dolphins are highly intelligent and often hunt cooperatively. They are often playful and inquisitive by nature.

Seals and Sea Lions

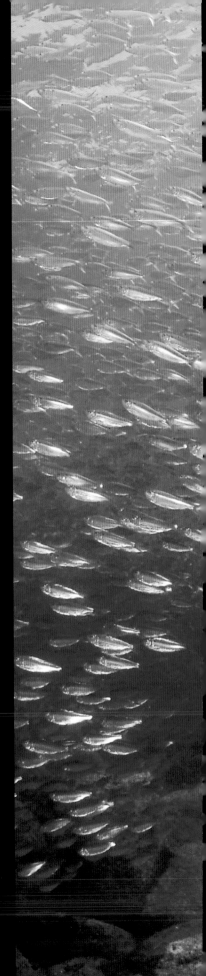

Seals and sea lions belong to a group of marine mammals known as pinnipeds ('fin-footed'). Their perfect adaptation to life in the water allows them to travel far, swim fast and dive deep in nearly all the world's oceans. Many species are concentrated in and around the polar regions, but they can also be found in temperate and tropical seas.

Evolved from land-based mammals, they retain some of the characteristics of their terrestrial ancestors: they are warm-blooded, breathe air through their lungs and give birth to live young which suckle milk from their mothers.

Diving

On land, pinnipeds are ungainly and cumbersome – either humping their bodies along the ground or else hobbling on all four 'legs'. In the water, however their streamlined shape and flipper-like limbs transform them into agile, graceful, almost balletic swimmers capable of diving hundreds of feet at great speed.

When diving, their metabolism reduces dramatically (their heart beats at $^1/_{10}$th of its normal rate) and they use oxygen stores in their large blood supply. Many seals and sea lions can dive to depths of 300 feet, for 20-30 minutes at a time.

A pinniped diver par excellence is the male Northern Elephant Seal (*Mirounga angustirostris*), which is capable of reaching depths of 5000 feet in the open ocean and remaining under water for up to two hours!

Breeding

Despite their ability to thrive in water, all seals and sea lions need to return to land to breed and rear their young. Dominant males, known as "beachmasters" will sometimes control and mate with up to 50 females. Territorial warfare between the males is common and often bloody.

In the high latitudes most pinnipeds will give birth on ice floes. In temperate and tropical zones they will often congregate in their hundreds at well-established breeding grounds. In the Pacific for example, sea lions head for the Galapagos Islands off the coast of Ecuador, feeding on fish and squid in the surface waters of the Humboldt Current as it meets the Equatorial Counter-current around the Islands. These creatures can also be found breeding on islands off the coast of California, and in much smaller numbers (if at all) on Honshu Island off Japan.

Northern Elephant seals breed on islands off the Mexican coast and along the Baya California Peninsula. In the Atlantic Ocean, Harbor Seals (*Phoca vitulina*), will head for beaches around Europe and the east coast of North America. The North Atlantic Gray Seal (*Halichoerus grypus*) has only recently started breeding on land (in Scotland) – its pups are white and therefore more easily camouflaged on ice than rock.

Predators

Natural predators of seals and sea lions include sharks, Killer Whales and the Leopard Seal (*Hydrurga leptonyx*), but it is man who has driven many species to the edge of extinction. Many populations have been decimated through hunting and drowning when caught in nets, although the protection of some species during the twentieth century has resulted in a gradual recovery.

Right: A California Sea Lion (*Zalophus californianus*) in pursuit of a shoal of fish.

Shelf seas

The shallow waters around the edges of the Earth's continents are known as shelf seas, the name referring to the continental shelf upon which they sit. A profusion of marine life exists here and man has exploited this over many centuries; the vast majority of commercially-caught fish in North America and Europe originate from the waters of the shelf seas.

The sediments washed down from rivers onto the continental shelf are rich in minerals and nutrients, the building blocks necessary to create plankton which sustain the rest of the marine food chain. Additionally, the debris which sinks down onto the shelf seabed from the bodies of dead plankton and larger marine organisms provides a rich source of food for the creatures that live there.

Formation and topography
During the last Ice Age, sea levels were much lower as a large volume of water was in a frozen state in the form of glaciers. At this time, the shelf seas of today would have been exposed as part of the continental land mass; it is only since the end of the Ice Age that they have become flooded.

These seas extend from low-tide mark to the edge of the shelf break, generally for about 45 miles, although they can be much wider – up to 550 miles, on the northern Siberian coast – or shallower, as on the Pacific rim and particularly along the edge of South America where the shelf runs out for a mere 3000 feet. This latter is known as a Pacific shelf and is associated with seismic activity in the form of volcanoes and earthquakes. The other type – the Atlantic – is characterized by a much broader and more stable gentle slope.

At the shelf edge the gradient increases dramatically to form a steep drop toward the sea bed. This is known as the shelf break and is where the continental land mass would have ended and the sea begun tens of millions of years ago.

Beyond the shelf break is the continental slope, often gouged with truly ancient river-valleys now filled with sediment flowing down off the shelf itself. Where the continental slope meets the ocean crust there is sometimes a gently sloping stretch called the continental rise.

Fishing
Fishing communities depend on many of the fish stocks which thrive in the shelf seas; Atlantic Cod (*Gadus morhua*), Haddock (*Melanogrammus aeglefinus*), and Hake (*Merluccius merluccius*), are all caught in northern hemisphere waters. Over-fishing has led to the depletion of some species; for example the Pacific Herring (*Clupea pallasi*), has been drastically reduced in numbers through commercial fishing. Other species important for the fisheries include snappers and the trevally, which are found in tropical and subtropical waters.

On the shelf sea bed a wide variety of marine life exists; sponges, sea squirts and mussels are fixed to the bottom and pump water through their bodies to filter out food particles. Other species will burrow or bury themselves in the silt and mud. These include anemones that will trap passing food in their tentacles, which wave free in the water. Carnivorous snails and sea slugs patrol the bottom as do a whole variety of invertebrates such as crabs and lobsters. Meanwhile skates and rays glide elegantly along the sea bed looking for snails and crabs.

Rays

Related to sharks, all rays are cartilaginous and give birth to live young. Many live on the sea floor in shallow waters, but some, such as the Manta Ray (*Manta birostris*), inhabit the open ocean.

Stingrays

Stingrays are to be found in all the world's oceans, but more commonly in tropical coastal waters, buried in the sand or mud of the sea bed. Their superb camouflage makes them hard to spot, and stings to humans are usually as a result of accidentally stepping on the rays.

Varying in size from 5 inches to 6 feet, the stingray is non-aggressive if left alone, but if provoked or disturbed it can deliver a powerful venom through its spine at the base of the tail. During an attack, the spine, which is extremely sharp or serrated, is erected and the tail is used to force it into the victim. Fatal attacks on humans, such as that on the Australian naturalist, Steve Irwin in 2006, are extremely rare.

As their eyes are on the top of their bodies, stingrays cannot use them efficiently to see their prey; instead they rely on smell and electro-receptors in a similar way to their cousin the shark. Their diet consists mainly of mollusks and crustaceans, which they crush with powerful teeth.

Manta rays

The Manta Ray, or Devilfish, is the largest of all the rays, measuring a formidable 23 feet across its wingspan and weighing up to 1.5 tons. It lives near the surface of the water in the open ocean, and has been seen to make spectacular leaps into the air, landing back in the water with a tremendous explosive noise.

It is characterized by its wing-like pectoral fins, a flat but enormous body and cephalic horn-like fins around its head. These latter it uses to sweep and channel the small fish and plankton that it feeds on into its mouth.

Placid nature

Despite its intimidating appearance, the Manta Ray is a placid creature if left undisturbed and will rarely attack large marine animals or humans. Indeed, it can often be seen with small fish called remoras attached to it as they hitch a ride to the next feeding ground. If harpooned or caught in nets however, its sheer size and body weight can cause a hazard – it has been known for a harpooned manta to take flight and pull the line and the boat for several miles.

Opposite: The Black Stingray (*Dasyatis thetidis*).

Below left: The massive "wing" of a Manta Ray (*Manta birostris*).

Below right: Remoras often hitch a ride on large fish such as the Manta Ray, scavenging scraps of food and also eating parasites.

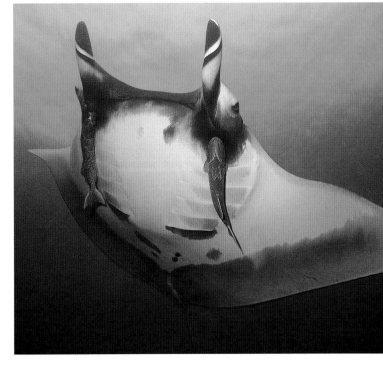

Seabirds

The seabirds of the open ocean, the pelagic hunters, are a group known as tubenoses and include petrels, albatrosses and shearwaters. Like other seabirds, they must come ashore to breed and rear their chicks; they have webbed feet enabling them to swim and land on water; and feed on fish, squid and plankton.

Feeding and migration

Predators of the surface waters, they have adapted their feeding habits to take full advantage of the conditions which abound in the open ocean, often undertaking long journeys to find an abundance of food.

A fine example of this is the Wilson's Storm-Petrel, or Wilson's Petrel (*Oceanites oceanicus*), which flies 20,000 miles north from its breeding grounds in Antarctica to the waters of the California Current in the Pacific Ocean. Here, during the northern hemisphere summer months, it will prey on the great stocks of fish that in turn have fed on the plankton blooms the current generates.

Below: A Blackbrowed Albatross (*Diomadea melanophris*) skims the surface of the ocean.

Diving

Once food is found, some birds, such as petrels, will dive in pursuit of their prey, using their wings or feet to propel them through the water. Others, shearwaters, for example, will plunge at high speed to snatch fish, their momentum carrying them through the water as far as is necessary. Frigate birds are capable of taking flying fish mid-flight and boobies will catch them as they return to the water. Frigate birds will also attack other birds in an attempt to steal their catch.

The albatross, found in all the world's oceans, is an extremely successful predator. Like other seabirds it can fly long distances with ease between feeding grounds. Thin wings, combined with a long wingspan, allow it to glide on air currents above the waves. The Wandering Albatross (*Diomedea exulans*), which is the largest of all flying birds, will fly tens of thousands of miles in search of food, resting by touching down on the sea at night. All albatrosses prefer hunting in the open ocean and use a variety of techniques to catch prey: sitting on the water and picking the food from the surface; attacking whilst flying close to the waves using their curved powerful beaks to pluck fish from the sea; or by joining with other birds in a feeding frenzy, for example where schools of fish have been whipped to the surface by dolphins.

Above: Blue-footed Boobies (*Sula nebouxii*) diving for fish off the Galapagos Islands.

THE
ABYSS

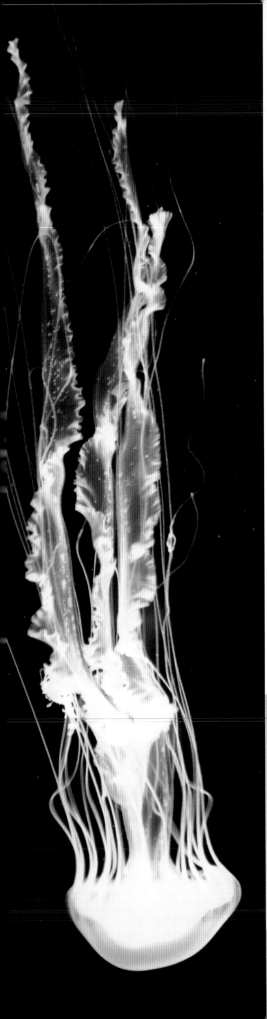

The deep ocean

Below 500 feet, and the teeming life of the photic or sunlit zone, lies the rest of the ocean, reaching depths of more than 33,000 feet over the submarine trenches, but averaging about 13,000 feet elsewhere. To put this in context, Mt Everest stands 29,028 feet high. In the deep ocean basins, the sunlit surface waters first give way to the twilight zone which stretches down to about 3,000 feet, and then from here, the gloom gives way to the deeper darkness of the bathypelagic or abyssal zone. Beyond 20,000 feet, and the ocean bed of the abyssal plains, lie the trench, or hadal zones, a habitat that is almost totally unexplored by man and certainly yet to yield many of its secrets. The abyss or deep ocean is characterized by intense cold, great pressure, a lack of light and a distinct scarcity of food, but still there is life to be found in these apparently hostile conditions.

Temperature variation

The temperature of the water in the open ocean can vary greatly in the first 1000 feet or so dropping from 68 – 77°F in tropical surface waters, to less than 40°F in the twilight zone. Below this, temperatures are fairly stable, with a range of about 39 – 30°F. Most deep-sea animals are cold-blooded and will have body temperatures close to that of the surrounding water, and as a consequence they will typically move more slowly, eat less food, live longer, and become sexually mature later in life than their warm water counterparts. On some parts of the deep ocean floor however, there are hydrothermal vents, which release water that has been warmed within the Earth's crust, and where numerous organisms thrive. They grow rapidly and are sustained by chemical processes in ways that are alien to almost all other life on the planet.

Although most changes in pressure occur relatively close to the surface they then become more gradual in the depths. Below 3,000 feet, the pressure is 100 times that experienced at sea level, and by 32,000 feet, it is equivalent to 8 tons per square inch. Yet despite this staggering statistic, many of the creatures of the abyss are able to withstand such forces with relative ease. This is because their body tissues are filled with fluids which will be at the same pressure as the water they live in. It is only when such animals are brought to the surface that the pressure equilibrium between their bodies and the surrounding water will change and they will die; a fact that has made studying many deep sea organisms all the more difficult.

Fading light

It is perhaps the lack of light in the abyss that has most affected life there. In the surface waters, many fish have adopted counter-shading as a form of camouflage, and whilst the twilight zone still affords enough light for some species to use this method, others have bodies which are transparent or silver, in order to reflect the available light. As the waters deepen and the light fades even further, many animals begin to take on brighter colors. This is because the different colors in sunlight are absorbed at different depths. Red is the first at around 20 feet, followed by orange, yellow and green. By 800 feet, all have been absorbed. Different colors of fish will therefore be more common at different depths, depending on the wavelengths that have been absorbed. A bright red fish in the twilight zone, for example, will be difficult to spot as all the red light will have been filtered out, and the animal will appear murky brown or gray, perhaps as little more than a dark shadow in the deep.

Opposite: Deep sea zooplankton.

Left: The darkness of the abyss lit up as a jellyfish floats by.

Finding food

Food in the abyss is extremely scarce; the lack of light means that photosynthesis cannot take place and therefore no plants can grow. Therefore, life is often dependent upon organic debris percolating down from the surface. On the ocean floor, starfish, sea cucumbers and other scavengers may rely almost entirely on this marine snow for their survival. Similarly, fish in these dark realms are usually small, with weak muscles, resulting in a lethargic existence; they too simply sit and wait for food to arrive. Others meanwhile, will undertake nightly migrations from the upper layers of the twilight zone to the surface waters, in order to feed on the abundance of plankton and other creatures that have gathered there. Of those that remain however, many are fearsome predators that possess huge mouths and stomachs; enabling them to swallow prey even larger than themselves. In a world where a meal may be difficult to find and may have to sustain an organism for several weeks, this can be seen as a distinct advantage.

Left: Close-up of Comb Jelly (*Ctenophora*) a relative of the Jellyfish.

Below: Comb Jelly (*Beroe Ovata*) which is found in waters from Cape Cod to Gulf of Mexico.

Tubular vision

In the twilight zone, where sunlight has almost, but not quite disappeared, many fish have adapted to see through the gloom. Most have very sensitive eyes, and some have developed tubular eyes with two retinas allowing them to see both distant and close objects in the poor light. However, below about 3,000 feet no light from the surface can penetrate and acute eyesight is of no benefit. Here, fish tend to have smaller, weaker eyes or else may be blind.

Inner light

A further adaptation is the ability of some deep sea creatures to produce bioluminescent light from within their bodies. In the twilight zone this may act as a form of camouflage, in much the same way as counter-shading, whilst in the abyssal depths, where no light penetrates, bioluminescence may be used to attract curious potential prey, help a predator to see its catch, or else enable different species to identify their own kind when breeding.

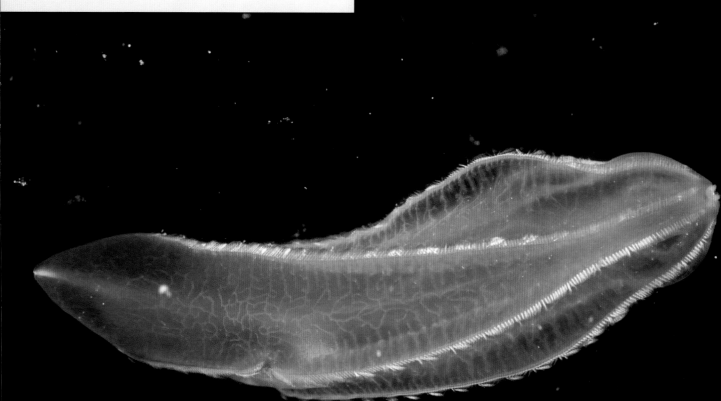

The twilight zone

Beyond the photic or lighted zone, at a depth of around 650 feet, the disphotic, mesopelagic, or twilight zone begins; a realm of near-darkness, which extends to a depth of about 3,000 feet, to the total darkness of the deep sea. Some light filters down through to the twilight zone, but there is not enough for photosynthesis to occur, and so the phytoplankton which form the basis of marine food webs in the ocean's surface waters are absent, and with the exception of a coralline red algae, which has been recorded at depths of 900 feet, no living plants are to be found here. Therefore productivity is low and food is scarce, and many of the animals that inhabit this zone must either migrate towards the surface to feed, or else rely upon sinking organic detritus.

Yet a lack of food is not the only difficulty faced by the animals that live here. The water temperature decreases rapidly with depth, to about 39 – 41°F, whilst conversely, the water pressure increases dramatically throughout the zone, and there is less dissolved oxygen than is available in the photic zone.

However, just as in other seemingly inhospitable environments a wide range of organisms inhabits the gloomy waters of the twilight zone, with an impressive array of adaptations for finding food, attracting a mate and evading predators, of which bioluminescence is just one.

Opposite above: Deep Sea Scallops (*Placopecten magellanicus*) dwell on the sea floor, but are capable of moving through the water by rapidly opening and closing their shells.

Opposite below: A mesopelagic shrimp.

Below: A transparent amphipod.

Many mobile invertebrates, such as tiny planktonic crustaceans, migrate up from the deep to the surface waters in order to feed at night.

Bioluminescence and other adaptations

Many of the organisms that dwell in the twilight zone, from simple invertebrates to fish, are capable of bioluminescence, that is, producing light in their bodies, and there are two main ways in which this is achieved. The first is by chemical means, whereby a substance called luciferin is combined and oxidized with an enzyme, luciferase, to produce light. This process takes place in specialized light organs that contain cells known as photophores. The second method is by regulating oxygen to symbiotic bacteria that live inside the body, which then glow.

Luring prey

Bioluminescence may be used for communication amongst members of the same species, to find potential mates or to keep members of a shoal together. It can also serve to locate or lure prey, or to deter predators. In some cases it is used to confuse and disorient an attacker, as seen in certain crustaceans and jellyfish. These may produce light in their bodies when touched, or be capable of emitting a cloud of glowing liquid into the water, as with some shrimps and squid.

It is also used as a form of camouflage, to break up an animal's outline. Species that use this method tend to lack light organs on their upper surfaces, so that they are hidden against the dark of the depths when viewed from above. They may, however, possess rows of photophores on their undersides, which produce blue-green light that camouflages them against the dim light descending from the surface. This strategy is known as counter-illumination, and is employed by some crustaceans, and also by fish such as the midshipman and hatchet fishes.

Free floating invertebrates

Another form of camouflage used particularly by the free-floating invertebrates that comprize the zooplankton, is transparency, which may make an animal difficult to see, regardless of from where it is viewed in the water. The various forms of jellyfish are probably the best known of the transparent marine invertebrates, but more complex organisms such as amphipod crustaceans, and even squid and octopus employ this method. Perhaps somewhat surprisingly however, many invertebrates in the twilight zone are also brightly colored in oranges and reds. Far from making them conspicuous, these colors actually also serve as a form of camouflage, as red light wavelengths are rapidly filtered out with the increasing depth of the water, making the animals appear dark.

Reflecting light

Many of the deepwater fish are darkly colored, whilst those found slightly higher in the water column may be silvery, in order to reflect what little light is present. Light being so scarce, several twilight zone inhabitants also possess enlarged eyes, to help them find food or avoid predators. Those of the amphipod crustacean *Cystisoma pellucidum*, for example, occupy most of its head, but some of the most unusual eyes are found amongst certain species of fish.

Opposite: A predatory viperfish.

Above: A mesopelagic squid.

Left: Jellyfish avoid detection by being transparent, but many are capable of dramatic bioluminescent displays.

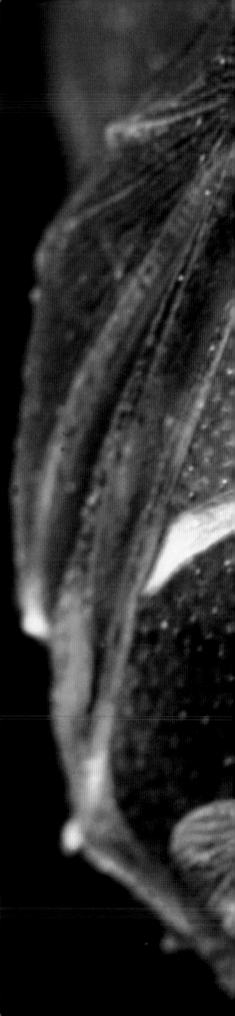

Fish of the twilight zone

Many fish, including hatchet fish, have large, tubular, upward-pointing eyes, which are designed to spot prey, such as planktonic crustaceans and small fish swimming above them, but those of the barrel-eyes, or spookfish, such as the Headlamp Fish, or Winteria (*Winteria telescopa*), which belong to the family *Opisthoproctidae*, are amongst the most pronounced, and provide them with excellent binocular vision, with which to accurately locate their prey in the darkness.

Some species also have partially translucent heads to allow more light to reach the eyes. However, the lateral vision of these fish is usually greatly reduced, and so other defences such as bioluminescence are employed to minimize predation. In the case of hatchetfish,they are also highly laterally compressed to reduce their silhouettes.

Food supply in the twilight zone

As food is in relatively short supply in the twilight zone, many predators do not expend unnecessary amounts of energy in hunting, but instead wait for passing prey, or attempt to attract it, often with bioluminescent lures. Such predators are often incredibly fearsome in appearance, with extendible jaws containing numerous needle-like teeth, probably in order to ensure that their victim does not escape once caught. Several species also possess stomachs that can be distended to accommodate very large prey, so that they can take advantage of any opportunity to feed.

Dragonfish

Dragonfish are similar in appearance to viperfish with eel-like bodies, large eyes, mouths and teeth, but many species, such as the Deepsea Dragonfish (*Grammatostomias flagellibarba*), also possess extremely long lures or barbels on the chin, which may be many times the length of their 6 inch body, at almost 6 feet. Unusually however, adult male dragonfish and closely related species often lack lures, teeth and even a functioning digestive system. Some species, such as the Black Sea Dragon (*Idiacanthus antrostomus*), which is also known as the Pacific Blackdragon, are known to be able to emit red light from under their eyes, enabling them to locate unsuspecting red-colored invertebrates.

Fangtooth

Right: A fairly small, but fearsome-looking fish is the Common Fangtooth, or Ogrefish (*Anoplogaster cornuta*). This species attains a length of just 6 inches, but it too possesses an extremely large mouth relative to the size of its body, which, as its name would suggest, contains fang-like teeth. In fact, there are sockets in its upper jaw in which the largest of its lower teeth are accommodated when its mouth is closed. As an adult, it feeds on small fish, but it is thought that juveniles mainly consume small crustaceans. The young of this species are quite different from the adults, with numerous long spines projecting from their heads, which originally led to them being classified as a distinct species. Similarly, juveniles of the Deepsea Stalkeye Fish (*Idiacanthus fasciola*) possess eyes on stalks, but these are retracted as the fish matures.

Viperfish

Sloane's Viperfish (*Chauliodus sloani*) usually grows to a length of about 12 inches, but is capable of swallowing fish bigger than itself. It possesses a large mouth and extremely long, recurved teeth, which are used to secure its prey and pass it to the stomach. This species uses bioluminescence, and has a glowing lure that extends from its dorsal fin, with which to attract its prey, and photophores in its mouth and along its body.

The Coelacanth: a living fossil

Until the discovery of a live specimen in 1938 off the coast of South Africa, it was thought that the Coelacanth (*Latimeria chalumnae*), had become extinct during the Cretaceous Period, some 60 to 70 million years ago, and similar species were known only from the fossil record. However, several of these fish have subsequently been encountered, which has even resulted in the identification of a distinct subspecies, *L. menadoensis*, in Indonesian waters.

The Coelacanth is a highly unusual species, which is thought to have remained unchanged for perhaps hundreds of millions of years, and to be closely related to the ancestor of all amphibians, reptiles, birds and mammals.

It has a simple, hollow notochord, a hinged skull, which probably enables it to consume large prey, and an organ in the head known as the rostral organ, which produces electromagnetic waves, and is used to detect prey, and may also be used in finding others of its species when breeding. The Coelacanth is known to give birth to live young. In addition to navigating with the rostral organ, its eyes are also highly sensitive to light, with a reflective layer known as the "*tapetum lucidum*," occuring behind the retina.

The Coelacanth is fairly large, attaining a length of around 6 feet, and may be blue or brown in color, with rough scales. It exudes mucus and oil from its body, and is thought to be able to enter a hibernation-like state when food is particularly scarce.

Hatchetfish

Hatchetfish make nightly vertical migrations in search of food, but it is thought that barreleyes tend not to. Some species are thought to remain at particular depths, which may relate to specific temperature zones.

Right: This hatchetfish has well developed eyes in order to utilize what little light may be available.

Opposite above: A viperfish in pursuit of its prey.

Opposite below: The Snipe Eel (*Nemichthys scolopaceus*)

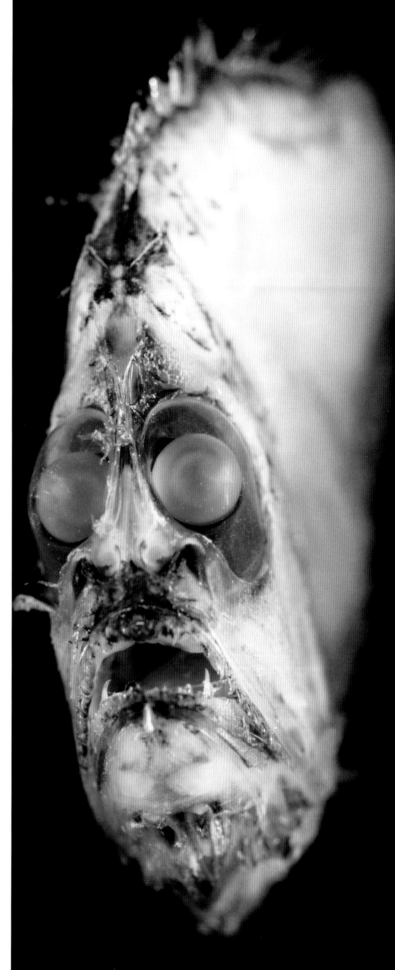

Ctenophores and Siphonophores

Comb jellies

Ctenophores are simple, gelatinous organisms related to jellyfish, and are also known as comb jellies as they possess rows of comb-like cilia, which they beat in order to provide propulsion through the water. In fact they are the largest animals that move in this way. Unlike Cnidarian jellyfish however, comb jellies lack stinging cells, or nematocysts, with which to catch their prey, and instead tend to ensnare their food, which typically consists of fish, crustaceans and other pelagic invertebrates, with sticky webs of tentacles. Others have enlarged oral lobes, which perform a similar function, whilst those of the genus *Beroe* simply suck other ctenophores into their very large mouths. In turn these organisms are consumed by larger jellyfish, fish and turtles, but most species are capable of bioluminescence, which is designed to deter or distract potential predators.

Ctenophores occur at a variety of depths, and may often comprize a large part of the zooplankton found in the photic zone. However, they are often also numerous in the twilight zone, and are also known to occur at much greater depths.

Super organisms

The siphonophores are also related to jellyfish, but are perhaps even more unusual than the comb jellies, being colonial animals that effectively function as a single organism, which is sometimes referred to as a super organism, with different individuals performing particular tasks. Some, the dactylozooids, form tentacles, and like the Cnidarian jellyfish, immobilize their prey with stinging cells, whilst others, such as the nectophores, gastrozooids, and gonozooids may form the bell that is used for locomotion, digesting food, or employed in reproduction respectively. Some colonies, particularly those that occur in the twilight zone, may be composed of vast chains of individuals, which may exceed an incredible 100 feet in length.

Left: Whilst most jellyfish possess stinging cells with which to catch their prey, some simply ensnare their food.

Opposite: Many whales feed on plankton at the sunlit surface, but others, such as the Sperm Whale (*Physter macrocephalus*) will dive to great depths in order to feed on squid and other animals.

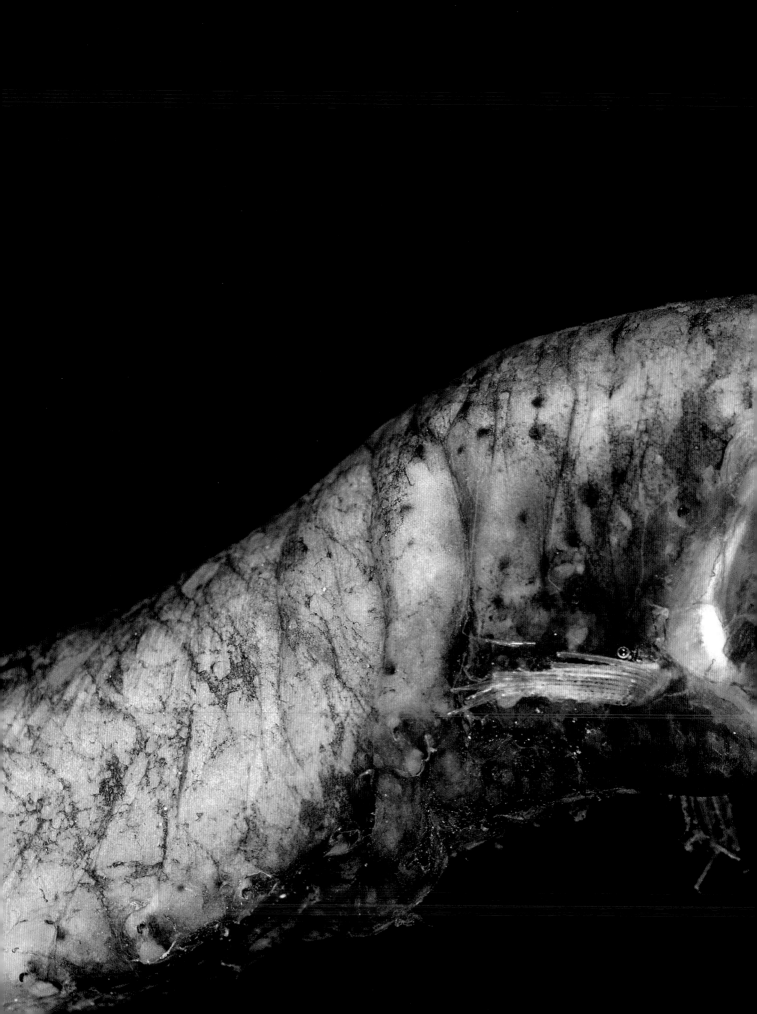

THE DARK ZONE

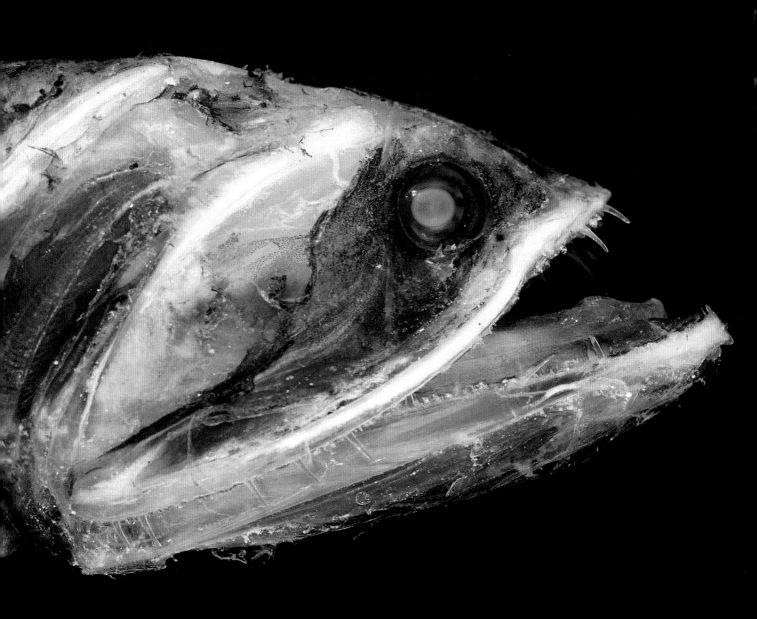

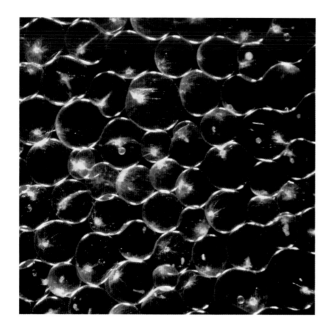

Perpetual darkness

Beyond a depth of around 3,000 feet, lies a realm of perpetual darkness, where no sunlight can penetrate, which is known variously as the aphotic, bathypelagic, or dark zone. This is generally considered to extend to a depth of about 13,000 feet, where it merges into the abyssal, or abyssopelagic zone. Almost 80 percent of the Earth's biosphere lies below the upper limit of the dark zone, and yet the difficulty in studying this space, particularly in terms of immense pressures, means that we know relatively little about it and its inhabitants. In fact it was long thought that nothing could survive in such an extreme environment, and it was not really until the late nineteenth century that such ideas began to be refuted. Perhaps unsurprisingly however, this huge volume of water is indeed sparsely populated, although there remains a surprising diversity of lifeforms. Although the known species may be relatively few and far between, it is believed that in this seemingly empty void, where the only light is produced by bioluminescent animals, or occasionally shines from deep sea submersibles, there are many fascinating animals yet to be discovered.

Deepwater cephalopods

With their well-developed eyes and nervous systems, the cephalopods, which includes the octopods, squid, cuttlefish and nautiluses, are amongst the most complex of the invertebrates, and are believed to be the most intelligent. They are found throughout the world's oceans, from surface waters to great depths, and are well represented in the dark zone.

All cephalopods are carnivorous, and are active predators, and whilst most animals in the dark zone are forced to conserve energy due to the extreme lack of food, perhaps by waiting for a passing meal or drifting with the currents, cephalopods have been observed swimming at surprising speeds even in deep water, and it is thought that even here they may be quite purposeful hunters, which probably rely on their well-developed senses to locate prey.

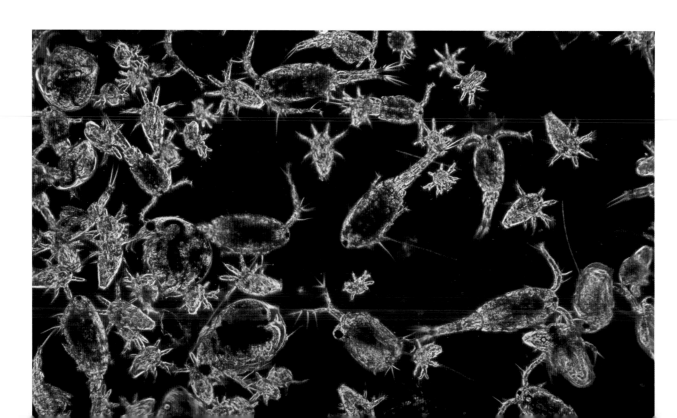

Vampire Squid

The Vampire Squid (*Vampyroteuthis infernalis*) whose scientific name literally means "vampire squid from hell," for example, had long been thought to simply drift around, waiting to literally bump into a source of food. Whilst it may indeed drift to conserve energy, it is also capable of surprising bursts of speed, and possesses the largest eyes relative to body size of any known animal, which no doubt help it both to find prey and to avoid predators.

Additionally, it is covered with rows of bioluminescent photophores, which presumably fulfil similar functions, and although it cannot discharge ink to deter or confuse an attacker, it is capable of releasing bioluminescent mucus instead. This species is one of the most unusual of all cephalopods, seemingly being somewhere between an octopus and a squid in form, with a unique arrangement of retractile fins and sensory filament-like tentacles, and it is placed in its own order, *Vampyromorphida*. It is also unique amongst cephalopods in being able to breathe and metabolize aerobically in the extremely oxygen-depleted waters of the "oxygen minimum zone," which typically occurs at between 1,600 and 3,000 feet. It is able to achieve this by means of an extremely low metabolic rate, and a highly efficient respiratory system.

Similarly unusual are the stauroteuthids, two species of deepwater octopus, which like the Vampire Squid, possess arms or tentacles that are joined and enclosed by an umbrella, or bell-like membrane. The two species, *Stauroteuthis gilchristi* and *S. syrtensis* have at times been observed to draw in their tentacles and inflate these membranes to form a balloon, but it is as yet unknown whether this relates to a feeding or defensive mechanism. They are however known to feed on small copepod crustaceans, and it is thought that mucus secretions may be used to ensnare their prey.

Giant squid

Attempting to study organisms such as these in their natural habitat has proved extremely difficult, and they do not survive long out of it, despite advanced techniques of capture, which involve maintaining water pressure around them. Amongst the most elusive, and also the most impressive, are the giant squid. These creatures were long supposed to be the stuff of legend, but several dead specimens have been discovered washed up on beaches since the late nineteenth century, when there was a long period of such strandings, and in 2004, the first photographs of live individuals were recorded. These huge cephalopods may attain a length of over 45 feet, and weigh more than a tonne, but despite their size, they have proven difficult to locate, and almost nothing is known of their behavior. It is known however, that they are preyed upon by the Sperm Whale (*Physeter macrocephalus*) and it is by following the movements of these whales that the squid have sometimes been successfully located. Some eight species have been described, belonging to the genus *Architeuthis*, but as yet it is not known how many distinct species there actually are.

Above: A giant squid consumes a tuna.

Opposite above: A magnified swarm of bioluminescent dinoflagellates.

Opposite below: Dark field photomicrograph of water fleas (*Cyclops* and *Daphnia sp.*) with first stage copepod larvae, known as nauplii.

Previous pages: The Elongated Bristlemouth Fish (*Gonostoma elongatum*).

Chambered nautilus

Unlike the octopods, squid and cuttlefish, which either lack shells, or possess greatly reduced internal shells, the Pearly, or Chambered Nautilus (*Nautilus pompilius*) is unique amongst the cephalopods in its possession of an external shell, and is regarded as a living fossil, which is thought to have changed little from the ammonites that are known from the fossil record for hundreds of millions of years. The shell is coiled, and consists of numerous liquid and gas-filled chambers, which aid buoyancy, whilst the animal itself resides in the terminal chamber, and another is added as it grows. A siphon passes from the nautilus through the gas-filled chambers, which is thought to allow the Pearly Nautilus to regulate its buoyancy, in order to move up and down in the water.

As in other cephalopods, the mollusk foot has become adapted to form tentacles, which are thought to be used to feed on invertebrates such as crustaceans, and it possesses relatively large eyes. Unusually, these have no lenses, and the Pearly Nautilus is thought to detect its prey primarily by smell.

It is known to feed at depth in tropical seas, but is also encountered close to the surface, and has sometimes been observed on coral reefs. This species is sometimes also known as the Emperor Nautilus, in order to distinguish it from the smaller subspecies *N. p. suluensis.*

Fish of the dark zone

Food is in even shorter supply in the dark zone than in the twilight zone above, with much of the organic material that descends from the sunlit waters being consumed well before it reaches the deep sea, and there are also fewer species of fish and other animals to prey on. However, most of the fish here are predatory, and like those found in the gloom of the twilight zone, they demonstrate various adaptations for finding and consuming other fish, such as bioluminescent lures, sharp teeth, and expandable stomachs.

In order to cope with the extreme pressure experienced in the dark zone, most fish here lack swim bladders and possess water-filled bodies with flexible tissues and relatively weak muscles. Most are also darkly colored, which effectively renders them invisible to predators and prey alike, and they tend to be fairly small, in order to reduce the demands on their metabolic systems. Some of the fish found in the dark zone have relatively large eyes, no doubt for picking up the bioluminescence of others, but in many species the eyes may be reduced, vestigial or absent.

Opposite: The Chambered Nautilus (*Nautilus pompilius*).

Below: This dragonfish possesses a bioluminescent chin barbel, with which to lure its prey.

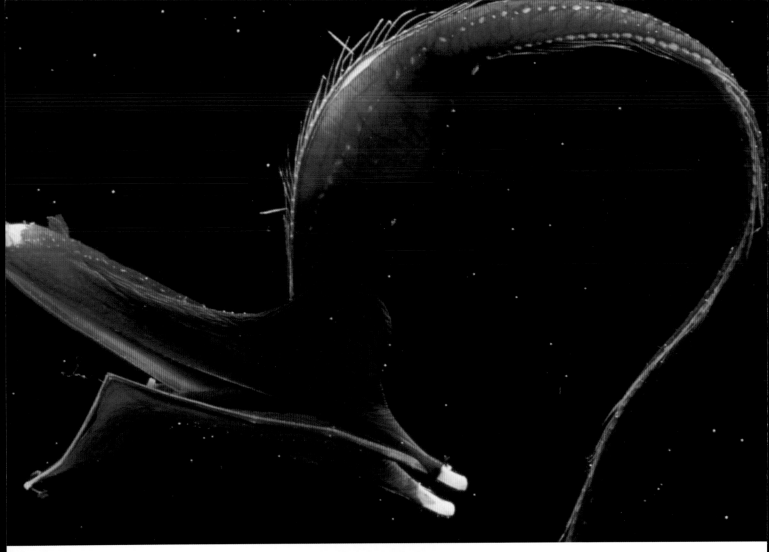

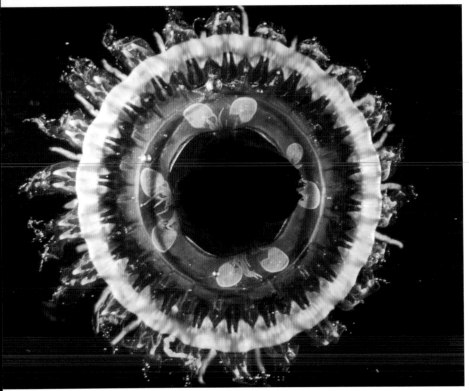

The Gulper Eel (*Eurypharynx pelecanoides*) possesses a huge, hinged mouth, with a pouch-like membrane in the lower jaw, and has a highly expandable stomach in order to consume large prey.

Above: The Gulper Eel.

Left: A deep sea jelly fish. Bioluminescence may be used both to attract prey and to deter predators.

Opposite: A deep sea hatchet fish reveals its bioluminescence.

Gulper Eel

The jaws of the Gulper Eel (*Eurypharynx pelecanoides*) are even more impressive. This species possesses a huge, hinged mouth, with a pouch-like membrane in the lower jaw, on account of which it is sometimes also known by the alternative names the Umbrella Mouth Gulper and the Pelican Eel. It also has a highly expandable stomach, which enables it to consume prey that is larger than itself. It is thought to feed on other fish and invertebrates such as cephalopods, which it may lure with the bioluminescent organ that is present at the tip of its long, narrow tail. It is also thought that it may feed much like a baleen whale, taking in huge gulps of water and sifting out its prey. It generally grows to a length of about 30 inches, but larger individuals may reach around 6 feet in length.

The Gulper Eel is the only member of the family *Eurypharyngidae*, although it is thought to be closely related to the onejaws, or monognathid eels of the family Monognathidae, such as the Paddletail Onejaw (*Monognathus ahlstromi*) and the swallowers of the family *Chiasmodontidae*, which includes the Black Swallower (*Chiasmodon niger*). The onejaws are so-called as they lack the normal arrangement of upper jaw bones, and instead possess a curved fang, which is believed to deliver venom into its prey, whilst the Black Swallower, which grows to a length of just 10 inches, is notable for the elasticity of its stomach, which provides it with the ability to consume prey up to a third longer than itself.

The Slender Snipe Eel (*Nemichthys scolopaceus*) is another highly unusual species, and as its name would suggest, its body is incredibly narrow and ribbon-like. It may grow to over 3 feet in length, and typically possesses a long, bird-like bill, which is lined with numerous small teeth. Both its jaws curve outward at the tips and so do not meet when the mouth is closed, but it is thought that this may enhance its ability to detect and capture its prey.

Bristlemouths

The bristlemouths such as *Gonostoma bathyphilum* also possess rows of very fine teeth, hence their name, and they are thought to be amongst the most numerous fish in the dark zone, and in fact, some have suggested that they may be amongst the most numerous of all vertebrates. Being rather small, with the largest species reaching about 3 inches long, these fish are likely to be one of the most important sources of food for many of the larger predatory fish that inhabit the waters of the dark zone.

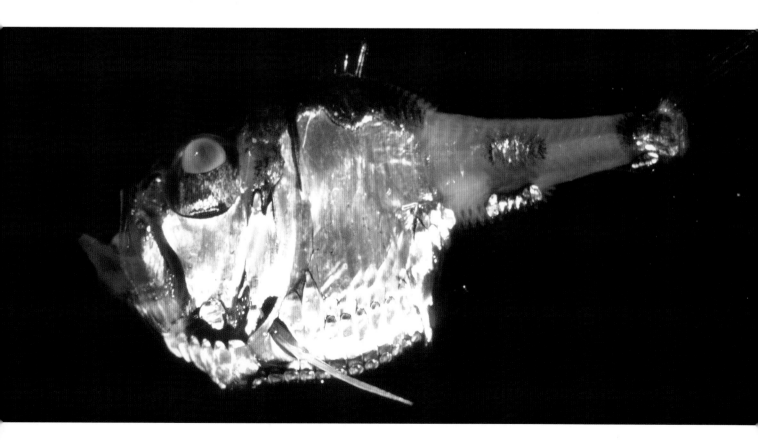

Reproduction in the dark

In terms of reproduction, finding a mate in these dark and sparsely populated waters is also problematic, but various adaptations are demonstrated to circumvent this difficulty. Fish may attract others with bioluminescence or pheromones, and in order to maximize the potential for breeding, many species are hermaphroditic, possessing both male and female gametes.

Anglerfish

Perhaps the most unusual breeding behavior of all is exhibited by certain types of deep sea anglerfish.

In all of the 110 or so known species, the males are dwarfed by the females, and are also somewhat underdeveloped in many respects. Remarkably however, in species such as the Humpback Anglerfish (*Melanocetus johnsoni*), Phantom Anglerfish (*Haplophryne mollis*), Triplewart Sea Devil (*Cryptopsaras couesi*) and Krøyer's Deep Sea Anglerfish (*Ceratias holboelli*), the males, which initially have relatively well-developed eyes and nostrils for seeking out a mate, become parasitic upon the females. In the case of Krøyer's Deep Sea Anglerfish for example, the male is just 6 inches in length, in stark contrast to the female, which is probably the largest of the deep sea anglerfish, attaining a length over 3 feet.

Once the male has located a female, he will attach to her hindquarters with his mouthparts, and will be nourished by ingesting her blood. Over time, the male becomes permanently fused to the female, their circulatory systems become continuous, and most of the male's organs degenerate, leaving only his sperm-producing testes intact. In this way, the female is able to guarantee a supply of sperm, to be used as required, and in some cases several males may attach themselves to a single female.

The anglerfish get their collective, common name from their method of feeding. This involves enticing fish and invertebrates toward their mouths with rod-like appendages, or lures, which extend from their heads, dorsal fins, and in some species, such as *Linophryne arborifera*, also from their chins. In the case of the Wolftrap Angler (*Thaumatichthys axeli*), which is also known as Prince Axel's Wonder-fish, a luminous barbel is even present within its mouth. The tips of these lures contain bioluminescent symbiotic bacteria, the glow of which attracts the prey, which is then snapped up by the anglerfish's large jaws.

Right: A female anglerfish (*Edridolychnus schmidti*) with two parasitic males attached.

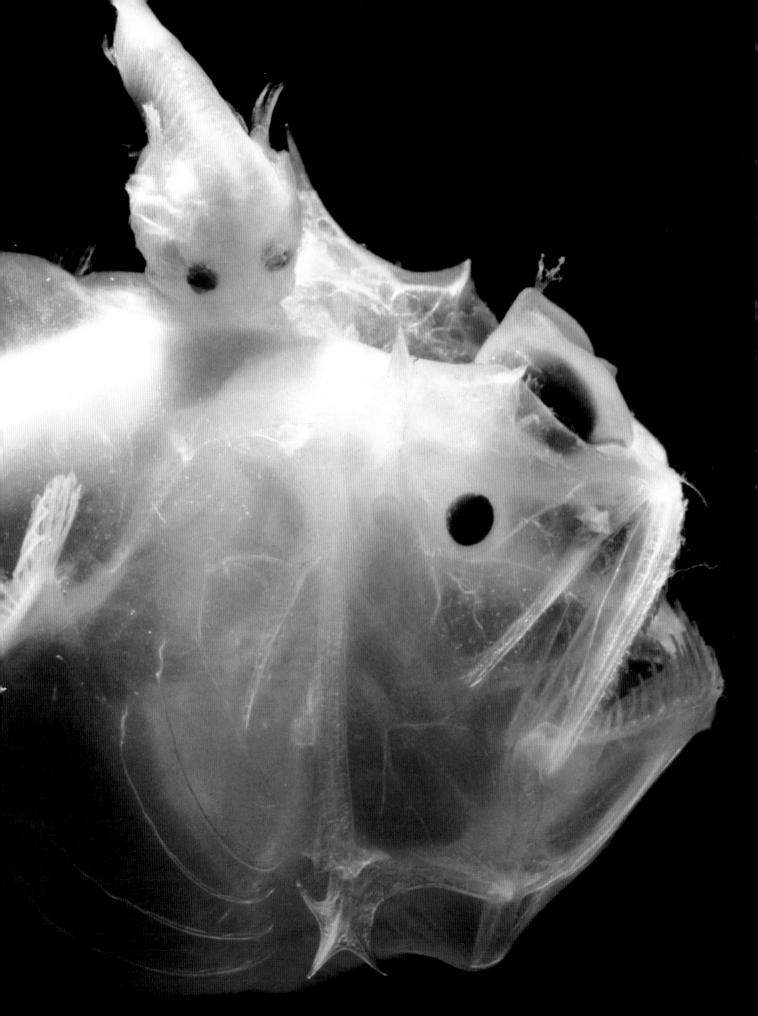

Deep sea bed & hadal trench

Moving into deeper water, away from the continental shelves and slopes, at a depth of around 10,000 feet, we first encounter the continental rise; a slope consisting of sediment that has been eroded from the continents and transported by rivers to the sea, and which has typically slipped down the continental slope as a result of the action of currents. Then, at a depth averaging about 13,000 feet, the abyssal plain, or deep sea bed begins. This vast, mostly flat expanse is Earth's largest habitat, and yet very little of it has ever been explored. These flat plains, which are comprised of clay and silt deposits, mainly stretch from the continental rise to the vast submerged mountain ranges of the mid-oceanic ridges, and are also punctuated by huge, isolated, volcanic seamounts and very deep trenches, the latter of which are also known as hadal zones, the word being derived from "Hades," the term for the ancient Greek underworld. The deepest of these trenches is the Marianas Trench in the Pacific Ocean, which is thought to extend to a depth of some 35,800 feet at Challenger Deep, its deepest point. Yet remarkably, even here, in the freezing, permanent blackness, where the pressure is over a thousand times greater than is experienced at the surface, thriving communities of organisms are to be found.

Marine snow

Along with the inorganic sediment that descends to form the abyssal plains themselves, a variety of organic detritus also makes it to the deep sea bed from the waters above, including the corpses of large animals, which are rapidly stripped by deep sea fish and invertebrates. However, the majority of food that reaches the depths is thought to be particulate; composed of the tiny dead and dying plants and animals that make up the plankton, combined with fecal waste, which forms flakes that fall as marine snow. Much of this never reaches the extreme depths, being consumed and decomposed as it passes through the sunlit surface waters and the twilight zone, but that which does represents a significant food supply for the benthic, or bottom-dwelling, inhabitants of the abyssal plains and submarine trenches, which feed on the biogenic ooze that it creates on the sea bed. It was once thought that this marine snow fell in an uninterrupted, continuous shower, but it has since been recognized that the rate of precipitation varies seasonally and geographically, according to the size and locations of the plankton blooms in the photic zone above, and that the benthic fauna tends to quickly take advantage of these sudden influxes of food.

Opposite: Deep sea brittle-star. Deep water brittle-stars and starfish can be found in large numbers at times, particularly if exploiting a large source of food.

Below: Hydrothermal vent panorama 8,530 feet deep off Mazatlan. Hydrothermal vents are underwater hot springs, which typically occur along the mid-ocean ridges.

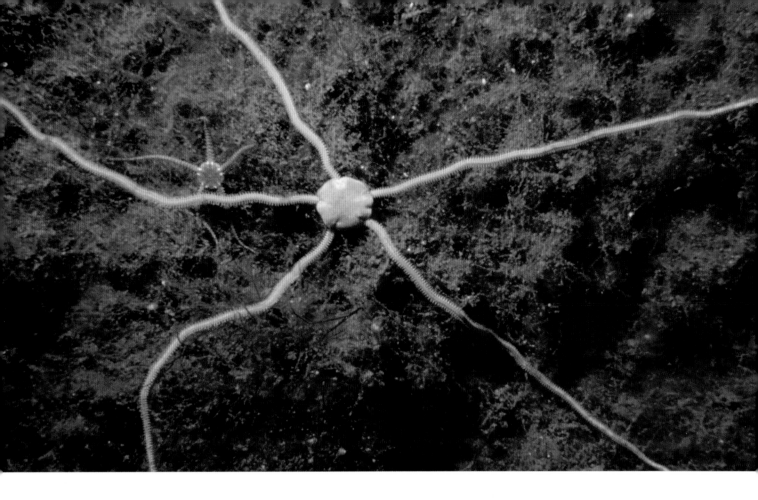

Undiscovered species

Until relatively recently, it was believed that the deep sea bed would be a virtual desert, perhaps entirely devoid of life, but what little of it that has been subject to exploration, and the numbers of formerly unknown species that such exploration has already revealed, suggest that there are potentially millions, and perhaps even tens or hundreds of millions, of as yet undiscovered species, dwelling on and within the sediment of the abyssal plains and down in the deepest trenches.

As in shallower waters with sandy or muddy substrates, a variety of infaunal animals, such as worms of various kinds, are to be found here, burrowing into the sediment itself. There are also numerous, generally larger creatures, which dwell on the surface, and make up the epifauna, including bivalve mollusks and isopod crustaceans. However, the larger surface fauna seems to be dominated by echinoderms, such as sessile sea lilies, starfish, brittlestars and sea urchins, and also holothurians, or sea cucumbers.

In fact, in places, the sea bed is littered with fecal casts and crisscrossed by the tracks and furrows left by sea cucumbers as they move across its surface, ingesting the sediment in search of organic matter. Some species, such as *Oneirophanta mutabilis*, walk on their tube feet, whilst others plough through the topmost layers of sediment, or even remain largely buried. Still others, like the flattened *Paelopatides grisea*, traverse the ocean floor with a rippling motion of the body, and some species are capable of swimming above it in this way. Perhaps somewhat surprisingly, sea cucumbers can sometimes be found in relatively dense aggregations in the depths of the trenches; something that is as yet not fully understood, but which may be related to breeding or feeding. In fact, food is often more abundant in the deep trenches, as they tend to occur fairly close to land masses, and so accumulate organic material from coastal habitats. In particular, they receive more decaying plankton, as the plankton generally blooms most densely in coastal waters.

The abyssal plains

Above, on the abyssal plains, sea cucumbers and their relatives tend to be found more widely spaced, although the mobile deep-water brittlestars and starfish may also be found in large numbers at times, particularly if exploiting a large source of food, such as a large fish or whale carcass. Sessile echinoderms, such as sea lilies, or stalked crinoids, are often found at great distances from each other. These creatures are attached to the sea floor or rocky outcrops by a stalk, and trap particles of falling marine snow with their feathery arms.

Feeding in the currents

Sea pens, which are related to jellyfish, corals and anemones, extend their polyps into the water column to catch food as it drifts past in the currents, and there are also corals and anemones to be found at these great depths. Deep-water corals, such as the solitary, soft, mushroom corals, and also the recently discovered Lophelia, have been found in cold waters at depths exceeding 3,300 feet, and although they lack the symbiotic algae, or zooxanthellae, common to the reef-building corals of shallow, tropical waters, large reefs of this incredibly slow-growing genus have been discovered. The deepest coral reef that is known so far has been found at a depth of around 9,800 feet.

Other sessile invertebrates include the highly unusual, carnivorous sea squirt, or tunicate, *Megalodicopia hians*, which possesses a gaping, mouth-like inlet; tube-dwelling polychaete worms; and deep-sea sponges. These sponges often provide sites of attachment and

Foraminiferans

Below: A variety of foraminiferans. These diverse, tiny, and in fact, mainly microscopic, animals are also protected by a test or shell, which may be comprised of calcareous secretions, or like the xenophyophores, built up out of minute particles from within the sediment. They also possess organelles, or outgrowths, known as psuedopodia, which may be finger-like, or branching and thread-like. These are used for both locomotion and feeding; and the foraminiferans typically consume miniscule fragments of organic detritus and bacteria.

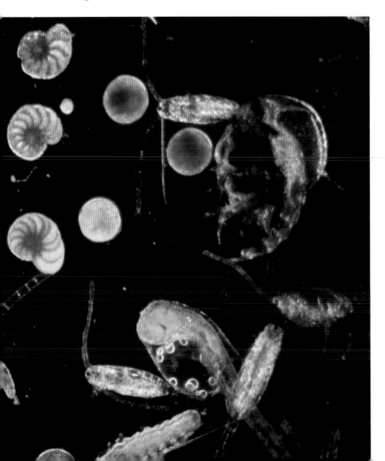

shelter for other organisms, as do another group of unusual, simple animals that were once thought to be sponges themselves; the xenophyophores. These are single-celled animals, which may be several inches across, and their living tissue is distributed amongst a structure known as a test, comprising a network of tubes, which is composed of sediment and the skeletons of planktonic animals. This test aids the xenophyophore in trapping particles of food, and also forms a relatively secure home for echinoderms, worms and crustaceans. Most xenophyophores live as epifauna, on the sea bed, sometimes in high densities, but an infaunal species, *Occultammina profunda*, has also been discovered.

Infauna

The infauna tends to be dominated by much smaller single-celled animals however, which are known as foraminiferans.

Worms are also numerous within the sediment, particularly nematode worms, which are commonly known as roundworms, and polychaete worms, or bristleworms. These also occur in a large number of different species, with a diversity of forms; from tiny detritivores and consumers of bacteria, to larger predatory species, and sessile tube-dwellers, which filter their food from the water column. There are also echiuran worms that dwell permanently within u-shaped burrows, and which extend an elongated probocis, which may exceed 12 inches in length, out of their burrows to collect sediment.

Deep sea bivalve mollusks tend to adopt a similar strategy, gathering detritus with a sensitive palp, quite unlike their siphon-feeding relatives that inhabit shallower waters. Others meanwhile are active carnivores, which burrow through the sediment in search of tiny crustaceans such as shrimp-like amphipods and the more numerous, but closely related harpacticoid copepods, which also live in the muddy ooze of the deep sea bed.

Swimming above the surface, somewhat more unusual crustaceans and mollusks are to be found, including deep water ostracods, which are also known as mussel, or seed shrimps, on account of their spherical, mollusk-like carapaces. Amongst the mollusks, there are species of squid that have been described and recorded, but as yet their classification and their relationships remains uncertain, despite the suggestion of Magnapinna as a genus. This includes a species nicknamed "big fin," which swims by flapping large fin-like appendages, rather than by water propulsion, and possesses extremely long tentacles, of around 27 feet in length.

Giant arthropods of the deep sea bed

Whilst most of the invertebrates found in the deepest parts of the ocean are relatively small, as a result of the distinct scarcity of food and in order to reduce metabolic demands, there are however some true giants, which are thought to be extremely slow-growing and long-lived, including giant sea spiders, which are related to the horseshoe crabs and more distantly to the terrestrial arachnids, such as mites, spiders and scorpions, and giant isopods, which are closely related and similar in appearance to terrestrial woodlice.

Sea spiders

Sea spiders belong to the class *Pycnogonida*, which is represented by around 500 species, which occur throughout the world's oceans, in a range of habitats, from sandy shores to the deep sea floor. Those inhabiting warm, shallow waters tend to be very small, perhaps just a fraction of an inch in size, but some of those that are found on the deep sea bed, particularly in the polar regions, may have bodies that exceed 2 inches in length, with legs up to 30 inches long. Sea spiders are carnivorous, feeding on small, soft-bodied invertebrates by means of an enlarged, straw-like proboscis, and remarkably, as their bodies are so small, their internal organs, including their digestive systems often extend into their long, walking legs. Their eggs meanwhile, are carried within smaller limbs, known as ovigers, with which they also clean themselves. In addition, sea spiders also possess a pair of pincers or chelicerae, and palps, which are sensory appendages. Newly hatched sea spiders possess only these last three kinds of limbs, with up to six pairs of the larger walking limbs developing later, through a succession of moults. This has suggested a relationship with arachnids, as mites are also known to develop in a similar way.

Opportunistic scavengers

Some nine species of giant isopod have been described, including *Bathynomus giganteus*, which is amongst the largest of all crustaceans, achieving a length of over 18 inches. They are found at depths of over 6,500 feet, and are thought to be opportunistic scavengers, although it is likely that they feed primarily on any live prey that they encounter, such as worms, echinoderms, smaller crustaceans, and perhaps also bottom dwelling fish. They possess seven pairs of legs, the first of which are adapted to form maxillipeds, which are used for manipulating food and bringing it to the mouthparts. These consist of four pairs of jaws, used for crushing and shredding their food. As food can be scarce on the deep sea bed, giant isopods are known to be able to survive for long periods without food, but they will tend to consume vast amounts when the opportunity arises, even to the extent of restricting their movement, or in the case of females, of losing eggs from their brood pouches. These eggs are known to be the largest produced by any marine invertebrate, and are carried by the female under special plates that develop at the top of the legs. When the young hatch, they are well developed, and do not pass through a larval stage.

Above: Anemones and corals are found even at great depths on the ocean bed.

Demersal fish

In addition to unusual invertebrates, there are also a number of highly unusual fish to be found close to and above the deep sea floor. Some have reduced muscles and skeletons on account of the immense water pressure, but they may still be quite robust. Additionally, they may also be eel-like, with elongated tails. This is thought to be an adaptation due to the lack of available food, and enables them to possess long, well developed lateral lines along their flanks, which are used in sensing other organisms in the total darkness. Perhaps somewhat surprisingly, many demersal or benthic fish also possess swim bladders, which enable them to achieve neutral buoyancy, in order that they can remain just above the sea bed. Unlike most fish found in surface waters however, these swim bladders may be liquid, rather than gas-filled, or else fatty oils may be combined with gasses within them to form an emulsion, which cannot be easily compressed. Several species also harbor other fatty deposits, often within the liver, which perform a similar function.

Rattail fish

The most abundant fish of the deep sea bed are the grenadiers, or rattails, as they are also known. As this name suggests, they have long tapering tails, however their heads and bodies are typically quite muscular and bulbous, providing them with a tadpole-like appearance. The rattails are quite closely related to cod, ling and hake, although they belong to a separate family, *Macrouridae*, which is known to contain almost 400 distinct species. These range in size from about 4 inches, to over 3 feet in length, as in the Giant Grenadier (*Albatrossia pectoralis*). Some are found at depths of just a few hundred yards, but others, such as *Coryphaenoides filicauda*, which lacks a common name, have been found at depths exceeding 20,000 feet. Other deep sea rat-tails of the same genus include Günther's Grenadier (*Coryphaenoides guentheri*), which is found in the Atlantic Ocean to depths of almost 10,000 feet, and the Abyssal Grenadier (*Coryphaenoides armatus*), which has been observed at depths of over 13,000 feet.

Brotulas

Closely related to the rat-tails are the brotulas, or cusk-eels, one of which, *Abyssobrotula galatheae*, has been recorded in the Puerto Rican Trench deeper than any other fish, anywhere on Earth, at over 26,000 feet; in other words, at a depth of over, or around five miles.

Some species of the gelatinous, eel-like snailfish, which closely resemble the rat-tails, with their large heads and tapering bodies, have also been recovered from great depths, at over 24,000 feet, whilst other eel-like species include deep water eel pouts, which are actually related to blennies, the primitive Spineback Eel (*Notacanthus sexspinus*) and deep sea hagfish. The Spineback Eel is thought to be related to the true eels, as it undergoes a leptocephalus larval stage, drifting with the currents in the water column as it grows. As an adult however, it feeds on worms and crustaceans taken from the bottom, and probably also on sedentary, colonial invertebrates such as sea pens and other soft, deep sea corals.

Rattail

Being mainly bottom feeders, the mouths of the rat-tail fish are usually positioned on their undersides. They are thought to feed primarily on sea cucumbers, crustaceans and other benthic invertebrates, particularly when they are young; as adults, many will also feed on other fish, and scavenge from the sunken carcasses of larger animals. Rattails swim slowly in order to conserve energy, but whilst it was once thought that they were likely to sit and wait for a passing, or falling meal, it is now believed that they may forage almost continually, using a range of sensory adaptations to help them secure a meal. These include barbels under the chin, which are sensitive to both touch and chemical changes in the water, and acoustic sensors on the head, which detect sound vibrations.

Above left: The Rabbitfish (*Chimaera monstos*). The more primitive chimeras more common at great depths. They are somewhat shark-like in appearance, but lack sharp, biting teeth, and instead possess grinding plates, which provide them with the alternative name, rabbit fish. Many species, such as the Smallspine Spookfish (*Harriotta haeckeli),* the Narrownose chimaera (*Harriotta raleighana*), and the Pacific Spookfish (*Rhinochimaera pacifica*) also possess a greatly enlarged, pointed snout, and a venomous spine, which is located close to the dorsal fin.

Above right: Hagfish possess a notochord and a cartilaginous skeleton, but lack both vertebrae and jaws. Instead, their mouthparts consist of a rasping disk, which is used to tear flesh from carcasses or slow moving prey, although they will also consume small invertebrates such as worms.

Cartilaginous fish with jaws, or the Chondrichthyes, are thought to have evolved from animals such as the hagfish, and these are divided into two major groupings or subclasses; Elasmobranchii, which contains sharks, skates and rays, and Holocephali, which contains the ghost sharks, or chimaeras.

Hagfish

The hagfish, which belong to the superclass Agnatha meanwhile, are the most primitive of all extant deep sea fish, and in fact, fish in general, and there is even some debate as to whether they should be regarded as fish at all, or even as vertebrates. Rather, they are sometimes classed as prevertebrates, as they may represent a link between invertebrates and vertebrates.

Sharks in the deep

The sharks, which have developed a largely pelagic lifestyle, are relatively scarce in the abyssal depths, although there are examples such as the Cookie-cutter Shark, named for the distinctive shape of its bite mark, and the Portuguese Dogfish (*Centroscymnus coelolepis*) which are found to depths of around 11,500 and 12,200 feet respectively. There is also a ray, Bigelow's Ray (*Rajella bigelowi*) which has been found at depths of up to 13,500 feet.

Blind in the abyss

Whilst most of these bottom-dwelling species are generally regarded as being rather unattractive, there are however, some quite elegant examples, such as the

Tripod Fish (*Bathypterois grallator*) and the closely related spiderfish, examples of which include the Longray Spiderfish (*Bathypterois longifilis*) and the Abyssal Spiderfish (*Bathypterois longipes*). These all possess highly elongated rays that project from the pelvic and caudal fins, which are used to stand on the sea floor and to detect the vibrations caused by potential prey or predators alike. Similarly, the pectoral fins also often possess long rays, which are held out sideways into the water to sense movement. Most of these fish possess tiny eyes and are thought to be almost entirely blind, although there are species with large eyes that may be sensitive to the bioluminescent lights. The Tripod Fish is known to dwell at depths of up to 11, 500 feet, whilst some of the spiderfish have been found at even greater depths, of around 16,500 feet. These fish typically face into the current and simply wait for a passing meal, and they are thought to feed on both invertebrates and smaller fish.

As with many deep water species, the Tripod Fish improves its chances of reproduction by being hermaphroditic, that is possessing both male and female gametes, but unusually, it is actually capable of self fertilization.

Hydrothermal vents and cold seeps: oases in the abyss

Of all the discoveries made in the oceans, or indeed anywhere on Earth, those of hydrothermal vents and cold seeps are amongst the most remarkable, for at such sites, communities of life thrive almost entirely independently of the energy of the sun. With incredibly rare exceptions, all food chains, and thus, life on Earth, are sustained directly or indirectly by the process of photosynthesis in plants, even on the abyssal plains, which receive the fallout of marine snow from above.

However, at the strange micro-environments created by hydrothermal vents and cold seeps, photosynthesis is replaced by chemosynthesis, whereby inorganic molecules are converted into life sustaining carbohydrates and proteins by bacteria, rather than plants, and the energy used to do so comes not from the sun, but from deep within the Earth.

Hydrothermal vents

Hydrothermal vents are essentially underwater hot springs, which typically occur along the mid-ocean ridges. At such locations, the movement of the Earth's crust results in deep cracks that allow seawater to enter, where it is superheated to temperatures of up to about

752°F by the underlying magma, before surging back out, laden with chemicals and minerals, which give the appearance of billowing clouds of black or white smoke. For this reason, the vents are known as either black or white "smokers". The former are the hottest, and carry iron and sulfide, which form black monosulfide, whilst the latter are cooler, and carry such white materials as calcium, silicon and barium.

Vent communities

Sulfide-oxidizing bacteria, and other primitive microbes known as archaea, which are capable of making their own food without sunlight, had been previously discovered in mud flats, the depths of mangrove swamps, and at terrestrial hot springs, but no one had imagined that they could be the primary producers, forming the basis of a food web and sustaining a whole host of other organisms. Yet this has been found to be the case at hydrothermal vents.

Vent communities typically contain a wide range of organisms, from various worms to bivalve mollusks, anemones, shrimps, white brachyuran crabs, squat lobsters, octopuses, and even fish, almost all of which were previously unknown to science, and are found only in these extreme environments. In fact, since the discovery of the vents, new species have been revealed at an astonishing rate, including organisms such as the Pompeii Worm (*Alvinella pompejana*), which are tolerant of some of the highest temperatures, greatest temperature

Hydrothermal vents

The water in the jets would normally form steam, but under the intense pressure of the deep ocean, it remains as a liquid. It is cooled almost instantly by the surrounding water as it emerges, depositing the mineral particles that it carries, which form chimneys, some of which can reach incredible heights before they eventually collapse. The tallest known, which was nicknamed "Godzilla," reached a height of around 135 feet before toppling; the growth rate can be prolific too, at up to about 20 inches in a single month.

The existence of such vents had long been hypothesized before their discovery, using the submersible, in 1977. However, the complex communities of life that they sustained were completely unexpected.

variations, and highest levels of acidity and toxic chemicals anywhere on Earth.

All of these creatures are sustained by the remarkable microbes, which may be ingested directly as food; by filter-feeding or grazing on the bacterial mats that they form on the rocky substrate surrounding the vents, or indirectly, as with fish that consume other vent dwellers such as worms and crustaceans. However there are more unusual feeding relationships to be found at the vents.

Giant tubeworms, known by the scientific name *Riftia pachyptila*, which grow to a length of around 6 feet, were discovered to contain vast quantities of bacteria, and yet possessed no mouths or digestive system. It was deduced that the bacteria lived symbiotically within them, inside specialized chambers, where they received shelter and the chemicals necessary for their growth, whilst synthesizing potentially toxic chemicals into food for the worms. Similarly, vent clams and mussels, such as *Calyptogena magnifica*, *Bathymodiolus elongatus* and *Bathymodiolus thermophilus*, were found to contain huge concentrations of these bacteria in their gills, which probably explains their prolific growth; the giant clams for example are able to attain lengths of about 12 inches, far larger than any others inhabiting the deep ocean.

Mid-Atlantic vents

Some vents are known to sustain only a small number of species, such as those discovered in the mid-Atlantic, which are dominated by species of shrimp, such as Rimicaris exoculata, which also feed on sulfide-fixing bacteria, and yet these too occur in their thousands.

Despite sustaining these thriving communities of life, it is known that each hydrothermal vent tends to exist for perhaps two or three decades, before they are closed by the continual spreading of the ocean floor. Quite how these vent organisms continue to populate new vents remains something of a mystery. It is thought that the planktonic larvae of vent species are probably produced frequently and in vast numbers, and set adrift in the hope of finding a suitable site for colonization. It is also suggested that decomposing whale carcasses may provide similar conditions, and represent a temporary haven for some.

Regardless of the transience of individual vents however, it is thought that these oases in the abyss have existed for hundreds of millions of years, and that the first life on Earth may have originated in conditions and environments such as these.

Above: Giant tubeworms, known by the scientific name *Riftia pachyptila*, grow to a length of around 6 feet.

Cold seeps

During the 1980s, similarly diverse and productive deep-sea ecosystems were discovered in areas where there were no hydrothermal vents, which led to the discovery of cold seeps; areas where methane gas, hydrogen sulfide and other hydrocarbons seep from fissures in the ocean floor at a similar temperature to the surrounding water. These may be released by archaea and bacteria breaking down organic material deep below the sea bed, originate from oil deposits, or be forced up from the seafloor by geological movements. As at hydrothermal vents, there are chemosythetic microbes, including archaea and eubacteria, at the surface, which form the basis of the seep ecosystem. These process the methane and other chemicals into food for a host of higher organisms, including mussels, clams and tubeworms, and just as at the vents, these microbes are often to be found living symbiotically within the bivalves and worms. Further up the food chain, crabs and fish are to be found here too.

Cold seeps are somewhat more stable and enduring than hydrothermal vents, and this, coupled with the lower temperature, is thought to enable some of the organisms that dwell alongside them to be incredibly long-lived. Some clams found at cold seeps are thought to be over 100 years old, whilst there are tubeworms estimated to reach 250 years.

MAN AND
THE OCEANS

The challenge of the oceans

In 1998, primitive tools were discovered on the Indonesian island of Flores, which could only have been brought there by prehistoric man, *Homo erectus*. It proved that sea voyages had been made at least 700,000 years ago – some 650,000 years earlier than previously supposed. Before this discovery the earliest ocean journeys were believed to have been from Indonesia to Australia some 50,000 years ago – the arrival of the ancestors of the Aborigine people.

Earliest encounters

Ocean journeys in this period really were voyages into the unknown and were fraught with danger, but they were still undertaken. It is not known exactly why – perhaps food supplies were in danger of running out, or the voyagers were escaping warring factions, or perhaps it was simply the lure of adventure. Instances of several very early voyages over great distances have been firmly established. Also around 50,000 years ago the Polynesians set out from the Philippines and New Guinea across the Pacific Ocean, traveling halfway around the world in search of new lands. Several different Indian tribes journeyed from South America to the Caribbean, although exact timings are not known. First were the Ciboney followed by the Arawaks, who were later almost completely wiped out by the more warlike Caribs that arrived toward the end of the fourteenth century, some one hundred years before Christopher Columbus.

Trading routes

These voyages were made only to get from one place to another, but as early as 1500 BC the Egyptians set out on regular trading expeditions around the Mediterranean. The Phoenicians took this one stage further, with their trade ships ranging as far as Britain, West Africa and around the tip of southern Africa to India. Phoenicia was not a nation, but an alliance of independent city-states, and in the sixth century BC the armies of Babylon wiped most of them out. Tyre, the remaining city, fell to Alexander the Great in 332 BC, but by this time the Greeks had taken over the Mediterranean trade routes. As the Roman Empire grew in strength it took over the Greek city-states, but Greek traders continued to flourish. The Romans also established sea trade routes, exporting glass, textiles, metals and pottery and importing incense from Arabia, silks from China, precious stones from India and spices from the East Indies and East Africa.

Further north, by the ninth century AD the Vikings were roaming across the north Atlantic, traveling from Scandinavia in great longships. Although historically they may be renowned for descending suddenly to rob coastal towns and villages, they were also great seafarers, colonizing both Iceland and Greenland and arriving in Newfoundland 500 years before the Spanish. It is possible they also traveled south to the Mediterranean and even around the tip of Africa to the Indian Ocean.

Seafaring nations

The discovery of the sea as an aid to trade was not limited to the people of Europe. At the same time as Phoenicia began to decline as a trading force across the Mediterranean, the Chinese had begun to trade around the Far East. By the fifteenth century Chinese sailors were skilled and adventurous, sending ships across the Indian and Pacific oceans. The Arabs also developed a seafaring tradition, trading along the northwest coast of India and across to Somalia and Ethiopia.

Below: For centuries, boats that sailed on the Indian Ocean were called dhows. While there were many different types, almost all of them used a triangular or lateen sail arrangement. This made them markedly different to the ships that evolved on the Mediterranean, which had a characteristic square sail.

Early seafaring craft

The Polynesians traveled across the Pacific in great double-hulled sailing ships that could carry up to a hundred people. In contrast, the Ciboney Indians had only light balsa wood canoes or rafts, perhaps using large palm fronds for sails. Very little is known about these early boats, although attempts have been made to reproduce them using materials and techniques that would have been available at the time to gain a better understanding of how they may have worked.

Ship development

By 1500 BC the Egyptians had developed a ship with a long central keel to provide longitudinal strength. Similar developments were happening around the same time in Crete, Greece and Phoenicia. The Romans took the earlier Greek and Phoenician designs and developed them still further. The trireme was a narrow war galley that used sail to travel, but had oars for use in battle. As its name implies, it held three tiers of rowers, and it was the fastest ship in antiquity, being able to exceed ten knots to chase and sink an enemy with its ram. During the battle of Salamis in 480 BC, the Greeks had only 380 ships, around half of which may have been triremes, but they were able to defeat the Persian navy of 600 ships. The hull was constructed of a light wood, such as pine, assembled with mortise and tenon joints. For trading purposes the Romans had the corbita, or merchant ship, which had a wider hull to accommodate more cargo. It was also built using mortise and tenon joints, with masts carrying square sails, and was steered by two side rudders connected to each other.

The Vikings

Viking longships, built from the eighth to the thirteenth century, were the next major step forward in ship design. They had a clinker-built hull assembled with iron rivets and one mast with a square sail – although when there was no wind the boat could be rowed with oars. To the starboard side was a single rudder. Like the Romans before them, the Vikings built long, narrow ships that were fast and maneuvrable for warfare and broader ships to carry cargo.

The Chinese developed the central rudder, watertight compartments and sails that could be operated from the deck – technical advances that were gradually incorporated into European ship design after Chinese ships began to arrive in the West in the fifteenth century. One of the major Western designs of this period was the carrack, which was a large and rather top-heavy floating fortress with very high fore and aft "castles" to stop the enemy boarding and allow attack from above, and rows of guns down each side. The similar but better-known galleon arrived in the sixteenth century, developed from the carrack but with a lower hull, which made it more streamlined and less likely to capsize. The galleon was used throughout the sixteenth century, for both exploration and trade, and was later adapted into the two-deck warship.

The clipper

The sailing vessel most associated with sea trading was the famous clipper, which was first built in America in the 1850s; it was known as a clipper because it "clipped" (shortened) established voyage times. The clipper did not have a large cargo capacity but it was very fast and it soon dominated the tea trade between China and England. The American Civil War gave the British a chance to develop their own version of the clipper, and their China tea clippers became the envy of the world. Ships raced to deliver the fresh tea crop – the average journey time from China to England was 111 days, but in 1866 the winners took only 99 days. However, by this time the steamship was gaining ground as a cargo vessel, and after the Suez Canal opened in 1869 the decline of the sailing cargo ship was swift.

Below: Dug-out wooden canoes have been used to navigate rivers and coastal waters since 8000 BC. The most advanced were developed in North America, with a frame of light wood separated from the bark covering by a plank sheathing.

Voyages of discovery

Most of the historic early voyages across the oceans were not meant to be great romantic adventures to find new worlds. Instead, they were mainly motivated by a search to find trade routes between East and West, after the established overland route was cut off by the capture of Constantinople by the Turks in 1453. Prince Henry of Portugal was an early pioneer of the navigation and exploration of the oceans – having quickly realized that traveling by sea could offer an alternative way to reach the East, he established a center to study marine science and navigation. All Portuguese ship captains were required to make detailed charts wherever they sailed and expeditions were funded, which initially opened up trading with West Africa. In 1487 a storm blew Bartolomeu Dias around the Cape of Good Hope, which revealed that there was a sea route to the south of Africa and the following year Vasco da Gama reached India this way.

Christopher Columbus

All these early voyages were based on traveling south to get round Africa, and then going east to India, but in 1492 an Italian, Christopher Columbus, set out to prove a more radical theory. He believed that he could reach Asia by sailing west, right round the globe, and he persuaded the King of Spain to fund an expedition. He set off across the Atlantic, but since no one knew just how big the world was, or that America existed between Europe and Asia, he mistook his first landfall for an island off the Asian coast instead of realizing that it was part of what is now the Caribbean. Five years later John Cabot set off from England and reached Newfoundland and in 1497 Amerigo Vespucci discovered South America, although it was not until 1507 that the new continent appeared on a map for the first time.

Magellan's epic voyage

In 1519 Ferdinand Magellan set off to be the first person to sail around the world. It took him a year to find a passage around the southern tip of South America, but then the Pacific on the other side proved to cover a much bigger area than had been imagined. It was not until 1521 that the exhausted sailors managed to make a landfall, on the island of Guam, and not long afterwards Magellan himself was killed in a local dispute. One of his captains finally made it back to Spain in 1522 – they had set out with five ships and 230 seamen, but returned with only one ship and 18 men.

Exploration continued throughout the sixteenth century, with new waters being charted and new territories discovered. Maps were continually improved and in 1569 Gerardus Mercator constructed his map projection of the world for navigation, which is still in use today. However, one of the big problems for early navigators was in determining their exact position at sea – without knowing this they could not chart voyages with any accuracy.

Right: Known to generations of schoolchildren as "the man who discovered America," Christopher Columbus was in fact trying to find a westward sea passage to the Orient when his fleet landed in the New World in 1492. This unintentional discovery was to change the course of world history and make him the most famed seafarer of all time. He tried to win backing for his explorations from a number of different countries. Finally King Ferdinand and Queen Isabella of Spain agreed to sponsor the expedition, and on August 3, 1492, Columbus and his fleet of three ships, including the Santa Maria, set sail for the journey across the Atlantic. This illustration shows King Ferdinand and Queen Isabella seeing Christopher Columbus off from the dock at Palos.

Navigation

The Polynesians were master sailors 50,000 years ago, navigating by the stars, and developing early maps using stick charts of bamboo and shells.

The concept of latitude and longitude had been developed in the third century BC by Eratosthenes, who was in charge of the great library of Alexandria in Egypt. The Greek explorer Pytheas used the North Star to navigate and developed a method of determining latitude. By 400 BC the Chinese had invented the magnetic compass. It was fairly easy to determine latitude at sea by using the stars, but longitude was much more complex. In 1714 the British Government offered a prize of $36,000 – an unimaginable sum in those days – to anyone who could devise a simple way of working out longitude. The final answer was a chronometer – a clock that was based around a spring escapement instead of a pendulum, and which remained accurate both over time and in all weather conditions. Using this, the navigator could see what time it was at home, work out what time it was where the ship was by studying the position of the sun, and by comparing the two work out his exact longitude. The chronometer was invented by clockmaker John Harrison, who had made the quest his life's work and finally received his prize when he was eighty years old.

The method of measuring latitude also became more accurate in the mid-1700s when the sextant was invented by John Hadley in Britain and Thomas Godfrey in America. This used a system of mirrors to measure the height of the sun above the horizon, and thus its latitude, and was accurate to 0.01 of a degree.

Above: A sextant is an instrument generally used to measure the angle of elevation of a celestial object above the horizon. Making this measurement is known as sighting the object, shooting the object or taking a sight. The angle, and the time when it was measured, can be used to calculate a position line on a nautical or aeronautical chart. A common use of the sextant is to sight the sun at noon to find one's latitude.

Right: Antique world map with navigational instruments, including a compass. A compass consists of a magnetized pointer that is free to align itself accurately with Earth's magnetic field. It is an old Chinese invention, probably first made in China during the Qin dynasty. The first person recorded to have used the compass as a navigational aid was Zheng He (1371-1435), from the Yunnan province in China, who made seven ocean voyages between 1405 and 1433.

Colonization of Australia

Throughout the seventeenth century the most formidable traders were the Dutch. The Dutch East India Company was founded in 1602 and although it was not interested in acquiring territory it encouraged its employees to look for new trading posts. In 1642 a skilled Dutch navigator, Abel Janszoon Tasman, set out to find the "great south land," which was later christened Australia. Several Dutch navigators had already discovered a land mass in the area, but no one knew if it was part of a bigger southern continent, the mythical *Terra Australis Incognita*. Tasman circumnavigated Australia, also discovering Tasmania on the way – he named it Van Diemen's Land but it was renamed in his honor in 1825.

The Endeavour

However, *Terra Australis Incognita* was believed to be much larger so its existence had still neither been confirmed nor denied, and in 1768 the British Royal Navy Lieutenant James Cook set out in a converted coal-ship, the *Endeavour*, to both observe the transit of Venus on June 3, 1769 from Tahiti, and then go on a voyage of discovery. He circumnavigated New Zealand and made a landing on the southeast coast of Australia, but returned to England, again without apparent proof of the mysterious new continent. On Captain Cook's return to the area the following year, he had Harrison's new chronometer to assist in navigation and after making several sweeps of the south he concluded that *Terra Australis Incognita* did not exist and that the land the Dutch had discovered and named New Holland was all there was to be found.

The eastern half of Australia was claimed by the British in 1770, and on January 26, 1788, a settlement and penal colony was established at Port Jackson and the British part of the continent was officially designated the colony of New South Wales. Settlement of the new colony was via penal transportation. Convicted felons were thrown on board ships and there they stayed in port, until the ship was full. The ships were not purpose-built to take convicts, so conditions were uncomfortable; the "passengers" stayed below decks with no bedding and poor food. The journey itself took eight months – six at sea and two in ports collecting supplies and carrying out repairs. Many convicts died on the voyage, or arrived sick from scurvy, dysentery or tropical fevers. If they arrived alive they worked, either on government projects such as road-building or mining, or on assignment to private individuals as unpaid labor. Women became domestic servants or farm laborers. More than 160,000 people were transported to Australia, with men outnumbering women by 6 to 1. The convicts were far more numerous than those that had come there of their free will. After they had completed their sentence, or as a reward for good behavior, the convicts could be pardoned. An absolute pardon was the freedom to return to Britain, if desired, and a conditional pardon meant the convict was free, but had to remain in Australia – by 1828, half the population of Australia was made up of freed convicts.

Transportation phased out

The western part of Australia was claimed by the British in 1829, and parts of New South Wales became separate colonies: South Australia in 1836, Victoria in 1851 and Queensland in 1859. Western Australia, Victoria and South Australia were free colonies – although labor shortages meant that Western Australia later began to accept convicts and Victoria took some from Tasmania. The Northern Territory was founded in 1863. Transportation to Australia was phased out between 1840 and 1868 but the Commonwealth of Australia was not established until 1901.

In 1768 a scientific voyage to Tahiti was organized to observe the transit of the planet Venus across the face of the Sun. The Admiralty gave Captain Cook the command of the ship Endeavour, on which the scientists traveled. During that voyage around the world from 1768 to 1771, Cook explored and charted the coast of New Zealand and also discovered the eastern coast of Australia. He claimed these lands for the British Empire and named one bay "Botany Bay" due to its many fabulous plants.

Scientific developments

Man has been to the Moon and the space programme continues to explore far-flung planets, which is rather ironic given that much of the Earth's surface remains unexplored – the part underwater, that is. The oceans cover 70% of our planet, a vast territory still waiting to be fully discovered. However, the sea can also be dangerous, both due to its influence on the weather and on its own power of destruction. Modern science has been studying not only how to exploit the ocean's resources, but also how to predict ocean changes and weather patterns that may cause problems inland.

The foundations of modern oceanography were laid by the ancient Greeks, who had a scientific interest in the sea. However it is only in the last century that the science of oceanography has really begun to advance. Captain James Cook was one of the forerunners of twentieth century oceanography. Between 1768 and 1780 he made three voyages through the Pacific and Atlantic Oceans, on which he gathered extensive data on ocean geography, geology, currents, tides and water temperatures, among other information. In 1807 President Thomas Jefferson established the US Coast and Geodetic Survey to create coastal charts of the entire United States and later that century marine biological stations were founded to study the new sea species that were being discovered. The British explorers Sir John Ross and Sir James Clark Ross went on expeditions to the Arctic and Antarctica respectively, on which they pioneered new methods of taking depth soundings and of collecting deep-sea samples of sediment, biota and water.

Voyage of the Beagle

Although perhaps better known for his theory of evolution, Charles Darwin was one of the early researchers studying the ocean. He was the naturalist aboard HMS *Beagle*, which voyaged along the South American coastline between 1831 and 1836 to create maps. Darwin not only studied living species, barnacles and fossils, but also did important work on how atolls and coral reefs develop.

The word "oceanography" was coined by two British biologists, W.B. Carpenter and C. Wyville Thomson, to cover the purpose of their round-the-world voyage in HMS *Challenger*. Between 1872 and 1876, *Challenger* traveled through all the oceans of the world – except the Arctic – measuring salinity, temperature and water density and taking deep soundings, grabs, dredges and trawls. They brought back tons of samples for further study. In all, 4,717 new marine species were discovered and seafloor sediments were documented for the first time. They also proved the existence of ocean circulation, although this was not mapped accurately for many more years.

Charles Darwin sailed on the naval survey ship, HMS *Beagle* on December 27, 1831 for what was to be a five-year journey. The most important part of the voyage for Darwin turned out to be the few weeks the *Beagle* spent in the Galapagos Islands. This was the beginning of Darwin's work which led to his theories about natural selection and led to the publication of his book, *The Origin of Species*.

When Captain Scott and his expedition arrived in Antarctica he would have seen very little plant or animal life. There are small amounts of lichen and moss, and some floating plants in the seas. Most of the birds in Antarctica are penguins. Some live on the drifting ice, while others live on land. The Emperor and Adélie penguins both breed and feed around its coasts.

Darwin studied plants and animals but was also very interested in the development of coral reefs, and was amongst the first to propose theories regarding their formation; theories that in fact turned out to be largely correct. There are only a few coral reefs around the Galapagos Islands, but there are also cooled, submerged lava flows, which support an extraordinary diversity of marine life, providing shelter to numerous invertebrates and fish.

Studying ocean currents

In 310 BC the Greek philosopher Theophrastus threw bottles into the Mediterranean to try to prove that it had been formed by water coming from the Atlantic. Although some of his theories were erroneous, he had hit on a method of studying water currents that has been in use in a similar way ever since. Until the mid-twentieth century, surface currents were measured by studying the passage of ships and the drift of the flotsam and jetsam of the ocean. In the 1770s American scientist Benjamin Franklin wondered why mail from America to Britain arrived faster than items coming the other way, so he compared the out-and-return journey times of ships crossing the Atlantic. This led him to publish the first chart of the Gulf Stream – the fastest current in the world.

These days it is not considered environmentally friendly to deliberately throw jetsam into the sea, but when cargo is lost from ships – perhaps a container is washed overboard during a storm – tracking the progress of its contents has provided valuable data.

However, there is now much more sophisticated equipment available to measure currents, including current meters, which are attached at varying depths on a fixed cable, and current drifters, which have remote signaling and are set loose in the current to send back data.

Probing the deep

Most of the early oceanographic research was carried out in coastal waters and near the surface, partly because these areas were easier to study and partly because it was initially believed that life could not exist below around 2,000 feet. By 1868 Carpenter and Wyville Thomson had proved that this concept was untrue. Initially the topography of the ocean floor had to be built up using single depth soundings, which gave an uneven and inaccurate result. Later, echo-sounding equipment was routinely installed on most larger vessels, so more detailed maps of the ocean floor could be compiled. More recently sophisticated computer equipment has been deployed, which has enabled high-definition maps to be made of some areas. Some state-of-the-art research vessels are also now equipped to drill in deep water to study the ocean's crust.

Plate tectonics

One important new concept that has been generally accepted since the 1960s is that of plate tectonics. This holds that the surface of the earth is made up of a series of huge, rigid plates, which move very slowly in relation to one another and change size and shape. At a few junctions – known as transform plate boundaries – the plates slide past one another. At divergent boundaries the plates move apart as new material is added from the Earth's molten center, and at the opposite convergent boundaries old material is consumed as the plates rub up against one another. This all happens so slowly that the motion is imperceptible.

Left: Diving in currents can be one of the most dangerous activities for a diver. The contour of the ocean bottom will change currents, often dramatically. Currents are usually generated by wind and tides or a combination of the two. Predicting conditions based on the local weather service is therefore of paramount importance.

Opposite: Red anenomes on the sea bed. The development of diving suits, manned submersibles and small submarines means that it is now possible to descend to the depths of the ocean and study the diversity of marine plants and animals at close range.

From the diving bell to the aqualung

People have dreamed about living underwater, but so far it has remained largely a dream. They have also long wanted to descend to the depths to explore – or to find sunken treasure. In Japan women dive without any aids to collect pearls or seafood, but even the most practiced can only hold their breath for a couple of minutes – although in this time they can reach depths of 100feet.

Edmond Halley

It is generally agreed that English astronomer Edmond Halley – after whom the famous comet is named – invented the forerunner of the modern diving bell in 1690. Halley designed and built a bell of wood in the shape of a truncated cone, with an open lower end 5feet inches diameter, and a closed top 3 feet across. It was weighted with lead and suspended carefully so it sank full of air. There was a clear glass port on the top for light and vision, as well as a cock to let out the heated, breathed-out air. About 3feet below the open end of the bell was a stage suspended by three weighted ropes. The air was replenished by the use of two large barrels, each weighted with lead to sink them, and with a bunghole in the bottom to let in water as the air condensed on the descent and to let it out when the barrel was drawn up full. Another bunghole was placed in the top of the barrel, to which a leather hose was attached. This hose was prepared with beeswax and oil and was weighted to hang below the bottom bunghole, so that no air could escape. When the hose was moved under the bell, a diver could pull up the end and the pressure of water through the bottom bunghole forced the air in the barrel up into the bell. The barrels could be lowered and raised via tackles and refilled on the surface, providing a continuous supply of fresh air. Using this technique, Halley stated that he and four other divers remained on the bottom for one and a half hours at a depth of 60feet.

The modern diving bell

The use of barrels to replenish the air in a diving bell continued for over a century, until in 1788 the noted British engineer John Smeaton constructed the first modern diving bell. Best known for his construction of the third Eddystone lighthouse, Smeaton used a force pump and tube arrangement and the bell had the pump mounted on its roof, so it could be totally submerged. The bell was actually a rectangular box of cast iron – referred to as a diving chest – accommodating two divers. One ingenious engineering element was a reservoir designed to ensure that any sudden failure of the force pump would not result in a shut-off of air and there was also a non-return valve to prevent air being sucked out through the tube. This diving chest was used for repairs on the foundation of Hexham Bridge in England.

Diving suit

Despite its technical ingenuity, the problem with the diving bell in general was a lack of mobility outside it for the diver. A further advance in underwater exploration came in 1819, however, when Augustus Siebe invented the first practical diving suit. Air could be pumped into the helmet through a hose, escaping through a gap at the waist of the diver's jacket. However, if the diver fell over the helmet quickly flooded and he could drown, so in 1830 the design was modified so it was completely airtight. Using it, divers could descend to 65 feet.

In 1943 French explorer Jacques-Yves Cousteau and engineer Émile Gagnan went one step further when they invented the Aqua-Lung, which revolutionized diving. Compressed air was carried in cylinders on the diver's back, connected via pipes to the diver's mouthpiece through an automatic pressure regulator, so for the first time people could swim feely underwater. Cousteau devoted his life to exploration of the underwater world and also designed an experimental colony to test the ability of people to live and work underwater. *Conshelf II* was sunk 32feet underwater in the Red Sea and five men lived inside for a month, going out every day to do experiments.

Above: Aqua-lung was the original name for the first open-circuit SCUBA (Self-Contained Underwater Breathing Apparatus) diving equipment. It was developed by Emile Gagnan and Jacques Cousteau in 1943. It consists of a high pressure diving cylinder and a diving regulator that supplies the diver with breathing gas at ambient pressure, via a demand valve.

Submersible craft

In 1620 Dutch engraver Cornelius Drebbel built a "diving boat," made of wood covered in greased leather to prevent leaks. It was powered by 12 rowers and made trips up and down the Thames at a depth of around 15feet. The passengers had to breath through tubes held up on the surface of the water by floats. The first submarine to sink a ship was the H.L. *Hunley*, one of a series of submarines built by Confederate forces in the American Civil War to give them an advantage over the much more powerful Union fleet. The H.L. *Hunley* was made from an old boiler and powered by eight men inside turning a crank; the captain sat at the front and steered, but the vessel could only move along just below the surface, as there was no periscope. One night in 1864 the submarine sailed up to the anchored USS *Housatonic* in the port of Charleston and rammed the ship underwater with an explosive charge on the end of a spar. The *Housatonic* quickly sank, but a wave from the explosion entered the hatch of the H.L. *Hunley* and swamped it, so the entire crew was drowned.

The modern submarine

The first practical modern submarine was built in 1900 by John P. Holland, an Irish-American. His initial design, twenty-five years earlier, had been for a one-man submarine propelled by cycle pedals, but the *Holland VI* was a major breakthrough in submarine design. For the first time, all the major components were present in one vessel – dual propulsion systems, a fixed longitudinal center of gravity, separate main and auxiliary ballast systems, a hydro-dynamically advanced shape, and a modern weapons system. The US Navy quickly purchased the pioneering craft. Technological advances continued in submarine design, culminating in the modern nuclear type. These submarines never need to resurface to recharge their batteries and can travel for 155,000 miles without refueling. They carry a crew of around 150 men and can dive to around 1,000feet; such craft can spend months at sea, never coming to the surface or landing at port.

Below: Atlantis commercial passenger submarine in Hawaii.

The vast ocean resource

When man first looked out to the ocean, he not only saw a beautiful expanse of glittering water stretching into the distance, but also an opportunity for food-gathering. At first this was limited to gathering seaweed and shellfish along the shore, and hunting seals and seabirds, but it was not long before fishing from boats was developed. Even today, on an average worldwide, fish and shellfish provide around 15% of the animal protein in the human diet.

The oceans contain millions of creatures, ranging from the largest on the planet – the blue whale, which can grow up to 100feet in length – to the microscopic shrimps called copepods. For centuries, man has taken fish from the sea, and many traditional techniques are still in use in the smaller island communities. Early man fished by wading quietly in shallow water and using a spear or bow and arrow to skewer the fish. Later more indirect methods of fishing were invented: nets were developed, which were thrown by hand from the beach, and traps were placed in shallow water. Fishing with a rod and line was also a basic skill – with feathers and shells used as bait, as well as worms and pieces of shellfish or fish. These communities lived close to nature so they had an intimate knowledge of their environment and of the habits of their prey and were able to use this knowledge to give them an advantage. For instance, it was discovered that some smells attracted fish, so strong-smelling substances were used to attract the fish to the shore. As on land, other animals and birds were also used to help man hunt: the Japanese trained cormorants to catch fish, placing a ring around the bird's neck to stop it swallowing its catch; Chinese fishermen used otters to round up fish and head them toward the net.

Early techniques to mechanized commercial enterprise

Such techniques were very successful, and often provided almost all the nutritional needs of an island community. They had very little impact on fish stocks as a whole, because they were local and the fishermen only took what they needed for their immediate needs. As communities grew bigger and more food was needed small fleets of trawlers roamed farther afield, going out to the ocean for a day or more at a time to look for shoals of fish that could be caught in a large net trailing behind the boat. Again this had little impact on stocks as a whole, since there was a limit to what a boat could hold and it had to return to base regularly to offload its catch.

Unfortunately this kind of fishing could not provide enough food for the exploding populations of the developing nations, and the technological advances in steam and diesel allowed large, ocean-going vessels to be built. Some fleets are now not so much commercial as industrial, containing hundreds of fishing boats, accompanied by factory ships that process the catch at sea. The fishing boats use open-mouthed trawl nets that are dragged just above the sea floor, or purse-shaped seine nets, which are bag-shaped nets pulled behind the boat and then closed around the catch. Long lines with rows of baited hooks are set to catch the larger fish, such as tuna. The fishing industry once also used drift nets, which were like huge curtains that sometimes stretched for more than 40 miles. These gigantic nets were left out for days at a time, but they not only snared the intended catch but also other sea creatures such as small whales, dolphins, turtles, seals and even seabirds. Caught in the net and unable to escape, these creatures often drowned and the dreadful loss of sea life prompted the United Nations to ban this type of net in 1992. Despite this, they are sometimes still used illegally.

Opposite: Tuna is of great importance to commercial fishing, but there are fears that certain species are being over-fished, which could seriously endanger them. Fish farming is now playing an increasingly important role in meeting the growing demand for food and helping to protect these threatened species. In this picture taken at a tuna farm in Baja, California, nearly all the tuna raised are sold to the Japanese market to be made into sushi.

Below: The oceans have provided coastal communities with food and a livelihood for thousands of years. They are home to a huge variety of plant and animal life. Microscopic plants drift in the sunlit surface waters, forming the basis of the ocean food chain.

Sophisticated technology

The gigantic fishing fleets have sophisticated technology aboard – sonar equipment can locate large shoals of fish below the surface and satellite remote sensing can pinpoint areas abundant in phytoplankton where fish are likely to be feeding. The fleets stay at sea for weeks or even months at a time, as the use of factory ships means that they do not have to return to base regularly to unload the catch. In just one day, a factory ship can salt hundreds of tons of herring fillet and freeze 100 tons of flat fish and process mixed fish into fish meal and fish oil. Apart from the massive stocks of fish that are removed from the sea each time, the biggest problem with such large-scale fishing is the waste that it causes. At least a fifth of the marine catch is thrown back into the water because it is too small or the wrong species. By-catch includes non-target fish species, invertebrates of no commercial value – for instance sea-pens, urchins and brittlestars – sea birds and marine mammals, including seals and dolphins. Unwanted fish and other animals are usually thrown back into the sea dead, injured, or so weakened that they are easily killed by predators.

Fishing quotas

By-catch is a problem that has been made worse by minimum catch sizes and allowable catch quotas imposed on commercially valuable species. Rules state that fish of certain species must be above a minimum size to protect immature breeding stock. However, as the size of fish cannot be determined before capture, immature fish are caught but then thrown back, often dead. Catch quotas are also imposed on valuable fish species in an attempt to protect stocks – once the quota has been reached, all other fish of that species must be discarded by law. But fishing then continues for other species, which will often live in the same areas, so the unwanted species are frequently caught only to be discarded. The worldwide yearly catch of all sea fish is between 60 and 80 million tons. There are around 20,000 species of fish, of which 9,000 are regularly caught, but only 22 species are taken in large amounts. Five groups of fish make up half the yearly catch: herrings, cod, jacks, redfish and mackerel.

Traditional fishing grounds

It was once believed that food from the sea was an unlimited resource, which could sustain the world for the foreseeable future. Unfortunately this idea has proved to be misplaced, as an exploding world population and dwindling stocks of fish, crustaceans and shellfish – mainly due to past overfishing – has placed many traditional fishing grounds in danger. There are only a few of these – half the world's annual catch comes from the North Pacific, North Atlantic and the west coast of South America.

Whaling

Whales have been hunted for over a thousand years, but today's methods are so effective that many species of whale are almost extinct. Following the collapse of one whale stock after another, the nations of the world tried to manage whaling to make it sustainable. Whilst some species had already been hunted to near-extinction, the new technology now meant that the whalers could catch and potentially threaten all whale species. In 1946 an agreement was reached to limit quotas to try to preserve stocks.

By 1972, the "allowable catch" in Antarctica had been reduced to less than 25% of that originally agreed by the International Whaling Commission (IWC). Blues and humpbacks had been placed on the endangered list and the fin whale soon joined them. Meanwhile, the decline in stocks along with the falling price of whale oil persuaded one nation after another to cease whaling so by 1969, only Japan and the Soviet Union were left – in Japan the popularity of whale meat was a big incentive to continue. In 1973–74, the total whale catch was about 32,000 and three years later it had dropped to some 22,000. However, in the 1980s, a total moratorium on commercial whaling was introduced, although several nations have ignored it. Norway resumed whaling in 1993 and both Iceland and Japan continue to whale for "scientific purposes" – although most of their catch ends up on the dinner table.

However, stocks are beginning to recover and whale sanctuaries have now been founded in Antarctica and the Indian Ocean. It has been estimated that over nine million people go whale-watching every year, and even some of the countries that still go whaling also offer whale-watching tours. Hopefully at some time in the not too distant future the whale will be worth more alive than it is dead.

Above: Edible crabs (*Cancer pagarus*) can have a diameter of up to 9 inches and weigh up to 6 pounds. They are found in the North Atlantic, North Sea and the Mediterranean and are heavily exploited for commercial purposes.

Shellfish

The importance and benefits of a low-fat diet have come to be recognized over the last twenty years or so, and shellfish is very low in fat so it has gained in popularity. It is also very rich in vitamins and minerals and, like fish, it contains Omega 3 polyunsaturated acids, which cannot be produced within the body.

The category of shellfish is usually understood to contain both crustacea (which have an outer shell like the lobster and crab), and mollusk (which are either soft bodied, like mussels and oysters, or cephalopods, like the octopus). The main types of shellfish commercially caught are oyster, mussels, cockles, scallops, lobster, crab, shrimp, prawn, crawfish, squid, octopus and cuttlefish.

Prawns are one of the most popular shellfish in the west, being used for sandwich fillings as well as in cooked dishes. Much shellfish is caught locally in shallow water but coldwater prawns are fished near Iceland, Greenland, Norway and Canada and tropical prawns come from Thailand, China, India and Ecuador. The UK exports most of its shellfish to France and Spain. Shellfish resources are currently exploited to their limit in many areas, and may be overfished in some places. They are under threat of further exploitation in the near future, so a combination of strict technical controls has been established to conserve stocks. The UK is proposing to establish a shellfish licence, which will maintain exploitation at current levels.

Farming the sea – husbandry and selection

If fish and shellfish are caught more quickly than they can breed and come to maturity, stocks will inevitably decline. Also, if a particular species is removed in large quantities from its natural habitat, the prey-predator balance can be upset, causing changes to whole ecosystems. Some species are already in danger, such as the whale.

One solution to the problem is to farm fish and shellfish, as the Chinese have been doing for 4,000 years. In other parts of Asia fish have been farmed throughout the centuries; shallow ponds are excavated near the shore, which fill with seawater on the incoming tide. The ponds are seeded with eggs and the tiny fish and crustaceans fed on larvae and plankton as they grow. Some of the most successful farmed species are salmon, oysters and mussels, all of which have a long history of cultivation. Exotic species, such as giant tiger prawns and sea urchins, yield excellent profits, but many other species are also farmed. These include scallops, prawns, shrimps, lobsters, and flatfish.

Some fish-farming involves the construction of artificial reefs to provide new habitats in barren areas. They are quickly colonized by shellfish and small fish, which can also attract larger fish to the area to feed. Mussels, oysters, lobsters, kelp, sea urchins and abalone have all been farmed on artificial reef sites. The reefs can be made of waste products, such as rubber tyres – millions of which are discarded each year – or can utilize structures such as decommissioned oilrigs, either sunk on site or installed in shallow water. This practise not only provides new fishing grounds, but also offers an excellent way of recycling waste materials.

It is not only fish and crustaceans that can be farmed – seaweed is also a successful commercial crop. Seaweed-farming is most widespread in the East, Southeast Asia, India, Africa and Latin America and over six million metric tons are produced each year. Many seaweed farmers are women and they can often earn more than their menfolk can by fishing.

Left: A diver inspects oyster shells with pearls in Manihi, French Polynesia. This region is renowned for its black pearls. These were once highly prized due to their rarity but this has changed as they are now cultivated. A pearl is produced by an oyster as a response to an irritant (such as a sand grain) in its shell. The oyster secretes layers of nacre around the irritant, eventually forming a pearl.

Marine pharmacology

About half of all drugs currently in use in the world have been derived from natural products, including many of the new anti-infective and anti-tumor drugs developed during the past twenty years. Plants found on land are still a principal source when developing new drugs, but recently there has been an increase in drugs developed from marine organisms. Using marine resources for medicinal purposes is not a new idea – in China, Japan and Taiwan seahorses have been used for centuries to create traditional treatments for sexual disorders, respiratory and circulatory problems, kidney and liver diseases, amongst other ailments.

Useful chemicals have been found in marine animals, fungi, algae and bacteria with a variety of beneficial characteristics including anti-bacterial, anti-coagulant and anti-viral properties. Recently new research has developed a cancer therapy that is made from algae and a painkiller that has been derived from the toxins in cone snail venom. Anti-viral drugs and an anti-cancer agent have been developed from a sponge found on Caribbean coral reefs, and currently a new drug based on extracts from an Indian Ocean sea hare is undergoing clinical trials for the treatment of breast cancer, tumors and leukaemia.

Marine organisms

At first marine organisms were collected at random and in huge quantities, in the hope that some useful compound might be extracted later, rather than as a result of targeted research. The disadvantage of this is that large quantities of material had to be processed to extract minute quantities of chemicals for testing. Genetic engineering has made prospecting for new drugs much more environmentally friendly – now it is routine to collect only small amounts of living material. The DNA is extracted from this and cloned into host bacterial cells, which produce large quantities of the chemical in the laboratory. This also means that the final drug can be made in the laboratory, rather than having to be extracted from the seafloor each time.

As has been found on land, it has become obvious that there are many beneficial substances to be discovered under the oceans – sometimes in the most unlikely of places. Vast tracts of the seas still remain untouched by human interference, so it is to be hoped that chances are high of discovering effective treatments for the new diseases that are developing on land.

Below: Starfish are believed to have medicinal properties and can be found on market stalls in places such as Bolivia.

Offshore minerals

When scientists on the HMS *Challenger* examined the ocean bed during the round-the-world expedition in 1872–6, they were surprized to find manganese nodules concentrated at depths of around 14,750 feet. About the size of a potato, they usually lie loose on the surface of the seafloor, and are as much as ten million years old. However even today it is not certain how they were formed. These nodules are mainly composed of manganese, iron, copper, nickel and cobalt, with traces of zinc, lead, titanium and vanadium, and although the manganese and iron are not of value the other metals are. Extraction has so far proved unfeasible, but their existence suggests that there are riches in the oceans that may well be worth the cost of extraction.

Valuable metal

Metals such as silver, copper and cadmium were also discovered in vast quantities at a divergent plate in the Red Sea during the 1960s, and have since been found elsewhere, such as at deep sea hydrothermal vents. It is not just the deep oceans that hold such riches however. In some areas of the world, beaches can be mined for gold, chromium, titanium, tungsten and even diamonds.

Of course perhaps the most obvious mineral that is easily available from the ocean is sodium chloride – more commonly known as salt. Salt has been extracted from seawater for thousands of years and the method is essentially still the same: the salt water is evaporated, leaving the crystallized salt behind. At least one third of the world's supply of salt is still produced in this way. In arid areas, desalination plants may work specifically to produce the valuable by-product of the process; fresh water.

Oil and gas

Oil and gas are fossil fuels, formed from the organic remains of dead plant material deep underground, and it has been estimated that as much as 90% of what is generated leaks from natural seeps. The remaining 10% is trapped under impermeable rock, in natural reservoirs under land or sea. Although oil and gas fields have been known to exist under the sea since the beginning of the twentieth century, the vast size of the reservoirs already discovered onshore meant that undertaking costly offshore drilling was not thought necessary. Unfortunately it has been estimated that in one year we now consume an amount of fossil fuel that took 1 million years to form – and consumption is ever rising – so it was not long before new fields had to be found to meet demand.

Gas under the North Sea

In the mid-nineteenth century, vast reserves of gas were discovered under the North Sea and even today this is still one of the biggest gas fields in the world. A few years later, oil was also discovered there, and there are now offshore gas and oil fields in many areas of the world, including the Indian Ocean, around the east coasts of North and South America, the west coast of Africa and even in the Mediterranean and the Arctic Ocean.

The drilling operations required to access these riches are carried out on a grand scale. Exploration wells can cost millions, with no guarantee of success. Commercial drilling can be carried out at depths of over 10,000 feet and drilling platforms are either floated or carried by transporter ships to be fixed in place for many months or years. The drilling operation itself is dangerous – in 1988 the Piper Alpha platform in the North Sea caught fire after two massive explosions. The first was due to a build-up of natural gas, and the second, larger, explosion was caused by a gas pipeline rupturing in the heat of the fire. The disaster was made worse because a nearby platform continued to pump gas into the inferno, even though the flames were visible for sixty miles, because the crew lacked the authorization to shut down. In all, 167 lives were lost.

Below: The Beryl Alpha oil platform. Oil platforms are massive structures – they must accommodate up to 300 crew — and are expensive to run as all essential supplies must be brought in by boat and crew members must be ferried back and forth. In addition the rig must be built to withstand local weather conditions, which may include hurricane winds in some areas.

Harnessing the ocean's power

If it could be harnessed effectively and economically, the power of the ocean could supply the global demand for energy. The beauty of such an energy source is that not only is it clean and safe, it would be renewed as fast as we could use it. In some ways we have used the power of water for many centuries – very early rafts were powered by the ocean currents on which they drifted, while inland streams of water were diverted through mill wheels to supply the power to grind corn. A more technologically advanced way of using water more efficiently is the hydroelectric dam, which produces electricity from the power of falling water.

Tidal power

In many places where there are strong tides, there were once tidal mills. Small examples existed for hundreds of years, but the same principle can be used on a much bigger scale. The tidal mill works in much the same way as a hydroelectric dam. The tide is temporarily held back by a barrier across an estuary, and then released through a series of turbines – power can be generated by both flood and ebb tides. The first such installation was the Rance barrage, near St Malo in Brittany, which opened in 1967. The estuary itself acts as a reservoir, and as a bonus the artificial lagoon that has been created has boosted water sports and other leisure activities in the area. The twenty-four turbines have chromium-nickel steel blades to prevent them being corroded by the salt in seawater.

Wave power

As well as the tides, the waves themselves are a potential source of energy, although research on how to harness it is still being carried out. A small pilot installation off the coast of Scotland was utilized successfully – but was then destroyed by a storm. The wave power plant works by channeling the wave into a submerged chamber, forcing air up through a turbine. Another type of wave power plant has giant rockers that float on the surface and are moved up and down by the force of the waves, pushing water through a shaft inside to drive the turbine. At present there are only a few such installations operating, but this is an area that is ripe for future expansion.

Other power options

In theory we could also harness the power of ocean currents by submerging turbines at strategic points such as at straits and around headlands. Pilot schemes have been successful, but we are some way away from having the technology to do this on a large scale.

Salvage

The law of salvage has ancient roots, and its main function is to encourage the rescue of vessels in peril at sea and the recovery of goods from shipwrecks on behalf of the owner. A crew on the scene after an accident at sea can claim salvage rights, as long as they voluntarily offer assistance to a vessel in distress; the crew of the vessel have abandoned ship; and the salvage operation successfully saves the cargo and/or the ship. Salvors do not accrue ownership rights to the goods they recover or to the vessel itself, but they do obtain a right to generous compensation for their work.

Left: Out at sea, waves usually rise and fall like giant ripples. They only form "white caps" when driven by strong winds, but when a wave surges up a beach, the water piles up until it topples over. Storm waves are loved by surfers but can seriously damage harbors, sea walls, seaside homes and farmland.

Maritime law

Maritime law is a very complex subject. Some rules have been introduced to protect travelers on the surface of the water, while others conserve the contents of the ocean depths.

Territorial limits

In the early seventeenth century a Dutch statesman, Hugo Grotius, wrote his book Mare liberum, which formulated the theory that the sea was international territory and that all nations were free to use it for international trade. In practice, the Dutch took this as a justification for using their superior naval power to break up existing trading monopolies and establish their own. England objected strongly to this, claiming sovereignty over the seas around what was to become the British Isles. In Mare clausum, published in 1635, John Selden claimed that the sea was just as capable of being claimed as terrestrial territories; as conflicting claims multiplied, maritime states finally agreed that territorial waters would be set radiating outwards from the shore. Finally, in 1702, Cornelius Bynkershoek developed De domino maris, which set the limit of each nation's territory at the distance a cannonball could travel from the shore – 3 nautical miles, which became the three-mile limit.

This settled matters until the 1950s, by which time two further factors had come into play: fishing stocks were becoming endangered, and mineral resources had been discovered under the sea. Trouble began to brew when Iceland extended its fishing limit to twelve miles in 1958, and then to fifty miles in 1972, which resulted in a four-year-long Cod War with nearby Britain as the traditional British fishing grounds were annexed by Icelandic fleets. It took many years for nations to agree on a common policy, but the Third United Nations Convention on the Law of the Sea (UNCLOS) – the most comprehensive international legal regime dealing with maritime affairs, which was adopted in 1982 and went into force in 1994 – accepts four main territory definitions at sea: territorial sea; the contiguous zone; the EEZ; and the high seas.

Coastal nations can proclaim sovereignty over an area extending up to twelve miles from the coastline. In this territorial sea zone, the nation has total control over any activity; ships belonging to other nations have only the right of innocent passage. Outside this area is the contiguous zone, which extends up to a total of twenty-four miles from the coast, in which the nation can enforce its customs, tax, immigration and sanitary laws. The Exclusive Economic Zone (EEZ) extends for up to 200 miles from the coast. Each nation has sole right over both the living and non-living resources of its EEZ, and can exploit the natural resources of the seabed and the water above, but is also responsible for its environmental protection. Beyond the EEZ zone, are the high seas, also called the Area, where no country has exclusive jurisdiction or sovereign rights.

Free passage

Ships and aircraft of any nation have right of "innocent passage" – which means they are not entering the area for purposes of hostile action, spying or to exploit resources – across territorial seas, and also right of transit through straits used for international navigation. The nations on either side of international straits can regulate navigation and other aspects of passage. Land-locked nations have the right of access to and from the sea, and freedom of transit through the territory of nations between them and the sea. In EEZs and on the high seas, all nations have freedom of navigation and overflight, but must comply with any legislation to manage and conserve resources.

Above: Under Rule 18, a power driven vessel must give way to a sailing vessel under sail, a vessel engaged in fishing whose fishing equipment restricts its maneuvrability, a vessel with restricted manoeuvrability, such as a dredge or tow boat and a vessel not under command – i.e. broken down.

Cable and pipe laying
The first transatlantic telegraph cable was laid in 1858, and many ocean floors are now covered in communication cables and oil and gas pipelines. Most of these cross the Atlantic between North America and Europe, but there are a fair number across the Pacific and the Indian Ocean. All nations, whether coastal or land-locked, are allowed to lay submarine cables or pipelines across the seabed without restriction in EEZs and on the high seas.

Wrecks

The oldest wrecked ship ever found was discovered off the coast of Turkey at Uluburun in 1984. It had sunk in about 1316 BC – over 3,000 years ago – and was carrying a cargo of copper, tin, glass, gold trinkets and jars of perfume. The lure of sunken treasure is strong and there are also many divers who like to explore wrecks for their interest value. The law of salvage does not apply to wrecks, which are designated as Underwater Cultural Heritage (UCH) and have their own law adopted in 2001.

Briefly, the UCH covers wrecks that are more than a hundred years old – which for the moment excludes relics from the two World Wars and even such iconic wrecks as the Titanic. Its main objective is the protection and preservation of the wreck in situ, so that valuable archaeological evidence is not lost. Many underwater sites are surprisingly well preserved, but when stable conditions are disturbed they can deteriorate very quickly. Divers who discover a wreck that is apparently over a hundred years old should leave it totally intact and report it to the nearest authorities. Only suitably qualified archaeologists are allowed to work on such sites and items should only be removed if the find is under threat – from cable laying, for instance – and if suitable provision has been made for their preservation.

Many nations do not agree with some of the legislation included in UCH. The US, UK and Russia are concerned about issues of sovereignty for sunken state vessels and the UK objects to the mandatory protection of all ships over a hundred years old, preferring its own approach of protecting only wrecks of "historical, archaeological or artistic importance." Divers have pointed out the difficulty of establishing if a wreck is unknown or not and ask how they can know how old it is without examining it. They are also concerned that the legislation, as it stands, prevents them from visiting known and accepted sites for recreational diving if they are more than a century old.

Below: Titanic set sail from Southampton on her maiden voyage to New York on April 10, 1912. Four days later she struck an iceberg about 400 miles off the coast of Newfoundland and within hours had sunk to the bottom of the sea. The remains of the Titanic were found in 1985 by Dr Robert Ballard, an oceanographer and marine biologist. This picture shows the bow railing silhouetted by the Mir2 submersible, which sits up on the anchor crane of the foredeck of the ship.

Man's impact

The oceans are essential to the survival of Earth – life originated in the seas and they now regulate our climate and provide much of our food. As well as being a rich resource they are also outstandingly beautiful, offering opportunities for a wide range of leisure activities or just quiet contemplation. Despite all this, the fragile ecosystem of the oceans has been in danger from humankind for many years and in many ways. Pollution, global warming, overfishing and simple overuse are all a threat to the seas around the planet, and it is important that man finds a way to regenerate and manage them in a sustainable way before it is too late.

The threat of pollution

Pollution of the oceans comes in many forms. A considerable amount of the vast quantity of waste that is generated by humankind on land finds its way into the sea, not to mention all the rubbish that goes straight overboard from ships in passage. The oil industry suffers regular spillages and industry creates vast quantities of toxins that must be disposed of in some way.

Rubbish

It has been estimated that 150,000 tons of plastic net and other fishing paraphernalia is either lost or jettisoned at sea and this poses a big threat to wild life, which can become entangled and die from drowning or exhaustion.

Each household in the west uses an average of 300 plastic bags a year – which is a staggering seven billion bags in total.

Much rubbish will degrade over time because of the action of sunlight and bacteria, but most domestic plastics and packaging that end up in the water do not. They will destroy the beauty of natural environments near towns and cities for hundreds of years to come unless they are physically removed. Most of these items are also light and can drift on the water, so they will find their way even to the most distant locations to deface previously pristine, untouched areas. In one recorded case an uninhabited island 300 miles from the nearest inhabited land and more than 3,000 miles from the nearest continent was found to have accumulated 950 items of rubbish on its shores. Fortunately in most countries of the world the policy toward domestic waste is now changing. Recycling and reuse are being introduced to cut down the amount of waste that is generated, and many countries that share a common sea have begun to cooperate to clear up their regional environments.

Below: The Pacific, Atlantic, Indian, Arctic and Southern oceans are all linked in one vast mass of water. Together they have a huge impact on our lives. They control the weather and prevent the planet from overheating. The oceans supply most of the oxygen that we breathe and are major sources of food and minerals.

Oil pollution

Natural substances, such as oil and gas, have always seeped into the environment in a small way and were dispersed without a problem, but since the beginning of the twentieth century the rate has been steadily increasing. Small oil spills happen all the time in shipping areas – during operations such as loading or discharging, for instance – and there is also run-off from land-based sources, such as cars and heavy industry. What is worse is that this spillage is not evenly spread over a wide area, but concentrated near oil production centers, along urban coastlines and following shipping lanes. It may be pollution at a relatively low level, but it is repeated continually over time and is doing untold damage to marine organisms in these locations.

Below: A major disaster happened in 1989, when the Exxon Valdez ran aground at Bligh Island off Alaska spilling 11 million gallons of crude oil and killing an estimated 250,000 sea birds, 2,800 sea otters, 300 harbor seals, 250 bald eagles and billions of salmon and herring eggs.

Some of the worst marine disasters have been caused by supertankers colliding, resulting in massive oil spillage. In 1967 the Torrey Canyon ran aground near Land's End in the English Channel, and released thirty-eight million gallons of crude oil into the sea. Only eleven years later the Amoco Cadiz ran into rocks off the coast of Brittany after its rudder broke and sixty-eight million gallons of crude oil was spilled, creating an oil slick eighteen miles long and eighty miles wide. Around 20,000 seabirds were killed and countless fish and other sea creatures were washed up on shore on both sides of the English Channel for weeks afterwards. On the other side of the world in 1979, the Atlantic Empress collided with the Aegean Captain off Tobago and forty-six million gallons of crude oil was emptied into the Caribbean seas.

Pollution from the oilrigs themselves also happens, when drilling accidentally releases pressure from the reservoir of oil beneath the seabed, causing a blow-out. The resulting out-pouring of oil can take time to stem – in the worst disaster of this kind, involving the drill rig Ixtoc I in the Gulf of Mexico in 1979, it took more than nine months to get the flow back under control. During this period a staggering 140 million gallons of crude oil poured into the sea.

Not all oil pollution is accidental – following the invasion of Kuwait in 1991, Iraqi forces attacked refineries along the Persian Gulf and left them pouring 240 million gallons of crude oil into the sea, causing an ecological disaster zone. The oil slick that resulted was the largest ever known, and on top of this 600 well heads were set ablaze, pouring black smoke into the air and depositing soot and sludge for thousands of miles around.

The burning of fossil fuels also releases greenhouse gas carbon dioxide into the atmosphere, which it is feared may be having an irreversible effect on the climate.

Sewage

Until relatively recently, most urban populations still dumped millions of tons of sewage into the sea, a great part of it untreated. Sewage is a rich mix of ingredients, including organic compounds, ammonia and nitrogen and it attracts bacteria, parasites and viruses. To some extent, sewage can be dealt with by natural biodegrading processes and some coastal cities continue to pump their human waste into nearby waterways, maintaining that nature deals with it perfectly well. Unfortunately, when concentrations reach a certain level, nature can no longer cope. This can happen quite quickly in closed seas with many coastal cities, such as the North Sea and the Mediterranean.

When nature loses ground against the tide of sewage the effect can be quite dramatic. The rich nutrients that sewage adds to the water encourage many organisms to flourish, so oxygen is rapidly depleted, plant life grows densely and the diversity of life in the area begins to drop quite quickly. Shellfish are soon poisoned and toxic phytoplankton may bloom – the so-called "red tides", which release toxins into the water, killing marine life and encouraging micro-organisms that cause diseases. These diseases do not just affect marine life – sewage contamination can lead to humans being infected with hepatitis, typhoid, dysentery, enteritis and cholera.

In Asia new strains of some of these diseases are developing and it is believed that this is directly related to the habit of dumping untreated sewage in nearby seawater. In 1988, a layer of toxic phytoplankton 33 feet thick spread along the straits between the North and Baltic Seas – millions of fish died and the beaches in the area were thickly coated with unpleasant slime. The incidence of red tides used to be fairly rare, but unfortunately they are now happening with increasing frequency, particularly in areas where there have been many years of chronic pollution.

Toxic waste

Seawater has always contained traces of metals and minerals, and even the heavy metals that are toxic to most life. These have seeped into the oceans naturally, from volcanic emissions or from vents around the edges of the tectonic plates. In small concentrations they do no harm, but if quantities are increased problems can ensue. Many industrial processes create by-products that are unwanted or even downright dangerous. Some can be disposed of easily and economically; others pose more of a long-term problem.

It is not just industrial waste that ends up in the sea. Following World War II, virtually the entire chemical arsenal of Nazi Germany was dumped, with much of it – at least 35,000 tons – ending up on the floor of the Baltic Sea. Hundreds of thousands of tons of chemical weapons from the Soviet Union, Britain and the United States were also dumped in the northern Atlantic, North Sea and elsewhere, including the Baltic. The poisonous weapons – including mustard gas, phosphorus, nerve gas, and other highly toxic chemicals – were joined by hundreds of thousands of unused bombs, mines and grenades.

Unpleasant substances find their way into the sea in other ways as well, via waste-water discharge outlets, atmospheric fallout or accidental spills. Heavy metals – such as mercury and lead – and radioactivity will poison or contaminate marine life and they can travel up the food chain, causing disease and infertility. Toxins in the sea have already seriously affected some coastal communities – the most famous case is Minamata in Japan. In the 1950s, fishermen and their families in this small town began to suffer numbness, speech, eyesight and hearing difficulties and loss of coordination. The symptoms were traced to a progressive degeneration in brain cells, and between 1953 and 1960, over 600 people died and thousands were left with permanent brain damage before the cause was established. A nearby factory had been discharging methyl mercury into the bay, which had contaminated shellfish that the affected people had eaten. This is not the only such case, but fortunately serious poisoning from seawater is now quite rare.

Below: All over the world, raw sewage is poured into the sea. This in turn feeds bacteria which multiply and deprive other sea creatures of oxygen. It also contains germs that can cause diseases. The problem is worse in developing countries where there may be no proper sewage treatment plants.

Chemical concerns

Two chemicals that are still of particular concern are DDT (dichloro-diphenyl-trichloro-ethane) and PCBs (polychlorinated biphenyls). DDT was introduced in the 1950s as a new wonder ingredient for pesticides and was initially celebrated for having many beneficial properties. PCBs arrived around the same time and are used in paints, plastics, adhesives and aerosols – to name just a few of the most common instances. DDT often found its way into the oceans via run-off from agricultural land into watercourses, which then took it down into the sea. Both DDT and PCBs also readily find their way into the atmosphere and from there into the ocean as a result of atmospheric fallout. DDT was banned in the West in the 1970s, but is still used extensively in developing nations. PCBs are used less than they once were, but are still found in many countries around the world.

Rather than learning from such mistakes, the chemical industry launches new "wonder" products all the time and these are inevitably introduced into the environment before their long-term effects can be studied properly. More than a thousand new chemicals arrive on the market each year and at least half are known to be hazardous or are classified as potentially harmful to human life.

Heat and noise

Physical pollution is not the only problem facing the ocean. Hot water from industry outfalls and cooling plants near the coast causes thermal pollution in the

ocean nearby, although this is usually dissipated quite quickly. As for noise, the sonar used to map the sea floor and the submarine explosions associated with drilling can adversely affect the traditional migration routes of whales and dolphins, since they use similar wavelengths to communicate with each other. Recently environmentalists have been trying to get the use of sonar banned near known migration routes and spawning grounds.

In the past, radioactive waste and toxic chemicals have often been sealed into containers and dumped far out to sea, but recently this practise has been actively discouraged. Containers can be damaged or break open, and despite the care taken leakages have caused major problems.

Unfortunately the toxic effects of DDT and PCBs were not realized at first – unlike more natural hydrocarbons they cannot be easily broken down by bacteria or chemical action so they tend to accumulate in the fatty tissue of living organisms. Again they travel up the food chain, becoming more concentrated as they go. When they reach the higher invertebrates they can cause abnormal growth and infertility, and dangerous levels have been detected in seals, polar bears, penguins and even deep-sea fish.

Environmental stress

The oceans are vast and large expanses remain untouched by humankind, but the seas around coastlines are often overcrowded and overused. Populations next to the sea are burgeoning – at least 70% of people in the world live close to the sea. In the latter half of the twentieth century the availability of cheap flights and other low-cost travel led to a rapid increase in global tourism.

Even events further inland can affect the coast. For instance, cutting down forests to release building land often leads to erosion of the soil, causing extra sediment discharge from land into the water. Sediment may not sound too serious since it is discharged into the sea naturally as well, but excess amounts can kill fish by blocking their gills, cloud water causing problems for other marine life and destroy mangroves and other wetlands. On the other hand, a reduced flow of sediment, perhaps caused by the installation of a dam inland, can lead to coastal erosion, as the sediment regularly washed away by the action of the waves is not replaced.

Coral reefs

Coral reefs are made up of the skeletons of billions of tiny living creatures called polyps, which feed on algae in the sea. Reefs are not just a beautiful and picturesque habitat for tropical fish – they are also an important part of the marine ecosystem. Reefs protect the coastline from erosion and provide sheltering lagoons around many islands and they can stretch for miles – the Great Barrier Reef off Australia is over 1,250 miles long and covers an area of 80,000 square miles. Some reefs have been in existence for more than 500 million years, but they are now being eroded by human activities at an increasing rate.

A major part of the problem are the very tourists who want to visit these beautiful marine habitats. Physical destruction of the reefs is caused by damage from boats and the removal of coral-reef limestone to provide building materials for the tourist infrastructure. Land clearance further inland causes sediment to be carried into the sea and deposited over

the living reef. This not only kills the marine life living in and around the area, but eventually also the reef itself. The tourist trade also escalates the amount of interaction that humans have with the reef – more scuba divers visit, fish are speared, shells, pearls and pieces of coral are taken as souvenirs. In some areas the influx may be so great in the tourist season that the reef does not have time to recover and regenerate between times.

A similar situation has developed in some areas on land, and recently many people have become interested in ecotourism, where such activities are developed to be sustainable and with an awareness of ecological needs. How ecologically sound these tours actually are needs to be carefully studied, however – in an ideal world numbers would be strictly limited and interaction with the local habitat only beneficial, but for the tour operator the need for profit is a powerful incentive to cut corners.

Although they are situated below the surface of the water, coral reefs are also being damaged by global warming. Reef-building corals are very sensitive to changes in water temperature and the stress induced by rapid increases in heat causes the coral to expel its symbiotic zooxanthellae plants, which live inside and provide the coral with its food and color. The affected area of reef appears white – an effect known as coral bleaching. If the situation continues, the coral will die.

Right: If destruction of the coral reefs increases at the current rate, it is estimated that 70% of the world's coral reefs will have disappeared within fifty years. This loss would be an economic disaster for peoples living in the tropics, and a tragedy for the rest of the world; and organisms such as this beautiful orange cup coral would be lost forever.

Global warming

At the turn of the twentieth century, the world is apparently hotter on average than it has been for the last 750 years. It is certain that the 1990s were the warmest decade since records began. Scientists worried about the effect of global warming in Antarctica, have been studying the Larsen ice shelf and its large ice cliffs. Rifts in the ice and the incidence of large sections falling into the sea indicate that the ridge may be breaking apart. Extremes of weather are becoming more common – hurricanes and flooding along North America's east coast have caused considerable damage in recent years, and some areas are now prone to heavy rain while others are suffering unusual drought. These changes are not all negative – some countries now have more amenable climates and growing seasons have been extended.

The rise in temperature is often attributed to the greenhouse effect – a term used to describe the Earth being kept warm by gases in the atmosphere around it trapping heat. Some scientists believe that this effect is becoming more pronounced as more gases are given

off into the atmosphere by man's activities. The main greenhouse gases are carbon dioxide and water vapor; carbon dioxide is given off by industrial installations and when fossil fuels are burned, and also when forests are burned in land clearance programs. Other greenhouse gases are CFCs (chlorofluorocarbons), which are given off by aerosol sprays and ice boxes, nitrous oxides from automobile exhausts and fertilizers, and methane from rotting vegetation and rubbish.

CFCs are also one of the main culprits in the damage to the ozone layer, which protects the earth from ultraviolet radiation – large holes in the ozone layer appear over Antarctica each spring and recently a small hole has appeared over the Arctic. Increased ultraviolet radiation reaching the Earth would not only cause more skin cancers and reduce the efficiency of the human immune system, but would also penetrate the sea and affect the production of plankton. The effects of this would be felt all the way up the food chain.

Above and left: One effect of global warming may be to change the world's pattern of rainfall. Many areas will become drier. In other areas there will be more severe storms such as gales and hurricanes. Stormy weather brings heavy rain and flooding which can devastate crops, destroy towns and lead to loss of life.

Rising sea levels

Much has been made of the fact that the level of the sea is rising, with the melting of the polar ice caps due to global warming cited as the main cause. If the ice caps at both the Arctic and the Antarctic did melt completely, the sea level would rise worldwide by an average of 262 feet. Even quite a small permanent rise in the level of the sea would have a serious impact on coastal cities and towns, which would need improved flood defenses to keep the water at bay. However, the impact may be more positive in some areas, restoring marshes and wetlands that have been lost over the centuries. It is by no means certain that the ice caps are melting though – in fact many scientists believe that we may be heading for a new ice age, although not for around 10–15,000 more years.

From 3,000 years ago to the start of the nineteenth century, the sea level was more or less constant, but since 1900 the level has apparently risen but only in some areas, in others it is falling. The height of the sea relative to that of the land has never been static and changes in level can be affected by many different factors, including volcanic activity and tectonic linked to the rise in sea level, but they are not necessarily cause and effect. In ice ages, the land is covered with water in the form of ice and snow. Ice is heavy, so the land slowly subsides, which means the relative sea level rises. When the ice melts the water runs off into the sea, so the water level rises even more but the land, free of the weight of the ice, begins to bounce back up – known as isostatic rebound – so the levels stabilize again relative to each other. Scandinavia, which was covered with a thick layer of ice only 10,000 years ago, is currently bouncing back at a rate of 3feet per century, while parts of Canada are moving upwards at 6feet per century. So although sea levels may be rising in some areas, in others they are falling in relation to the land.

Another factor that needs to be taken into account is that most of the measurements that show a large increase in the height of the sea level are taken by satellite, but in many cases these figures are not matched by the data collected by tide gauges on land. The satellite data may be faulty, the calibration may be incorrect or the equipment may be giving a false reading. It is also not clear how much seasonal variations are affecting the results.

Index

ACKNOWLEDGEMENTS

The Publishers would like to thank Oxford Scientific Films and Gettyimages
for providing the copyright photographs for this book.

©Oxford Scientific Films:

Pg 12 Phototake Inc; Pg 17 Oliver Grunewald; Pg 31 (bottom) Vince Cavataio; Pg 35 (top) Bill Brennan; Pg 42 (left) Harold Taylor; Pg 43 Harold Taylor; Ph 48 Ron Dahlquist; Pg 50 Steve Turner; Pg 51 Richard Herrmann; Pg 53 (top) Patricio Robles Gil; Pg 54 Green Cape Pty Ltd; Pg 55 Ed Robinson; Pg56 Gerard Soury; Pg 58 Bill Paton; Pg 60 Niall Benvie; Pg 62 Chris Knights; Pg 64 Ian West; Pg 66 Sue Scott; Pg 67 (top) Olaf Broders; Pg 67 (bottom) Bob Gibbons; Pg 68 Rodger Jackman; Pg 69 Paul Kay; Pg 70 Mark Webster; Pg 71 (bottom) Chris Knights; Pg 72 Mark Webster; Pg 73 Gerard Soury; Pg 76 Ian West; Pg 78 William Gray; Pg 79 Oxford Scientific; Pg 80 Tony Tilford; Pg 81 (top) Oxford Scientific; Pg 81 (bottom) Oxford Scientific; Pg 82 (top) Paul Kay; Pg 83 Oxford Scientific; Pg 84 Gustav Verderber; Pg 85 Colin Milkins; Pg 86 Paul Kay; Pg 87 (top) Paul Kay; Pg 87 (bottom) Oxford Scientific; Pg 89 (top) Fredrik Ehrenstrom; Pg 89 (bottom) Tobias Bernhard; Pg 90 Howard Hall; Pg 91 (bottom right) Terry Button; Pg 91 (bottom left) Chris Sharp; Pg 92 Richard Herrmann; Pg 94 David Boag; Pg 95 (right) Rodger Jackman; Pg 96 Oxford Scientific; Pg 97 (top) David Boag; Pg 98 Sue Scott; Pg 99 Oxford Scientific; Pg 101 Paul Kay; Pg 102 (top) Barrie Watts; Pg 102 (bottom) Harold Taylor; Pg 103 Barrie Watts; Pg 104 Paul Kay; Pg 106 Richard Herrmann; Pg 107 (left) Paul Kay; Pg 107 (right) Oxford Scientific; Pg 108 Richard Herrmann; Pg 109 Paul Kay; Pg 110 Kathie Atkinson; Pg 112 Sue Scott; Pg 114 Randy Morse; Pg 115 Paul Kay; Pg 117 Karen Gowlett Holmes; Pg 118 (top) Tobias Bernhard; Pg 120 (top) Gerard Soury; Pg 121 Karen Gowlett Holmes; Pg 122 Doug Wechsler; Pg 123 (bottom) Bob Gibbons; Pg 124 Sue Scott; Pg126 Tobias Bernhard; Pg 127 David B Fleetham; Pg 128 Paul Kay; Pg 130 Tammy Peluso; Pg 131 (top) Richard Herrmann; Pg 131 (bottom) David Fleetham; Pg 133 Daniel Cox; Pg 134 Oxford Scientific; Pg 135 Gerard Soury; Pg 136 (top) Sue Scott; Pg 137 Tobias Bernhard; Pg 139 Gerard Soury; Pg 142 William Gray; Pg 144 Kathie Atkinson; Pg 147 Kathie Atkinson; Pg 148 Mark Jones; Pg 149 (top) Waina Cheng; Pg 149 (bottom) David B Fleetham; Pg 150 (bottom) Mark Webster; Pg 151 David B Fleetham; Pg 152 Mark Deebie & Victoria Stone; Pg 154 Tobias Bernhard; Pg 155 Tobias Bernhard; Pg 156 Oxford Scientific; Pg 157 (top) Mary Plage; Pg 157 (bottom) Phillip J DeVries; Pg 158 Berndt Fischer; Pg 159 (top) Partridge Prod Ltd; Pg 159 (bottom) Mike Birkhead; Pg 162 Doug Allan; Pg 164 David Fleetham; Pg 165 Gerard Soury; Pg 166 Doug Allan; Pg 167 Doug Allan; Pg 168 Gerard Soury; Pg 169 (bottom) Norbert Rosing; Pg 170 Mark Hamblin; Pg 171 Patricio Robles Gil; Pg 173 (right) Ben Osborne; Pg 178 (bottom) Gerard Soury; Pg 178 (top) Doug Allan; Pg 180 David B Fleetham; Pg 186 (top) Konrad Wothe; Pg 186 (bottom) Tim Jackson; Pg 187 Steve Turner; Pg 204 Richard Herrmann; Pg 225 David B Fleetham; Pg 226 Oxford Scientific; Pg 227 Harold Taylor; Pg 228 Thomas Haider; Pg 232 David B Fleetman; Pg 234 Karen Gowlett- Holmes; Pg 235 Richard Herrmann; Pg 239 Tammy Peluso; Pg 241 Howard Hall; Pg 248 Tobias Bernhard; Pg 252 Chris & Monique Fallows; Pg 253 Godfrey Merlen; Pg 258 David Fleetham; Pg 259 Herb Segars; Pg 261 (top) Zigmund Leszczynski; Pg 262 Oxford Scientific; Pg 263 (bottom) David Fleetham; Pg 265 Norbert Wu; Pg 266 Oxford Scientific; Pg 267 Paulo De Oliveria; Pg 268 Tobias Bernhard; Pg 269 Thomas Haider; Pg 270 Paulo De Oliveria; Pg 272 (top) Oxford Scientific; Pg 272 (bottom) Roland Birke; Pg 273 Bob Cranston; Pg 274 W Gregory Brown; Pg 275 Paulo De Oliveria; Pg 277 Mark Deebie & Victoria Stone; Pg 278 Clive Bromhall; Pg 280 Scripps Inst. Oceanography; Pg 285 (left) Paulo De Oliveria; Pg 285 (right) Joanne Huemoeller; Pg 287 Scripps Inst. Oceanography; Pg 290 David A Land; Pg 299 David B Fleetham; Pg 301 Richard Herrmann; Pg 305 Mark Webster; Pg 307 Sharon Green; Pg 310 Bennett Productions; Pg 312 (bottom left) Jan Callagan.

©Getty Images: Pg 21 (top); Pg 21 (bottom); Pg 23 (top); Pg 24; Pg 29; Pg 30 (bottom); Pg 31 (top); Pg 33; Pg 34; Pg 291; Pg 292 (right); Pg 293 (top); Pg 293 (bottom); Pg 294; Pg 295 (bottom left); Pg 303 (left); Pg 308 (top left); Pg 308 (bottom); Pg 311; Pg 314 (top).

This book would not have been possible without the help of
Jane Benn; Oliver Higgs; Mark Brown; Richard Betts and Murray Mahon.